the christmas table

the christmas table

RECIPES AND CRAFTS TO CREATE YOUR OWN HOLIDAY TRADITION

by Diane Morgan

PHOTOGRAPHS BY E.J. ARMSTRONG

CHRONICLE BOOKS

SAN FRANCISCO

dedication

In loving memory of John Ashby Conway, a profoundly important culinary mentor. And to Alma Lach, my other significant culinary teacher, for her generosity of spirit and keen knowledge of food.

Library of Congress
Cataloging-in-Publication Data

Morgan, Diane, 1955 - The Christmas table :
recipes and ideas to create your own magical
holiday / by Diane Morgan;
photographs by E.J. Armstrong. p. cm.
ISBN 978-0-8118-6093-2 (alk. paper)
1. Christmas cookery. 2. Christmas
decorations. I. Title.
TX739.2.C45M675 2008
641.5'686—dc22
2007042024

ISBN: 978-0-8118-6093-2

Manufactured in China.

Lead Food Stylist: Charlotte Omnes
Food styling: Patty Wittmann, Diana Isaiou
Prop Styling: Kim Holderman
Designed by Alicia Nammacher
Typesetting by Connie Bigelow
The photographer wishes to thank
the whole gang for a really fun shoot—
and Joe Holdsworth for humoring
us with coffee and chocolate . . .

10 9 8 7 6 5 4 3 2 1

Chronicle Books LLC
680 Second Street
San Francisco, California 94107

www.chroniclebooks.com

acknowledgments

In the spirit of Christmas, when family and friends are remembered and acknowledged for making life so special and every day a blessing, I have a long, important list of people deserving a big thank-you gift, wrapped with sparkling paper and tied with a huge bow:

To Bill LeBlond, my editor at Chronicle Books and dear friend, for all his expert guidance, support, and time. It's a professional relationship beyond compare and one I cherish deeply.

To Lisa Ekus, my agent, for her amazing advice and enthusiasm. And to Jane Falla and everyone else at The Lisa Ekus Group for their dedicated support.

To Amy Treadwell, Peter Perez, Leslie Jonath, Andrea Burnett, Jennifer Tolo Pierce, and the others at Chronicle Books, who have inspired, supported, publicized, and otherwise kept my projects on track. You are all delightful to work with. To Sharon Silva, many thanks for copyediting my book with such care and precision. To Alicia Nammacher, thank you for your beautiful, festive design. A huge thank you to E.J. Armstrong and her staff.

To Cheryl Russell, my fabulous assistant, I don't know what I'd do without you! We've cooked together for so long, and tested and retested so many recipes, that I can hardly keep track of how many books we have worked on. You make developing and testing recipes both a pleasure and loads of fun—it seems like Christmas every time we're in the kitchen.

To my friends Harriet and Peter Watson, you have given me the biggest gift of all: your friendship and unwavering support. You have eaten more test recipes and given me honest feedback for more books than I can recall. I can't hug and thank you enough. You bring me joy and much laughter even when really big deadlines like this one are looming. Our families sharing the holidays together represent the essence of the Chrismukkah spirit.

Many thanks to my friends, family, and colleagues: David Watson, Paola Gentry and Eric Watson, Richard and Barb LevKoy, Larry LevKoy, Irene LevKoy, Domenica Marchetti, Charlie and Jeanne Sosland, Bruce and Ellen Birenboim, Steve and Marci Taylor, Sukey and Gil Garcetti, Roxane and Austin Huang, Margie Sanders, Priscilla and John Longfield, Karen Fong, Sherry Gable, Alicia Buoni, Brijesh and Ann Anand, Deb and Ron Adams, Summer Jameson, Kam and Tony Kimball, Mary and Jack Barber, Sara and Erik Whiteford, Tori Ritchie, Josie Jimenez, Joyce Goldstein, Laura Werlin, Monica Bhide, Denise Bina, Judith Bishop, Carolyn Burleigh, Ericka Carlson, Lisa Hill, Cathy Whims and David West, Lisa Donoughe, Kathy Campbell, Barbara Dawson and Matthew Katzer, Tony Gemignani, Braiden Rex-Johnson, Alma Lach, Michael Wehman, Janine MacLachlan, Julie Hasson, David Lebovitz, Janie Hibler, Lisa Morrison, Lorinda and Ray Moholt, Andy Schloss, and the wonderful folks at McGonigle's Meat Market.

For their creative talent and amazing guidance when it comes to holiday decor and flowers, I want to thank David and Leanne Kesler of The Floral Design Institute and Christine Belluschi of Klorafil, Inc., both of Portland, Oregon. You three are brilliant, talented, and so much fun to work with.

Thanks to Adair Lara, for her talent, humor, and time shooting my author photo.

Special thanks to Antonia Allegra and Don and Joan Fry, for their professional guidance and encouragement. Whether in France or at the Greenbrier, it is always treasured time when we are together.

Finally, my husband and two children are the most treasured gifts of my lifetime. This book wouldn't have been nearly as much fun to write without my loving and nurturing husband, Greg, sharing in all I do. To Eric and Molly, my children, thank you for all your love and caring every step of the way.

contents

introduction

"Good tidings to you wherever you are," and welcome to *The Christmas Table*! This book—in one neatly bound package—is all about bringing you comfort and joy with helpful ideas to simplify, organize, and plan your holiday season.

Christmas is a spirited and creative time of year, with an abundance of family, friends, and, of course, food, food, and more food! For many, Christmas begins the day after Thanksgiving with the start of holiday shopping (not for me, I'm napping!). It actively emerges in my home in early December, accompanied by a steady stream of Christmas cards and invitations to holiday parties.

Slowly, but surely, poinsettias appear in my sunroom; blood oranges and pomegranates replace the display of squashes in my kitchen; and the fragrant scent of evergreen is everywhere. For me, Christmas is a season to savor, not fret over. It is a precious time when food, memory, and other strands of our lives can come together in powerful and fun ways. That is why I wanted to write this book.

The Christmas Table is filled with more than seventy recipes for glorious things to eat. But sitting at my Christmas table, surrounded by those dearest to me,

I rejoice that food does so much more than keep our bellies full. It nourishes our hearts and souls as well. Legendary food essayist M.F.K. Fisher wrote almost prayerfully about "a communion of more than our bodies when bread is broken and wine is drunk."

The process of writing this book was wonderfully nostalgic. I thought back to my childhood in Pittsburgh, helping Grandma Becky and Grandma Rose make rugelach and sugar cookies for Christmas. I remembered the adults happily drinking my grandfather's famous homemade eggnog, while the children gulped down Shirley Temples (we sensed there was a secret grown-up ingredient in the eggnog). We were an enthusiastic, exuberant, and hungry crowd.

I was transported to the year my daughter performed in *The Nutcracker*, and to the pastry class I took more than a dozen years ago where I made my prized Swiss gingerbread village. (My handiwork, still intact with marzipan snowmen and chalets dusted with confectioners' sugar snow, remains a cherished holiday decoration to this day.) I recalled reading *The Polar Express* on Christmas Eve to two sleepy-eyed but oh-so-excited children (now young adults), and hours spent sweeping up the glitter and glue from ornaments they proudly made at school.

The season is also about our broader communities. For several years my family "adopted" a needy family for Christmas through a local social-service agency. We would buy clothes and bedding and toys, and arrange gift baskets overflowing with cooking utensils, spices, rice, beans, sugar, flour, coffee, pasta, pots, and pans. During dinner we would share stories and reminisce about this wonderful buying spree. Then we'd all join hands, lower our heads, and fall silent. Of course, this was a spirited group, and the solemnity soon gave way to that all-important holiday digestif—laughter.

As with all my book projects, I harvested interesting tidbits of information along the way. For example, I now know (and you will, too) that the cultivation and processing of sugarcane began in the South Pacific several thousand years before the birth of Christ, but the so-called "honey without bees" didn't reach western Europe (by way of India, Persia, China, and other parts of the globe) until the Middle Ages. Gingerbread? In seventeenth-century Germany and France, only professional bakers were permitted to make gingerbread, restrictions that were relaxed at Christmas and Easter. Sugarplums? They were intensely sweet, boiled round candies similar to comfits—not plums at all. Ethnic holiday foods? Kutya, tamales, fattoush, stollen, glögg, empanadas, buñuelos, and natilla are traditional holiday foods on an international array of Christmas tables. And you'll find more tidbits and fun facts sprinkled throughout the book.

I have also included detailed information on seasonal foods and ingredients, specialized equipment and tools, holiday decor, and menus and timetables for all types of entertaining. Ease into the holiday spirit with a Deck-the-Halls Decorating Party (page 210), Christmas Open House (page 212), or Christmas Eve Supper (page 214). Or, blend interfaith traditions with Chrismukkah—The Hybrid Holiday Meal (page 220).

All of the recipes in this book were family- and friend-tested and come with training wheels: cook's notes and do-ahead tips that eliminate guesswork about presentation, what can be frozen, how far in advance a recipe can be made and refrigerated, and how the recipe can be broken down into manageable steps. In addition, you will find great recipes from some of my professional colleagues who, in the spirit of the season, generously allowed me to adapt them for this book. These include Radicchio Caesar Salad (page 63); Saffron-Scented Fish Stew (page 56); and Gingerbread Bundt Cake with Crème Anglaise (page 137).

You'll also discover main-course classics with a holiday twist, such as Whole Roast Salmon with Farro-Herb Stuffing (page 96) and Roast Loin of Pork Stuffed with Apricots and Dried Plums (page 87). There are festive side dishes, too, including Potatoes au Gratin with Fresh Thyme and a Parmesan Crust (page 116), Wild Rice with Roasted Chestnuts and Cranberries (page 108), and Fa-La-La-La Latkes (page 114). Leftovers? They can be a busy cook's best friends. The Leftover Favorites chapter gives you many mouthwatering, next-day ideas, such as Lamb and Pita Sandwiches with Yogurt-Mint Sauce (page 200), Hot Beef Borscht (page 198), and Macaroni and Cheese with Ham (page 202).

I devote an entire chapter to holiday breakfast foods, including some that can be prepared the night before and one that uses a packaged mix! (Spending more time around the tree on Christmas morning sometimes trumps scratch baking, even in my household.) So enjoy a leisurely and yummy morning with Panettone French Toast (page 152), Overnight Cinnamon Bread Custard (page 159), and Cranberry Muffins with Brown Sugar–Almond Streusel (page 160).

And, of course, Christmas is full of sweet delights, as are the recipes in the Holiday Dessert chapter. (Alas, no fruitcake recipe here.) Friends call the Eggnog Cheese-cake with Candied Kumquats (page 124) a dream come true. They are equally rhapsodic about the Bûche de Noël (page 131). The chapter on The Great Cookie Exchange is certain to satisfy even the most discerning cookie doyenne. Chocolate-Dipped Shortbread Stars (page 172) are a perennial crowd-pleaser at my home, and the Coconut-Orange Snowballs (page 169) are delicious and fun to make.

For sentimental reasons, the Food Gifts from the Kitchen chapter holds special meaning for me. For years, friends and colleagues have asked me to share my recipe for Christmas pecans, and up until now I steadfastly held out, preferring only to give them as gifts. The recipe is on page (184). Enjoy!

So now I ask for a gift from you, which is to derive pleasure from creating your own magical holiday. Be playful in the kitchen. Have fun decorating your home. Take time to appreciate the sights and smells and sounds of the season. And above all, treasure everyone around your Christmas table.

Merry Christmas and *dona nobis pacem*.

the twelve planning tips of christmas

The first verse of "The Twelve Days of Christmas" begins, "On the first day of Christmas, my true love gave to me—A partridge in a pear tree."

If my true love gave me a partridge in a pear tree on Christmas Day, all I would be thinking is, "Sweet, but that's another mouth to feed and another pet to clean up after." Or, better yet, "What do I stuff it with?" Now, if my true love gave me a cook, a baker, and a cleanup crew—that would be a gift. And, speaking of gifts, it wouldn't be so bad to rewrite the last verse and forgo the twelve drummers drumming in favor of twelve days of sunning. (After all, who doesn't need peace and quiet after the houseguests leave?) Pick a beautiful, warm sunny spot, with a waitstaff delivering icy margaritas—it would all be bliss to me.

But what if Santa isn't that generous or attentive? Or, your true love thinks a joint gift of a riding mower is the best present of all? Or, your in-laws decide that, since you have the largest house and love to cook, it makes sense for all of the family to gather at your place?

Grab a pen and pad of paper because your gift from me is The Twelve Planning Tips of Christmas. Consider this a self-help guide for the Christmas-challenged. I have thought through all that I do when planning for the holidays and have assembled a list of tips that will bring joy, organization, and a can-do spirit to the hassles and triumphs of holiday entertaining.

1 *Choosing a Style*   >>>   The Christmas season is a time to celebrate, and there are many ways to entertain. Throw a party that fits your lifestyle, budget, energy level, and time frame. Ask yourself lots of questions: Do you like to entertain formally or informally, with lots of guests or just a few? Do you have the time to organize an open house, or would a casual buffet dinner be less stressful? How many times over the holidays do you want to entertain? Do you have the kitchen space and living space to accommodate a few guests or a large group? Make it comfortable, manageable, and enjoyable for everyone—including you.

One year, my husband and I decided to host his company party at our home for nearly seventy guests, and then hold an open house the next afternoon for friends, family, and neighbors. It sounds crazy but it worked. I decorated once, and all the flowers and greens were fresh. I made enough food for both parties, duplicating the menu in many instances. All the dishware, glassware, and linens were rented and saved me money because I utilized them twice. And we rearranged furniture to make room for a bar, a buffet, and people milling about, and it worked for both parties. I hired a kitchen helper, a server, and a bartender, and paid my children to answer the door and take coats. We were a team for two parties and everything went smoothly. After the first party we cleared and washed the dishes, vacuumed, and freshened the bathrooms, and we were ready for the second party. I am not recommending this double-party plan as a yearly tradition for celebrating the holidays, but it was a wonderful way to see many friends and colleagues—and to reciprocate their past invitations—in just two days.

2 *Setting the Scene*   >>>   Of course, entertaining is about food and drink, but it is also about setting a mood, especially at Christmastime. Decorating is a personal expression of your style and traditions. Your home doesn't need to look like a holiday scene in a glossy magazine spread; after all, a team of stylists creates those photographs. However, simple seasonal elements can make an event more memorable. Every year, I decorate the mantle with fresh greens and hang the holiday stockings that we've had since the children were toddlers. I carefully transport the Swiss gingerbread village I made a dozen years ago from the storage room to the dining room to decorate the buffet. It's these sentimental elements that make the holiday special. Add pretty votives to the table, select Christmas music to play in the background, place a wreath on the door, set a red amaryllis on the counter in the kitchen, and then put a second one in the guest bathroom. Decorating doesn't need to be elaborate—just enough to create a warm, inviting ambience.

3 *Making a List—Checking It Twice* >>> I don't know what I would do without a series of lists for holiday entertaining—any entertaining, for that matter. Plan the guest list and send out invitations at least three, but preferably four, weeks in advance. Plan the menu and decide on what flowers you need to buy, and then make lists based on the different stores you will be shopping at, such as the butcher shop, the bakery, the wine store, the florist, and the supermarket. Write down the errands you will need to tackle each day on a separate sheet of paper. Keep a pen handy to cross off items you've purchased and errands you've completed. You'll feel great satisfaction when everything is checked off. Finally, write a timeline for your holiday menu, organizing it exactly the way the Christmas menus are detailed on pages 210 to 221. It will keep you from being harried and frazzled.

4 *Planning Ahead—Food* >>> If your holiday entertaining requires a turkey, goose, ham, standing rib roast, beef tenderloin, leg of lamb, or crown roast of pork, you'll make your butcher happy and yourself less crazed if you order it two weeks ahead. You're more likely to get exactly what you want with advance planning. If turkey is on your menu, allow about four days for a frozen turkey to thaw in the refrigerator. If you're serving a fresh bird, pick it up one or two days before you roast it. Fresh birds are commercially refrigerated just above freezing, which means they often have icy juices in the chest cavity. A day or two in a home refrigerator eliminates the problem.

5 *Planning Ahead—A Well-Stocked Holiday Pantry* >>> A smart host keeps jars of olives, pickles, and other delectable spreads on the pantry shelf during the holidays for spur-of-the-moment entertaining. Stonewall Kitchen makes terrific condiments to spread on crackers or crostini. Containers of nuts and boxes of crackers, chips, and bread sticks make it easy to assemble snacks or party nibbles without a lot of fuss. I buy some interesting cheeses at holiday time, and keep ready-to-eat crudités, such as baby carrots, radishes, and celery hearts, in the refrigerator.

6 *Planning Ahead—Kitchen Equipment* >>> Once you have decided on a menu, check your cupboards to determine whether you have all the pots, sauté pans, baking pans, and other equipment you'll need to make the recipes. Invest in a few things you think you'll use again and again. I bought a sturdy roasting pan and V-shaped roasting rack a number of years ago and use it throughout the year, but especially at Thanksgiving and Christmas. Quality baking sheets are a must-have for making holiday cookies and appetizers. Specialty bakeware, such as a Bundt pan or a springform pan, is required for specific desserts, and it's hard to substitute another pan. Borrow one if you can, or buy one and add it to your kitchen arsenal. A food processor and stand mixer make certain tasks a snap, but a strong arm and a whisk work, too. (Small kitchen appliances make great Christmas gifts!)

7 *Planning Ahead—Tableware* >>> Check to make sure you have the serving bowls, platters, and utensils you'll need for serving your menu. Also, assess your china, glassware, and silverware and count to see if you have enough of everything. For a large party, rent what you need, or use disposable plates and utensils, buying sturdy brands that won't collapse under the weight of the food. I certainly don't have the dishware to host a party for fifty, but several years ago I did buy twenty-four white china appetizer and dinner plates during the holiday sales. They are basic, yet great-looking, and were relatively inexpensive. They're handy to have for cocktail parties and buffet dinners. Think about the napkins, tablecloths, or place mats you will be using. Are they clean? Do they need to be pressed? Do you have enough? Simple white linen napkins can be made festive by tying them with holiday ribbon (page 225).

8 *Setting the Table* >>> Whether you are setting up a buffet or serving a sit-down dinner, set your table the day before the party. It takes longer than you think; you'll have one less thing to do on the day of the party; and any last-minute details you forgot will become obvious. For a buffet, I like to arrange the bowls and platters in place to make sure everything will fit, plus I write each recipe name on a Post-it and stick it on the serving piece. That way, my kitchen helper or I can easily retrieve the right bowl or platter when needed. Mix and match the serving pieces to create variety and interest. I might place cookies on a silver platter I inherited from my grandmother and set it right next to the white china cake plate I bought at Target.

9 *Organizing the Bar* >>> Cheers to the holidays, and cheers to the host who has thought through all the details of setting up a bar, with beverages, glassware, stirrers, shakers, and so on. It takes planning! First, decide the style of party, and then decide what you are going to drink and match it with the appropriate glassware. Not every party needs to have a full bar with hard liquor and cocktail fixings. It is perfectly acceptable to offer a single special-occasion cocktail, such as the Pomegranate Martini on page 53, and have wine and beer on hand. For a full bar, add scotch, bourbon, gin, and vodka, plus tonic, soda water, and other mixers, along with soft drinks and

sparkling water. Or, serve Champagne at the start of the party and follow with wine. For a large party, especially an open house or formal cocktail party, have someone staff the bar, whether a paid bartender, a friend, or your spouse. Have plenty of cocktail napkins at the bar, and keep a roll of paper towels underneath in case of spills. Watch out for overindulging guests, and have a few designated drivers or the telephone number for the local taxi service.

10 *Coordinating a Team of Cooks* >>> During the holidays, families often designate one home for entertaining but divide up the cooking responsibilities among many. This is a wonderful way to share in the spirit of the holiday, as long as someone is coordinating the effort, usually the host family. My suggestion, especially with the ease of e-mail, is for the host to put together a menu, get everyone to agree to it, and then put the name of who will prepare each item next to it on the menu. That way there is no confusion about what is being served and who is cooking it. In addition, to prevent oven gridlock, determine if guests are bringing food hot and ready to serve or whether it needs to be baked before serving. Because we live only fifteen minutes from close friends with whom we share many holiday meals, I once whisked a turkey from my oven, tented it with foil, and let it "rest" while we drove to their house for dinner. The bird was ready to carve when we arrived, and the bird didn't crowd the side dishes out of our friends' oven.

11 *Recruiting Kitchen Elves* >>> Santa has helpers, so why shouldn't you? Let there be a steady stream of happy, helping hands in the kitchen to make baking and cooking a joy. Don't just fill the house with the sweet smells of gingerbread or the savory scent of roast turkey and stuffing. Have it overflowing with laughter and with stories of Christmases past. However, if you're pressed for time and have tasks without willing helpers—and, of course, have a budget that allows it—hire some helpers. A maid service can clean when you can't; a culinary school student, needing money and experience, can chop and prep while you attend to other duties. Think through what it takes to make the holidays as stress-free as possible and then decide how many elves you need. That can be a gift to you.

12 *Making Merry Memories* >>> The twelfth planning tip of Christmas is the most important: celebrate the true sprit of the holiday, remember to make the season a memorable time for family and friends to be together, and laugh—even if a drink spills, an ornament breaks, or a latke burns. Here's a toast to organization and planning—now, may I please have a second cup of wassail punch (page 50)?

foods of the season

Here is a list of seasonal foods and special ingredients for the recipes in this book, with tips on preparation and some preferences.

BLOOD ORANGES
There are three types, or cultivars, of blood orange: the Tarocco, native to Italy; the Saguinello, native to Spain; and the Moro, from Sicily. Available from December to May, blood oranges are small to medium-sized fruits with dramatic crimson, blood red, or red-streaked flesh and deep red juice. The skin can be pitted or smooth and is often tinged with red, and the flesh contains a moderate amount of seeds. The tangy-sweet juice is a perfect cocktail ingredient. The fruit can be peeled and eaten fresh, used in salads and sauces, or made into marmalade. Although primarily grown in Mediterranean countries, especially Italy, citrus growers in California, Texas, and Florida are now cultivating them in the United States.

BREAD CUBES
Not all bread cubes are created equal. My preference is to make my own for stuffing— it's simple and can be done ahead—using good artisanal bread. I cut the bread into $1/2$-inch cubes, which I prefer to the typically smaller store-bought cubes. Dry bread cubes purchased from an artisanal bakery are my next choice, and commercially prepared bread cubes are an acceptable third option. If you purchase the latter, look for unseasoned bread cubes and packages that haven't been crushed (or you will have lots of bread crumbs instead).

Making your own bread cubes is a quick and easy task with delicious results. There is no comparison between home-made bread cubes and the cellophane-packaged ones available in supermarkets. I usually prepare mine a day or two before Christmas. Buy a loaf of artisanal or country-style white bread, trim off the crusts, cut the bread into $1/2$-inch cubes, and spread the cubes on rimmed baking sheets in a single layer. Toast the cubes in a preheated 400°F oven until just beginning to brown, about 10 minutes. Let cool completely and store in an airtight container until ready to use. Artisanal bakeries are springing up in every city and town around the country. Check out their breads for making bread cubes. If you are short on time, these same bakeries often sell toasted bread cubes made from their day-old loaves, especially during the holidays.

BRUSSELS SPROUTS

Cute, like miniature cabbages, Brussels sprouts are typically sold loose, but some markets, especially farmers' markets, sell them on the stalk. Look for tightly packed heads with fresh green leaves, and avoid leaves that are yellowed or speckled with black spots.

CELERY ROOT (CELERIAC)

This brown, knobby vegetable with creamy white flesh belongs to the same family as celery but is bred for its root, rather than its stalks and leaves. Texturally, it is similar to potatoes when cooked but has a unique flavor reminiscent of celery and parsley. Look for firm roots that are medium to large (by the time you peel the small ones, there is hardly anything left). Use a paring knife, rather than a vegetable peeler, to remove the rough outer peel. Like potatoes, celery roots begins to oxidize and discolor quickly after peeling, so immediately immerse the peeled chunks in cold water.

CHESTNUTS

Fresh chestnuts are always in the market at Christmastime. They are fun to roast and delicious to eat, but tedious to peel. There are about 36 chestnuts in a pound, yielding about 2 1/2 cups peeled nuts. I often buy peeled chestnuts in vacuum-sealed packages, cans, or jars (see the Cook's Note on page 110) for use in soups, stuffings, and the like. They are a time-saver, though not a money-saver.

CHICKEN STOCK AND BROTH

I'm one of those cooks who always has homemade chicken stock in the freezer. It's a habit: Every time I roast a whole chicken, I make a small batch of stock by tossing the neck, giblets, and wing tips into a saucepan with a bit of chopped yellow onion, celery, and carrot; a small bay leaf; a few black peppercorns; and cold water to cover. I simmer it for an hour, strain it, and I have stock. It's easy and never feels like a chore—at least to me. Canned broth is a good substitute. Look for a brand that is low in salt; I prefer Swanson's low-sodium, fat-free organic broth.

CHOCOLATE

I'm a self-avowed chocoholic and have tasted my way through many fine brands. I tried not to have a disproportionate number of chocolate desserts, cookies, and food gifts in this book. That said, it is Christmas—a time to enjoy chocolate. All the recipes in the book were tested with Valrhona, Callebaut, or Scharffen Berger chocolate. In some recipes, where the knockout taste of a bittersweet chocolate is deserved, I call for dark bittersweet chocolate that indicates at least 64% cacao on its label. That means the chocolate bar contains a minimum of 64% by weight of ingredients—chocolate liquor, cocoa butter, cocoa powder—derived from the cacao bean, with the rest of the bar made up primarily of sugar and vanilla. (The ratio of chocolate liquor to cocoa butter within a cacao percentage varies among manufacturers.) Taste test for yourself and decide whether you like semisweet, bittersweet,

Clockwise from far left.
Red Swiss Chard; sautéed
Brussels sprouts with garlic
and Parmesan; radicchio;
natural pistachios

or extra-bittersweet chocolate for your desserts. They are all interchangeable. I also recommend chopping the chocolate before melting it for better texture and consistency. You can leave the chocolate bar in the wrapper and break it with your hands, or you can use a meat fork or carving fork to break apart the bar and then finely chop it with a knife. If you make a lot of chocolate desserts, invest in a chocolate fork, available from www.bakers-catalogue.com. All of the chocolate brands mentioned are available in specialty stores or by mail order. You will also enjoy checking out www.chocosphere.com.

CRAB
There are lots of crab varieties, both fresh- and saltwater, and what is available in your fish market will largely depend on where you live. In the Pacific Northwest, I mostly see Dungeness, which is prized for its sweet, succulent flesh. King crab and snow crab are also found in the northern Pacific. In the East and South, blue crab, rock crab, and stone crab are most readily available. For the recipes in this book, I'm using fresh-cooked lump meat or flaked meat from the body and/or claws, depending on the variety. It's expensive but also the tastiest, and is much preferred over canned crabmeat.

CRANBERRIES
These are the small, red, tart berries of a plant that grows in bogs on low, trailing vines. They come in 12-ounce packages—look for bright red, firm berries—and are always available fresh at Christmastime. Check the recipe carefully to see how much you need, and buy extra bags for the freezer. A 12-ounce package is equivalent to about 3 cups berries. Cranberries are delicious in muffins, scones, and coffee cakes.

EGGNOG
A classic beverage of the season, eggnog is a smooth, creamy, ultrarich blend of milk or cream, beaten eggs or egg yolks, sugar, nutmeg, and usually, though not always, a liquor or combination of liquors, such as dark rum, brandy, or bourbon. Some eggnog recipes are made with separated eggs: a custard is made from the milk, sugar, and egg yolks and then stiffly beaten egg whites are folded in. Other recipes use only the egg yolks: a rich, eggy custard is made and then stiffly beaten cream is folded in. Homemade is best, but during the holidays prepared eggnog is found in the dairy section of supermarkets—*sans* liquor, of course.

FLOUR
All of the recipes call for either cake flour or all-purpose flour. Depending on the flour specified, I use Softasilk brand cake flour or Gold Medal brand unbleached all-purpose flour to test my recipes. What is most important about flour when baking is not the brand, per se, but how the flour is measured. The proper way to measure flour is to spoon it into a dry measuring cup and level off the top with the blunt side of a table knife. Scooping flour right from the bag or from a canister with a measuring cup and then leveling off the excess means the flour is more compacted, which I find results in a less tender cake, cookie, or pastry. Weighing flour yields the most accurate measure, but because most American home bakers rely on volume measures, recipes do not typically include weights.

GOOSE
Serving a fresh goose for Christmas takes some planning, unless you have a hunter in the family, because you'll

need to order it from a butcher or specialty market. Frozen goose is available throughout the year, also from specialty markets. If frozen, thaw the goose in the refrigerator, allowing two to three days for the bird to defrost fully Geese can weigh from 8 to 18 pounds. A 10- to 12-pound goose is the average size available and will serve six. Check out www.nickyusa.com for ordering game meats and poultry.

HAM

A ham is cut from the hog's hind leg. A whole ham, which includes both the shank half and the butt half, can weigh 14 to 18 pounds. Unprocessed ham is referred to as fresh ham. Country hams are traditionally dry-cured and salted (and sometimes smoked). They must be soaked and simmered extensively before baking. Partially cooked hams from smokehouses in New England and the Southeast are available by mail order or online. City hams are fully cooked hams that have been cured either by immersing the ham in a wet brine (wet-curing) or by injecting the meat with a brine solution (injection-curing), and then smoked. The ham recipe in this book calls for a fully cooked, smoked ham. The best are labeled "ham" and contain no added water. Others are labeled "ham with natural juices," and "ham–water added," or, the least expensive and least desirable, "ham and water product." A fully cooked ham is ready to eat and only needs to be heated through.

MÂCHE

This is a tender, dark-leaved winter salad green with a tangy bite. It is also known as corn salad, field salad, field lettuce, and lamb's lettuce. The spoon-shaped leaves are velvety soft and grow in little rosette-like clusters. Mâche needs to be treated with care: buy it no more than a day or two before you plan to serve it, swish the leaves in a bowlful of tepid water to clean them, and pat them dry with paper towels. Roll the leaves in fresh paper towels and seal them in a plastic bag to keep them fresh. At the market, I often see greenhouse-grown mâche sold in sealed bags.

NUTS

Nuts are used extensively during the holiday season, in both savory and sweet dishes. Store raw nuts in a tightly sealed container in the freezer to keep them as fresh as possible. Toasting them brings out their delicate flavor, and toasted nuts enhance any dish to which they are added, making the minimal extra effort worth it. Spread the nuts in a single layer on a rimmed baking sheet and bake on the center rack in a preheated 350°F oven until lightly browned and fragrant, 5 to 7 minutes; then pour onto a plate to cool. If you need ground nuts for a recipe, you can purchase them already ground or buy shelled nuts and grind them at home in a food processor fitted with the metal blade, using the pulse button to control the coarseness.

OYSTERS

Three primary species of oysters are sold in the United States, whether naturally grown or cultivated in beds: Pacific or Japanese oysters, found on the Pacific seaboard; eastern or Atlantic oysters, from the Atlantic seaboard; and the small and delicious Olympia oysters from Washington's Puget Sound. Fresh oysters are available year-round, debunking the myth that you should only eat oysters during months spelled without an *r*. Quick processing and advanced refrigeration techniques in trucking and storage keep the oysters fresh even during hot weather.

However, experts think the best time to eat oysters raw is in the fall and winter because they spawn during the summer and the meat tends to be softer. I use fresh, shucked oysters that I buy from my fishmonger. The best are sold in clear, screw-top jars, so you can see that the oysters are tightly packed, plump, have good color, and the oyster liquor is clear, not cloudy. Ask to smell the oysters if you question their freshness. They should smell sweet and briny fresh, not fishy at all.

PANETTONE

Traditionally served at Christmastime, this towering Italian sweet yeast bread is made with citron, raisins, anise, and, sometimes, pine nuts. It is sold in Italian markets and some supermarkets, often in colorful packaging that details its origins.

PARSNIPS

Cultivated in Europe since ancient times, parsnips were brought to America in the 1600s. Resembling a carrot, this creamy-white root vegetable has a complex flavor that makes it taste sweet, herbal, and earthy. Parsnips are available year-round, but their flavor is best in fall and winter. Look for well-shaped, medium-sized roots that are firm with no spots or shriveled skin, and no sprouting at the tops. Store and cook parsnips as you would carrots; they are delicious roasted, braised, steamed, or boiled for mashing.

PEARL ONIONS

These tiny, papery white or yellow onions are used in side dishes, soups, and stews. They are more flavorful when fresh, but frozen peeled pearl onions will do in a pinch.

PERSIMMONS

Bright orange with a smooth skin, persimmons need time to ripen. You'll most likely see two Japanese varieties in the market: The Fuyu is bright orange, squat, and tomato-shaped, and can be sliced when ripe and eaten like a tomato. The Hachiya is heart-shaped with a pointed bottom and has a smooth, bright orange-red skin. It has a more astringent taste when ripe and should almost feel like mush when ready to eat. Persimmons are in season in late fall. You can buy Hachiyas in quantity, allow them to ripen on your counter-top, and then scoop the soft, jellylike flesh from the skin and purée and freeze it. Persimmon pudding is a fond holiday dessert for many.

POMEGRANATES

The pomegranate, one of only seven fruits mentioned in the Old Testament, is round, about the size of a large orange, and has a smooth, glossy red to red-pink skin that feels leathery. Inside is a complex set of compartments made up of tiny, shiny, rubylike fleshy edible seeds surrounded by spongy, bitter, cream-colored membranes. The seeds are the only edible part of the fruit.

To remove the seeds, fill a medium bowl with water and place it in a sink. Cut off the crown of the pomegranate with a stainless-steel knife (a carbon-steel knife can turn the juice bitter), and scoop out some of the center membrane, or pith, with a spoon. Use a knife to score the skin into quarters, and then cut through enough of the membrane to see the seeds. Immerse the pomegranate in the water and break apart the quarters with your thumbs. Use your fingers to peel away the white membrane and pop out the seeds. They will sink to the bottom of the bowl and the membrane will float to the top. Discard the membrane. Drain the seeds, spread them on a double-thick layer of paper towels to absorb the excess moisture, and they are ready to use. (I wear an apron and disposable surgical gloves when preparing pomegranates, because the juice stains both hands and clothing.)

RADICCHIO

This Italian red-leaved salad green belongs to the chicory family. There are two forms commonly found in the marketplace: *radicchio rosso di Chioggia* looks like a small head of cabbage with burgundy leaves and white ribs; the leaves of *radicchio rosso di Treviso* are long and tapered like the inner leaves of romaine lettuce and are burgundy with white ribs, though the color can range from wine red to pink. It is the distinctive color and complex bitter flavor that makes radicchio so appealing in salads, as well as baked, sautéed, or grilled. Look for crisp leaves with no brown spots. Breaking the heads apart and soaking the leaves in cold water for an hour crisps them. Wrap the drained and dried leaves in paper towels and store in a plastic bag in the refrigerator for up to two days.

SALMON

I could write pages and pages on salmon—and, in fact, I did just that in my cookbook, *Salmon* (Chronicle Books, 2005)—but here are only brief descriptions of the types used in the recipes in this book.

Cold-smoked salmon: Often called lox, this is brine-cured, cold-smoked salmon that has been smoked in temperatures ranging between 70° and 90°F for anywhere from one day to three weeks, depending on the style of smoking and tradition. In the Pacific Northwest, we often see smoked salmon in the marketplace that has been cured with a sweet brine and smoked with alder wood. It is very different from the Jewish deli-style smoked salmon, known as Nova or Nova Scotia lox, that I ate growing up. This lox has a silky, tender flesh and is slightly salty. It is sold either pre-sliced, or as my father preferred, sliced by hand when ordered.

Hot-smoked salmon: This salmon is typically first soaked in a flavored brine and then smoked in temperatures ranging from 120° to 180°F for anywhere from a couple of hours up to a day or more. The flavoring of the brine and the wood used to smoke the fish tend to have distinct geographical styles.

Fresh salmon: Whether a whole fish or a fillet, fresh salmon is labeled, according to United States Department of Agriculture (USDA) regulations, either "wild" or "farmed." Beyond that, you might see little white signs stuck in the ice or on the package indicating the fish's origin, upbringing, and whether or not it is organic. Wild salmon will be Pacific salmon from California, Oregon, Washington, British Columbia, or, most likely, Alaska. (Or, caught by a sport fisherman with a privileged license to fish for the few wild Atlantic salmon left in the rivers that feed the Atlantic Ocean.) Farmed Atlantic salmon might be labeled organic if it is actually farmed salmon originating from the North Atlantic, off the coasts of Ireland, Nova Scotia, and Scotland. Europe has had organic certifying agencies in place since 1998. Salmon farms with organic certification must operate in adherence to a strict set of standards. My preference is always to buy wild salmon because I discern a textural difference in the fish: wild salmon has a more muscular flesh than farmed salmon, which is softer and seems a bit flabby to me.

Farmed salmon is available year-round, while wild salmon is seasonal, with the peak between mid-May and mid-September. However, many Pacific fishermen and processors freeze their salmon within forty-five minutes of catching it and are therefore able to keep fish markets supplied with wild salmon all year. Look for moist, glistening skin on fillets, and if the salmon is whole, look for eyes protruding bright and clear. It should smell fresh, not fishy. Don't be afraid to ask to sniff the fish before purchasing it.

SALT
I keep several types of salt in my kitchen. Within easy reach of my stove and prep counter are a bowlful of kosher salt and another filled with fine sea salt. I buy Diamond Crystal kosher salt, in the red box, at specialty-foods markets and many supermarkets. The sea salt I use is from the Mediterranean. Ordinary table salt includes an anti-caking agent that leaves a chemical aftertaste, so I don't use it in my kitchen. At the table, I offer a finishing salt, such as *fleur de sel*, for sprinkling on foods.

SATSUMA TANGERINES
My favorite variety in the mandarin orange family, small Japanese satsumas always feel like a gift when they first appear in the market in late November. They are sweet, seedless, and juicy and have a loose skin that is easy to peel.

SHRIMP
In the United States, shrimp is the most popular food from the sea. The sweet crustacean is divided into two broad categories, warm-water shrimp and cold-water shrimp. Within those categories are hundreds of species. From the cold northern waters come the small shrimp often referred to as bay shrimp. The most common shrimp from warm waters include gulf or Mexican whites and pinks; gulf browns; tiger shrimp; and rock shrimp. Shrimp are marketed according to size and indicate the number per pound, such as jumbo (11/15), extra large (16/20), large (21/30), medium (31/35), and small (36/45). Beyond size, shrimp are typically sold either in the shell with the tail attached and the head removed, or peeled and deveined. They are also marked either fresh or frozen. However, unless you are buying shrimp right off a boat or from a water-filled tank, almost all shrimp have been processed and flash-frozen, because they deteriorate quickly after harvesting. So, "fresh" shrimp in the market have actually been thawed prior to sale. Buy shrimp that glisten and smell clean, fresh, and "of the sea." If you smell any hint of ammonia, it means the shrimp are old and deteriorating. I prefer to buy my shrimp uncooked with the shell on. Cooking shrimp in the shell is easy and the results are more flavorful.

TURKEY
At one time, fresh or frozen was the only choice you had when it came to buying a commercially raised whole turkey. Now there are lots of choices, and quality and taste differences exist among them. Here are my thoughts on what is available in the marketplace.

Standard turkeys: These mass-produced, conventionally raised birds are sold either fresh or frozen during the holiday season. This is a perfectly acceptable turkey, easy to obtain without a lot of forethought from any large supermarket and reasonably priced.

Self-basting turkeys: Sold fresh or frozen, these turkeys have been "enhanced" with fat of some sort, in addition to natural and artificial flavorings. The theory behind this product is that the bird doesn't need to be basted, saving the cook time and energy. Good idea in theory, badly executed in practice, primarily because the enhancer is flavored vegetable oil, which I don't consider an enhancer. This is my least-favorite turkey on the market. Do not brine a self-basting turkey. These birds have already been injected with a salt solution.

Free-range turkeys: These are the turkeys that get to run around the barnyard, so to speak. They aren't necessarily raised outdoors, but they are raised in spacious, open environments. Many of them are labeled "organic" as well, and are more expensive than other turkeys. If you order from a knowledgeable butcher or have a specialty-foods store you trust, ask the staff who raises the turkeys they sell and if the birds are both free-range and organic, or just free-range. These can be delicious, moist, and flavorful birds, and I believe they are usually worth the price.

Kosher turkeys: Although usually sold frozen, these birds are often available fresh in large supermarkets at Thanksgiving and Christmas. They have been inspected,

slaughtered, and cleaned under strict rabbinical supervision, which makes for an expensive bird. If you will be serving observant Jewish guests, this is the turkey to buy; otherwise, opt for a non-kosher, free-range bird. Do not brine kosher turkeys. They have already been salted in the koshering process.

WILD RICE

Long considered the "caviar of grains," wild rice is native to North America and, despite the name, is not a true rice. The grains are long, slender, and black, with a unique nutty, almost smoky flavor. They come from a reedlike aquatic plant that was found only in the wild until relatively recently, but nowadays is naturally cultivated. Local Indians still gather wild rice by hand, paddling their canoes through the rice beds of Minnesota. Wild rice is also grown in the southern states and in rural mountain valleys in Northern California.

WINTER SQUASHES

These are squashes that are allowed to mature on the vine and are stored for winter use. The skin is hard and inedible, and the flesh needs to be cooked before eating. Hubbard, butternut, pumpkin,

delicata, and acorn are some of the more common winter squashes in the market.

YAMS

Confusion reigns in the grocery store when it comes to sweet potatoes and yams. Technically, true yams are a thick, starchy tuber native to Africa, Asia, and many parts of the Caribbean. They are unrelated to potatoes, including sweet potatoes, which are roots, not tubers. Yams are mostly found in Asian grocery stores, and rarely in traditional American supermarkets. However, when you shop for sweet potatoes in a typical grocery store, you'll find two types: yellow-fleshed labeled "sweet potatoes," and dark-skinned and orange-fleshed labeled "yams." Those dark-skinned ones are technically sweet potatoes, too, and are mostly grown in North Carolina and Louisiana. The two types can be used interchangeably; however, orange-fleshed sweet potatoes are higher in beta-carotene and sugar, so they caramelize nicely. Their yellow-fleshed counterparts are higher in starch, so they are better for baking. For the recipes in this book, I prefer Garnet yams.

special equipment + tools

Cooking for the holidays doesn't require a lot of fancy equipment, but some kitchen items will make your life easier. Following is an alphabetical list of the tools and equipment I have used to make the recipes in this book. Review the list to see what you'll need before you begin your holiday cooking and baking. Not every tool, pot, pan, or appliance has to be top-of-the-line quality, though some items are worth the extra investment because they'll last a lifetime. I mention where quality makes a difference and where spending more saves money in the long run.

For Roasting Meats and Poultry >>>

BULB BASTER
This tool certainly makes basting meat and poultry easier, but a large spoon will work in a pinch. Buy either a stainless-steel or a heat-resistant plastic baster. I prefer the latter because I can see through it. Glass basters are a mistake, as they inevitably break.

CARVING BOARD
Different from a cutting board, a carving board has a "moat" that collects meat juices and a "well" that traps them. This is handy for carving all kinds of meats and poultry. My favorite type is a wooden board that is reversible, so you can use the flat side for chopping and dicing.

CARVING KNIFE AND FORK
A carving set is lovely if you are presenting a whole bird or a whole piece of meat and carving it at the table, but it is not critical. If you don't have one, you do need a very sharp utilitarian carving knife and carving fork. After working hard to roast your holiday turkey or prime rib, you want to cut smooth, even slices. A good knife is a lifetime investment.

FINE-MESH SIEVE
Doing double-duty for cooking and baking needs, I have three sizes of fine-mesh sieves. I use the large- or medium-sized

sieve for straining stocks, soups, or sauces, depending on the volume to be strained. I use the small one for dusting confectioners' sugar over cakes, pastries, and tarts.

GRAVY STRAINER

This useful tool looks like a measuring cup with a spout that originates near the bottom. You pour in pan juices or gravy, the fat naturally rises to the top, and the relatively fat-free liquid that settles to the bottom is easily poured out through the spout. Although handy for making gravy and sauces from pan juices, this strainer is definitely not essential.

KITCHEN TWINE

Buy the proper twine to truss your bird or tie your roast. It should be 100 percent linen, which resists charring. Flimsy string won't do, and dental floss can tear the skin and chars (I've seen it used!). You'll be surprised how often you will reach for twine once it is in the kitchen.

MEAT THERMOMETER

The small-dial, thin-shaft instant-read thermometer is the most accurate way to judge the doneness of meats, poultry, and fish. You must not leave the thermometer in the food, however. Instead, you

insert it, give it a few seconds to register the temperature, and then out it comes. For safety and sanitation, always wash the thermometer before reinserting it in any food. I prefer an analog thermometer to a digital one, as the readings on digital models tend to jump wildly from one temperature to another.

OVEN THERMOMETER

If you doubt the accuracy of your oven's thermostat, buy an oven thermometer before you start cooking and baking. Once you know how far off the thermostat is, you can adjust the temperature dial accordingly. Whether your oven is brand new or old, it doesn't hurt to have an oven thermometer to double-check its accuracy.

PROBE THERMOMETER

This thermometer is made up of a probe with a thin wire connected to a transmitter. You insert the probe into the food, put the transmitter on a counter next to the oven, and program the transmitter with the desired temperature. The newest versions have a transmitter and wireless remote, so you can walk up to 120 feet away and the pager will beep when the food is done. These thermometers

are cool, but Internet reviews have been mixed. If you like reading manuals and figuring out how to program gadgets, this is the tool for you.

ROASTING PAN

These are usually about 4 inches deep and made of stainless steel or aluminum, sometimes in a nonstick finish (makes for easy cleanup). The best ones are extra heavy and have sturdy, upright handles. Measure your oven before you buy! A medium pan, about 16 by 12 by 5 inches, is adequate for a turkey weighing up to 20 pounds or even a seven-rib prime rib. The best pans cost about one hundred dollars and will last a lifetime, but for years I managed with a black-and-white-speckled, enamel-coated steel pan I bought at a hardware store for under twenty dollars. I don't recommend using disposable foil pans because they buckle easily. If you must use them, buy two for double thickness.

ROASTING RACK

A V-shaped steel rack, preferably nonstick, elevates meats and poultry for faster cooking and keeps the pan drippings away from the meat. Buy one with tall, vertical handles on two sides; they make lifting the meat much easier. The noncollapsible V-shaped racks are by far my favorite. A high-quality, medium-sized rack costs about twenty dollars. Before you buy, make certain the rack fits inside your roasting pan! A flat wire rack is a better choice for baking a ham, which is too broad for a V-shaped rack.

SERVING PLATTERS

Whether you are serving a whole turkey, goose, leg of lamb, or standing rib roast, it is important to make sure you have a platter large enough to accommodate it. You don't need to spend a fortune for a china platter. Shop at outlet stores and discount shops, where you can have fun mixing and matching serving pieces.

For Soups, Salads, and Side Dishes >>>

BAKING PANS

Count how many baking dishes you'll need for your planned menu. Usually I need at least three 9-by-13-inch baking dishes or pans. The classic clear-glass dishes are great, though I prefer the look of white porcelain. There are lots of attractive possibilities on the market, and they vary in price. Buy what fits your budget.

DUTCH OVEN

I get my upper-body workout when I lift up my 6-quart Dutch oven made of enameled cast iron. That heft is what makes it a great pot. Look for a Dutch oven with a tight-fitting lid and a heavy, flat bottom that can be used on the stove top or in the oven. This is the ideal pan for soups, stews, short ribs, and brisket.

GRATERS, PEELERS, ZESTERS, AND JUICERS

All of these handy tools make cooking and baking a lot more fun. If you don't own a rasp-like zester by Microplane, buy one. It is one of my favorite kitchen gadgets. It outperforms other tools for zesting citrus, and works well for grating whole nutmeg and Parmesan cheese. I prefer two-piece juicers, either manual or electric, because the cup part catches the juice and makes it easier to measure.

MIXING BOWLS

I require a steady supply of mixing bowls while cooking and baking for the holidays. My favorites are nesting sets made of stainless steel, though I also have a set of glass ones to use in the microwave. Stainless-steel bowls are inexpensive, easy to wash, and last a lifetime. Buy several in each size.

POTATO RICER, POTATO MASHER, OR FOOD MILL

If mashed potatoes or yams are on your holiday menu, you need to have a ricer, masher, or food mill on hand. The food mill and the ricer are the best tools for lump-free potatoes. The advantage of owning a food mill is that it is also great for puréeing fruits and vegetables. The old-fashioned masher produces a coarser mash. (If you are contemplating using a food processor, don't. You'll end up with potato glue.)

SAUTÉ PANS AND SKILLETS

When cooking for the holidays, I most often reach for my 12- and 14-inch sauté pans. Sautéing vegetables for a crowd calls for a big pan, and the 14-inch size is ideal. Buy sauté pans that come with lids and have ovenproof handles. That way, you can use them to make frittatas and other dishes that you finish under the broiler. I use my 10-inch sauté pan for sautéing aromatics. As for skillets, I reach for my 7-inch, nonstick omelet pan for toasting pine nuts, and my large cast-iron skillets for making deliciously crisp potato pancakes. It helps to have a variety of sizes and finishes. Cast iron is ideal when you want beautifully

Clockwise from far left: Small fine-mesh sieve for dusting; large fine-mesh sieve for straining; pastry bag and star tip

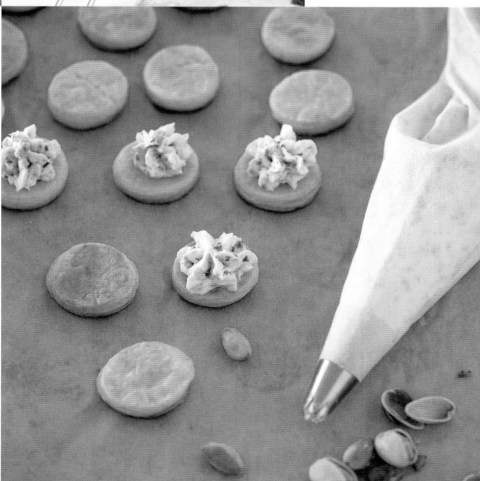

browned, seared foods. It is also inexpensive when compared to, say, All-Clad three-ply stainless-steel pans with an aluminum core.

STOCKPOT

This tall, narrow pot is used for making soups and stocks. I own a 12-quart, multiuse stockpot with a strainer insert and shallow steamer pan. It can be used for cooking pasta, too. Three-ply stain-less-steel stockpots with an aluminum core are terrific for even heating and slow simmering, but they are expensive and an investment. An inexpensive aluminum stock-pot works well, too, as long as the stocks don't contain an acidic ingredient, such as tomatoes or citrus juice.

TONGS

Tongs are an essential tool for turning foods and for moving them around in a pan. They should be about 10 inches long, strong, made of stainless steel, and ideally spring loaded. I like tongs that lock in a closed position for easy storage. OXO tongs have comfortable cushioned, non-slip handles and are rounded, rather than serrated, at the top.

WHISK

A whisk is indispensable for mixing sauces and salad dressings, whipping heavy cream for a dessert, and the like. A stainless-steel wire whisk is best because it won't rust. I have an 8-inch and a 12-inch whisk and find both sizes handy.

For Baking >>>

BUNDT PAN

A Bundt pan is a tube pan with fluted or scalloped sides. Bundt is a registered trademark for a pan created in 1950, by H. David Dalquist, the founder of Nordic Ware. Bundt pans are made of cast aluminum and have a nonstick finish. A 12-cup pan is the standard size for most cake recipes. Cakes made in the new silicone tube pans don't bake as evenly

or brown as well as they do in this classic pan.

RIMMED BAKING SHEETS

I couldn't live without my heavy, nonstick aluminum rimmed baking sheets made by Chicago Metallic's Commercial Line. They are workhorses in my kitchen for baking cookies, pastries, crackers, and the like. I buy rimmed baking sheets as opposed to classic cookie sheets because they offer the most versatility. Use a silicone heatproof spatula to lift baked items, so you don't scratch the surface of the pan.

COOLING RACKS

Have two racks on hand, or enough to cool an average batch of cookies. These don't need to be expensive; any sturdy wire rack will do.

FOOD PROCESSOR

A food processor is a time-saver all year long but especially during the holidays, when you want to make a pâté, cheese dip, pastry dough, or the like. I prefer the KitchenAid processor because the lid's safety mechanism is much simpler to use and clean. Unless you use it to make bread dough, you don't need a giant machine. The standard 11-cup model is what I have always owned, and it meets

my preparation needs. A mini–food processor is handy for chopping ginger, garlic, and similar items. It's what I use to mince all the ginger for the Gingerbread Bundt Cake with Crème Anglaise on page 137.

GRIDDLE

If your family loves pancakes, French toast, and grilled sandwiches, it is worth investing in a cast-iron griddle that fits over two burners. It heats evenly and browns food nicely. Lodge makes a preseasoned griddle that will last a lifetime.

LOAF PANS

I own glazed ceramic, shiny aluminum, and black baker's steel loaf pans. All of them bake differently. For most yeast breads, I prefer the black baker's steel pans for a rich, dark brown crust on the sides and bottom of my breads. For quick breads, such as the Apricot, Ginger, and Walnut Tea Bread on page 195, I like to use my shiny aluminum or glazed ceramic pans precisely because the sides and bottom brown nicely without darkening and forming a crust. The shiny aluminum pans are the least expensive.

MUFFIN PANS

You will need 12-cup miniature muffin pans if you plan to make

Spicy Crab in Wonton Cups (page 36) or Wild Mushroom Croustades with Caraway and Dill (page 46). Buy the shiny aluminum ones; they are inexpensive. I have four pans to make batch cooking quicker. (Don't put the pans in the dishwasher; it dulls the finish.) For the Yorkshire Pudding with Chives (page 107) and the Cranberry Muffins with Brown Sugar–Almond Streusel (page 160), you will need a 12-cup standard muffin pan. I have a nonstick muffin pan made by Chicago Metallic and prefer it over my older aluminum one.

PARCHMENT PAPER AND NONSTICK BAKING LINERS

I recommend using nonstick baking sheets, or lining a baking sheet with either parchment paper or a nonstick baking liner—Silpat is the best-known brand—to create an excellent nonstick surface. Parchment paper is less expensive, but good-quality nonstick baking liners will last for years with proper care.

PASTRY BAG AND DECORATING TIPS

If you like to decorate your baked goods for the holidays, buying a reusable waxed canvas pastry bag makes sense. You can also buy disposable pastry bags at cookware stores, decorating-supply shops, or online. Either buy individual decorating tips for hors d'oeuvres or desserts, or buy a set of tips to have for a lifetime. Ateco brand pastry tips are popular with pastry chefs and are what I use. The bakerscatalogue.com Web site is a good source for these items.

PASTRY BRUSH

Natural bristle brushes have long been the standard for pastry brushes, but silicone brushes, which are new on the market, make cleanup a snap. I have found that egg wash applied to pastries with a natural bristle brush goes on more evenly.

ROLLING PIN

For pie and tart makers, high-quality tools make baking a pleasure. Invest in a heavy, thick pin made of hardwood or marble and at least 12 inches long. It's a tool for a lifetime. American-style rolling pins have handles, while French-style pins do not. They work equally well.

SPRINGFORM PAN

This pan is great for cheesecakes and other cakes that are difficult to unmold. Springform pans come in aluminum, stainless steel, or nonstick. I prefer the aluminum ones. For this book, you will need a 9- or 10-inch pan with 2-inch sides.

STAND MIXER

I've had my KitchenAid stand mixer made by Hobart for almost thirty years. It is sturdy, heavy, and dependable. I bought an extra mixing bowl and an extra whip attachment, so I could swap out a used bowl or beater without needing to stop and wash the dirty one. This is especially helpful if you are making a cake that requires the yolks and whites to be beaten separately. The new KitchenAid mixers are being manufactured in China and don't seem to be as dependable as the old ones, so it is worth looking at other brands. A good mixer should be a lifetime investment. That said, you can get by with a handheld mixer for all of the recipes in the book.

TART PANS

Before you start baking, check the recipe to make sure you have the correct-sized pan. I keep 9- and 11-inch ones on hand. The traditional aluminum tart pans with removable bottoms are the best for even browning. When ready to serve dessert, slip off the sides of the pan, slide the tart off the base onto a pedestal cake stand, and you have a buffet-ready presentation.

1 seasonal hors d'oeuvres + holiday drinks

Welcome your holiday guests with the ambrosial scent of ginger and sweet apples as you hand them a steaming hot toddy or a cup of spice-infused wassail. They'll be hungry, too, and here's a collection of treasured seasonal hors d'oeuvres that are sure to please both them (delicious) and you (plenty of do-ahead tips and recipes that freeze well). ❋ For an open house, make several of the recipes and add some store-bought additions, such as cured meats for a charcuterie plate, assorted cheeses and breads, and pickled and fresh vegetables for a crudité platter. For a cocktail hour before dinner, select two or three appetizers and add assortments of olives and nuts. Enjoy tempting palates with Spicy Crab in Wonton Cups, Wild Mushroom Croustades with Caraway and Dill, or Pistachio and Chive Goat Cheese on Puff Pastry Wafers.

spicy crab in wonton cups

The flavor of fresh crabmeat is so good on its own that my primary goal in developing this hors d'oeuvre was to use a minimum of ingredients. I wanted to highlight the crab flavor and texture, not mask it. Although I keep a jar of *sambal ulek*—an Indonesian hot chile paste—in my refrigerator at all times, I thought it might be too obscure to use in this recipe. When I went shopping to buy *sambal ulek*, my Asian market was out of stock, but my local supermarket had it in the Asian-foods section—yours probably will, too.

WONTON CUPS
20 WONTON WRAPPERS (FROM ONE 14-OUNCE PACKAGE), EACH CUT INTO 3-INCH SQUARES
3 TABLESPOONS ASIAN SESAME OIL

CRAB FILLING
8 OUNCES FRESH-COOKED CRABMEAT, PICKED OVER FOR SHELLS AND WELL DRAINED
1/4 CUP MAYONNAISE
1 TEASPOON MINCED FRESH CILANTRO
1 TEASPOON SNIPPED FRESH CHIVES
1/4 TEASPOON FRESHLY GRATED LEMON ZEST
1/4 TEASPOON *SAMBAL ULEK* (SEE COOK'S NOTE), OR MORE TO TASTE
20 LITTLE FRESH CILANTRO LEAVES FOR GARNISH

To make the wonton cups, position a rack in the center of the oven. Preheat the oven to 350°F. Have ready two 12-cup miniature muffin pans. Working with wonton wrappers at a time, brush the top side of each wrapper with sesame oil, and press, oiled side down, into a muffin cup. Repeat with the remaining wrappers. Brush the bottom of each wonton cup with a little sesame oil. Bake until the wontons are golden brown, about 10 minutes. Let cool completely in the tins, then remove carefully. Store in a tightly covered container at room temperature until ready to fill. (The cups can be made up to 2 days ahead.)

To make the crab filling, place the crabmeat in a medium bowl and use your fingers to flake the crabmeat. Using a rubber spatula, gently stir in the mayonnaise, minced cilantro, chives, lemon zest, and *sambal ulek*. Taste and adjust the seasoning, adding a bit more *sambal ulek*, if desired. Cover and refrigerate until ready to fill the wonton cups. (The crab filling can be made up to 1 day ahead.)

To assemble and serve, place the wonton cups on a serving platter. Spoon about 2 teaspoons of the crab filling into each cup, and garnish with a cilantro leaf.

Makes 20

COOK'S NOTE
Sambal ulek, *also spelled* sambal oelek, *is an Indonesian condiment made from chiles, salt, vinegar, and sometimes garlic and tamarind. Sold in jars, it is a fiery paste with bright flavors—a little goes a long way. Other Asian chile pastes with garlic can be substituted, but this one is a favorite of mine. If refrigerated after opening, it will keep indefinitely.*

blue cheese pastry buttons

When I am developing recipes and thinking up menu ideas, I often reflect on memorable meals I have had in restaurants. Sometimes, for inspiration, I open my restaurant journal and look at the notes I've taken and the pictures I've drawn. While coming up with appetizers for this book, I thought back to the delightful *amuse-bouche* I ate years ago when my husband and I lived in Chicago. One cold December night, we splurged on a celebratory dinner at Le Perroquet, and the "gifts from the kitchen" were these savory shortbreads topped with a blue-cheese butter rosette.

2/3 CUP UNBLEACHED ALL-PURPOSE FLOUR, PLUS MORE FOR DUSTING

1/2 TEASPOON KOSHER OR SEA SALT

1/8 TEASPOON FRESHLY GROUND PEPPER

3 TABLESPOONS UNSALTED BUTTER, CHILLED AND CUT INTO SMALL CUBES

2/3 CUP (ABOUT 3 OUNCES) GRATED SHARP CHEDDAR CHEESE

3 TABLESPOONS SOUR CREAM

BLUE CHEESE BUTTER

1/2 CUP CRUMBLED BLUE CHEESE, AT ROOM TEMPERATURE

2 TABLESPOONS UNSALTED BUTTER, AT ROOM TEMPERATURE

In the work bowl of a food processor fitted with the metal blade, combine the flour, salt, and pepper. Pulse to combine. Scatter the butter, Cheddar cheese, and sour cream over the flour mixture and pulse just until the mixture begins to form a ball. Remove from the work bowl, flatten into a disk between 2 sheets of plastic wrap, and refrigerate for 45 minutes.

Position 1 rack in the center and another rack in the lower third of the oven. Preheat the oven to 350°F. Have ready 2 rimmed baking sheets, preferably nonstick. For pans without a nonstick finish, line the pans with parchment paper or use nonstick baking liners.

While the dough is chilling, make the blue cheese butter. Wipe the work bowl of the food processor clean with a paper towel. Combine the blue cheese and butter in the work bowl and process until well combined. Remove to a small bowl and reserve. (The blue cheese butter can be made up to 2 days in advance and refrigerated in a covered container. Bring to room temperature before using.)

To shape the pastry buttons, lightly dust a work surface with flour. Lightly dust the top of the dough with flour. Using a rolling pin, roll out the pastry 1/8 inch thick. Use a 1 1/2-inch round fluted cookie cutter to cut out the crackers. Gather up the scraps, reroll the dough, and cut out more crackers. Place the crackers about 1/2 inch apart on the prepared baking sheets. Use a fork to prick the dough all over before baking.

Bake the crackers, switching the pans between the racks and rotating them 180 degrees halfway through baking, until lightly browned on the bottom, 10 to 12 minutes. Remove the crackers to wire racks to cool. Store the crackers in an airtight container at room temperature until serving. (The crackers can be made up to 3 days ahead, but will taste freshest if you rebake them for 3 minutes on the day you serve them.)

To assemble the hors d'oeuvres, spoon the room-temperature blue cheese butter into a pastry bag fitted with a small open star tip and pipe a small rosette in the center of each cracker. Arrange on a serving tray and serve at room temperature.

Makes 60

sake oyster shooters

You'll need twelve to twenty-four 4- to 5-ounce oversized shot glasses for serving this appetizer. I bought inexpensive contemporary shot glasses at a restaurant supply house near where I live. They make a festive statement when passed on a tray at a cocktail party, and if your guests are anything like mine, they'll come into the kitchen looking for refills. I've found many other ways to use these glasses for entertaining, such as filling them with cold soup in the summer for appetizer "soup shots," serving miniature portions of chocolate pudding topped with a whipped cream rosette, and turning my brunch oyster shooters into Bloody Mary shooters with oysters and a tiny celery stick.

1 1/2 TEASPOONS WASABI POWDER

1 TABLESPOON WATER

1 JAR (8 FLUID OUNCES) YEARLING-SIZED FRESH OYSTERS (ABOUT 24)

2 TABLESPOONS FINELY SNIPPED FRESH CHIVES

1/3 CUP VERY FINELY DICED ENGLISH CUCUMBER

1 BOTTLE (750 MILLILITERS) SAKE, ICE COLD

In a small bowl, combine the wasabi powder and water and stir until smooth. Set aside.

For each shooter, put 1 oyster in a shot glass and top with about 1/8 teaspoon wasabi mixture, 1/4 teaspoon chives, and 3/4 teaspoon diced cucumber. Pour 1 ounce sake over the top. Serve immediately.

Makes 24

pistachio and chive goat cheese on puff pastry wafers

The better the goat cheese, the better the spread. Look for artisanal and farmstead goat cheeses—almost every farmers' market I've been to has some local purveyors. However, please don't think that commercial goat cheeses won't work. I developed this recipe using several different supermarket brands and all were good. I prefer to buy pistachios in the shell because they are fresher, and it seems to me that shelling your own is ample justification for the cook to munch a few. Take off any loose pistachio skins while you're at it. I like to pipe a rosette of goat cheese on top of each wafer for a festive look, but it works equally well (and certainly tastes as great) to place a teaspoonful dab on each wafer with a butter knife.

PUFF PASTRY WAFERS

1 SHEET FROZEN PUFF PASTRY DOUGH, FROM A 17.3-OUNCE PACKAGE ($1/2$ PACKAGE)

ALL-PURPOSE FLOUR FOR DUSTING

1 LARGE EGG, BEATEN

PISTACHIO AND CHIVE GOAT CHEESE TOPPING

1 CLOVE GARLIC

$1/4$ TEASPOON KOSHER OR SEA SALT

5 OUNCES FRESH GOAT CHEESE, AT ROOM TEMPERATURE

3 TABLESPOONS UNSALTED BUTTER, AT ROOM TEMPERATURE

$1/3$ CUP SHELLED NATURAL PISTACHIO NUTS, FINELY CHOPPED

3 TABLESPOONS SNIPPED FRESH CHIVES

FRESHLY GROUND PEPPER

35 SHELLED NATURAL PISTACHIO NUTS FOR GARNISH

Remove 1 pastry sheet from the puff pastry package and thaw at room temperature for 30 minutes. Tightly seal the remaining pastry sheet and return it to the freezer for another use. (Or, double the recipe and make 70 pastry wafers.) Position a rack in the center of the oven. Preheat the oven to 425°F. Have ready 2 identically sized rimmed baking sheets. Line 1 pan with parchment paper, and have ready a second sheet of parchment paper the same size.

Unfold the pastry sheet and place it on a lightly floured cutting board. Using a rolling pin, roll the pastry just enough to remove the fold marks. Using a 1$3/4$-inch round cookie cutter, cut out about 35 rounds. Place the rounds on the parchment-lined baking sheet. Brush the tops of the rounds with the beaten egg, being careful the egg doesn't run down the sides. Cover with the second sheet of parchment, and place the second (empty) baking sheet on top, so the baking sheets nest together. (This will keep the pastry even and prevent it from rising too much, creating crisp wafers.) Bake until crisp and light golden brown, about 15 minutes. Remove the top baking sheet and piece of parchment and let the wafers cool on the pan on a wire rack. (The wafers can >>>

pistachio and chive goat cheese on puff pastry wafers
CONTINUED

be made up to 1 day in advance and stored in an airtight container at room temperature.)

To make the goat cheese topping, combine the garlic and salt in the work bowl of a food processor fitted with the metal blade and process until the garlic is finely minced. Add the goat cheese and butter and process until well mixed and smooth. Scatter the nuts and chives over the top, add a few grinds of pepper, and pulse 2 or 3 times until combined. Taste and adjust the seasoning. (The goat cheese spread can be made up to 2 days in advance, covered, and stored in the refrigerator. Remove from the refrigerator 1 hour before piping or spreading on the wafers.)

To assemble the hors d'oeuvres, spoon the goat cheese topping into a pastry bag fitted with a $5/8$-inch open star tip and pipe a rosette onto the center of each wafer. Alternatively, use a butter knife to apply a delicate dab of the goat cheese topping to the top of each wafer. Top each rosette or dab with a pistachio. Arrange on a platter and serve at room temperature.

Makes 35

cucumber cups with smoked salmon and chive pâté

These delicate and refreshing hors d'oeuvres look chic passed on an elegant tray. This is the time of the year that I pull out my silver trays, inherited from my grandmother or received as wedding gifts, and polish them for holiday entertaining. (Actually, my husband does the polishing and enjoys the chore. Lucky me!) Line the tray with some long sprigs of dill or a banana leaf (often sold fresh or frozen in Asian or Latin American grocery stores). The contrast of the dark green leaf against the sparkling silver is the perfect backdrop for these glistening cucumber cups filled with creamy pink salmon pâté flecked with minced chives and dill. All you need is a glass of Champagne!

5 OUNCES FRESH GOAT CHEESE, AT ROOM TEMPERATURE

4 OUNCES SMOKED SALMON (LOX), CHOPPED

1/4 CUP HEAVY (WHIPPING) CREAM

PINCH OF CAYENNE PEPPER

3 TABLESPOONS SNIPPED FRESH CHIVES

1 TEASPOON MINCED FRESH DILL

2 ENGLISH CUCUMBERS, ENDS TRIMMED

36 TINY SPRIGS FRESH DILL FOR GARNISH (OPTIONAL)

To make the salmon pâté, in the work bowl of a food processor fitted with the metal blade, combine the goat cheese, salmon, cream, and cayenne and process to form a smooth paste. Transfer to a small bowl and use a rubber spatula to mix in the chives and minced dill. Set aside while you form the cucumber cups. (The salmon pâté can be made up to 2 days in advance and refrigerated in a covered container. Remove from the refrigerator 45 minutes before piping the rosettes.)

To make the cucumber cups, cut the cucumbers crosswise into 1/2-inch-thick slices. Using a 1 1/2-inch fluted pastry cutter, flute each slice to create an attractive edge and at the same time remove the skin. Using a small melon baller, scoop out the center of each slice to make a cup, leaving a 1/4-inch-thick layer as a base. Blot the cucumber cups with paper towels. (The cups can be arranged in layers in a covered container lined with a double thickness of paper towels and refrigerated for up to 1 day.)

To assemble the cucumber cups, place the salmon pâté in a pastry bag fitted with a 1/2-inch open star tip and pipe a rosette into each cucumber cup. Garnish with a tiny sprig of dill, and arrange on a serving platter. Serve immediately, or cover loosely with plastic wrap and refrigerate for up to 1 hour.

Makes about 36

polenta crostini with fig and kalamata olive tapenade

Quick-cooking polenta poured into a loaf pan and chilled turns into delectable crostini when sliced, cut into squares, and then broiled. The crisp corn base makes an enticing counterpoint to the rich, savory fig and Kalamata olive tapenade. This appetizer is ideal for holiday entertaining, because both the polenta and the tapenade can be made in advance. It also takes no time to unmold, slice, and broil the crostini, and that, too, can be done a couple of hours ahead. If you are pressed for time, skip making the fig tapenade (though it is wonderfully delicious) and buy a prepared topping. A favorite is Stonewall Kitchen's Sun-Dried Tomato and Olive Relish.

POLENTA CROSTINI

OLIVE-OIL COOKING SPRAY

3 CUPS WATER

1 CUP INSTANT POLENTA

1 TEASPOON KOSHER OR SEA SALT

1/2 TEASPOON FRESHLY GROUND PEPPER

1/4 CUP FRESHLY GRATED PARMESAN CHEESE, PREFERABLY PARMIGIANO-REGGIANO

2 TABLESPOONS EXTRA-VIRGIN OLIVE OIL

FIG TAPENADE

1 1/2 CUPS STEMMED AND FINELY CHOPPED DRIED BLACK MISSION FIGS

1/2 CUP WATER

1/2 CUP KALAMATA OLIVES, PITTED AND CHOPPED

1/3 CUP PINE NUTS, TOASTED (SEE COOK'S NOTE, FACING PAGE)

2 TABLESPOONS BALSAMIC VINEGAR

2 TABLESPOONS EXTRA-VIRGIN OLIVE OIL

2 TABLESPOONS SMALL CAPERS, RINSED AND BLOTTED DRY

1 1/2 TABLESPOONS CHOPPED FRESH OREGANO

1/2 TEASPOON KOSHER OR SEA SALT

1/2 TEASPOON FRESHLY GROUND PEPPER

To make the polenta crostini, generously grease an 8 1/2-by-4 1/2-inch loaf pan with olive-oil cooking spray. Set aside.

In a 2 1/2-quart saucepan over medium heat, bring the water to a boil. Stir in the polenta, salt and pepper and continue to stir constantly until the polenta has thickened, 5 to 7 minutes. Adjust the heat to low if the polenta is bubbling too vigorously. Remove from the heat and stir in the Parmesan cheese. Pour the polenta into the prepared loaf pan and smooth the top so it is level. Place a sheet of plastic wrap directly over the polenta to prevent a skin from forming. Set aside until cool, and then refrigerate for at least 2 hours to allow the polenta to firm up. (The polenta can be made up to 2 days in advance.)

To make the fig tapenade, place the figs and water in a small saucepan and bring to a simmer over medium-low heat. Cook until the figs have softened and the liquid has evaporated, about 7 minutes. Transfer the figs to a medium bowl. Add the olives, pine nuts, vinegar, olive oil, capers, oregano, salt, and pepper. Mix gently to combine. Transfer to a serving bowl, cover, and set aside at room temperature for 1 hour to allow the flavors to meld. (The tapenade can be prepared up to 5 days in advance, covered, and stored in the refrigerator. Remove from the refrigerator 45 minutes before topping the crostini.)

To finish the crostini, position an oven rack 4 inches below the heat source and preheat the broiler. Unmold the polenta onto a cutting board, and cut crosswise into 1/3-inch-thick slices. Cut each slice into thirds to form rectangles. Arrange the pieces on a rimmed baking sheet and brush the tops with the olive oil. Broil until lightly golden and crisp, 3 to 5 minutes. Let cool to room temperature before topping. (The polenta crostini can be broiled up to 3 hours before serving. Set aside at room temperature.)

To assemble and serve, place the polenta crostini on a large platter. Spoon a small dollop of the fig tapenade in the center of each rectangle. Serve immediately, or cover and set aside at room temperature for up to 45 minutes.

Makes about 75

COOK'S NOTE
To toast the pine nuts, place a small, heavy skillet over medium–high heat. When it is hot but not smoking, add the pine nuts and toast, stirring constantly, until nicely browned, 3 to 5 minutes. Transfer to a plate and set aside to cool.

wild mushroom croustades with caraway and dill

Croustades are petite French toasted bread cups that hold savory fillings—ideal for holiday entertaining. In one bite you taste a robust indulgence of diced wild mushrooms sautéed with a little onion, flavored with fresh herbs and caraway, and swirled with a touch of cream. I like to mix cremini mushrooms with shiitake, chanterelle, or oyster mushrooms, depending on what is available at the market. If any of the mushroom filling is left over, add it to risotto or use it as an omelet filling. Once you've made the croustades and see how easy they are to form and bake, create your own fillings, such as caramelized onion, Chinese-inspired shrimp and green onion, or artichoke and Parmesan. I love the mushroom filling with whole-wheat croustades, but using a simple white bread is the most traditional.

CROUSTADES
24 THIN SLICES SOFT WHOLE-WHEAT BREAD
(SEE COOK'S NOTE, FACING PAGE)
1/2 CUP (1 STICK) UNSALTED BUTTER, MELTED

MUSHROOM FILLING
1/4 CUP PURE OLIVE OIL

1 SMALL YELLOW ONION, MINCED

1 1/2 TEASPOONS CARAWAY SEEDS

1 1/4 POUNDS ASSORTED WILD AND CULTIVATED
MUSHROOMS SUCH AS CREMINI, SHIITAKE,
AND CHANTERELLE, IN ANY COMBINATION,
WIPED OR BRUSHED CLEAN, STEMS TRIMMED,
AND CAPS FINELY CHOPPED

1 1/2 TEASPOONS KOSHER OR SEA SALT

FRESHLY GROUND PEPPER

2 TABLESPOONS MINCED FRESH FLAT-LEAF PARSLEY

1 TABLESPOON MINCED FRESH DILL

1 TEASPOON MINCED FRESH THYME LEAVES

1/2 CUP HEAVY (WHIPPING) CREAM

48 TINY SPRIGS FRESH DILL FOR GARNISH
(OPTIONAL)

To make the croustades, position 1 rack in the center and another rack in the lower third of the oven. Preheat the oven to 400°F. Have ready four 12-cup miniature muffin pans. (If you only have 2 miniature muffin pans, make the croustades in 2 batches.)

Using a rolling pin, roll out the bread slices thinly. (You want to flatten the bread without tearing or squishing it.) Using a 2 1/2-inch round biscuit cutter, cut out 2 rounds from each slice. (Save the leftover pieces for croutons or bread crumbs, if desired.) Lightly brush each bread round with melted butter. Press the bread rounds into the muffin cups, buttered side down, so they fit snugly and the bottoms are flat. The top edges will be pleated. Bake the croustades, switching the pans between the racks and rotating them 180 degrees halfway through baking, until completely dried, crisp, and the top edges are golden brown, 17 to 20 minutes. Let cool in the pans on wire racks, then remove from the pans. (The croustades can be made up to 3 days in advance and stored in an airtight container at room temperature.)

To make the mushroom filling, in a large skillet over medium-high heat, warm the olive oil and swirl to coat the pan. Add the onion and sauté until just beginning to soften, about 3 minutes. Add the caraway seeds and stir constantly until fragrant, about 1 minute. Add the mushrooms and sauté, stirring frequently, until they just begin to soften, about 2 minutes. Add the salt and a few grinds of pepper and continue to sauté until the mushrooms give off their juices, about 5 minutes longer. Add the parsley, minced dill, thyme, and cream to the pan and cook, stirring constantly, until the liquids are almost evaporated, 1 to 2 minutes longer.

Remove from the heat. (The filling can be used immediately or cooled, covered, and refrigerated for up to 3 days. Warm the mushroom mixture before filling the croustades.)

To assemble and serve the croustades, place the croustades on a serving platter. Spoon a rounded teaspoon of the warm mushroom filling into each cup. Garnish each cup with a dill sprig.

Makes 48

COOK'S NOTE

What you need to make these croustades is supermarket whole-wheat bread—nothing fancy here, just bread with a soft texture and crust. Once rolled, brushed with butter, and baked, the bread cups firm up and make cute, crisp shells perfect for holding the savory mushroom filling.

merry bloody mary with a fennel salt rim

Here's my favorite brunch drink to serve along with Gravlax (page 155), buttered pumpernickel or toasted bagels, and condiment bowls filled with diced shallots, cucumbers, capers, and dill. The fennel salt is the secret ingredient that sets this drink apart.

FENNEL SALT (SEE COOK'S NOTE)

1 LEMON WEDGE

ICE CUBES

2 OUNCES (1/4 CUP) ABSOLUT PEPPAR VODKA

4 OUNCES (1/2 CUP) TOMATO JUICE

1/4 TEASPOON EXTRA-HOT PREPARED HORSERADISH

2 DASHES OF WORCESTERSHIRE SAUCE

CELERY STICK WITH LEAFY TOP

Spread a little fennel salt on a small saucer. Rub the rim of a highball glass with the lemon wedge, and then invert the glass onto the fennel salt to coat the rim. Fill the glass with ice. Reserve the lemon wedge.

Fill a cocktail shaker with ice and add the vodka, tomato juice, horseradish, and Worcestershire sauce. Cover, shake vigorously, and then strain into the prepared glass. Squeeze the lemon wedge over the drink, and then drop it in. Garnish with the celery stick. Serve immediately.

Serves 1

COOK'S NOTE

Fennel salt is available at specialty markets and kitchenware stores selling gourmet ingredients. To make your own, toast 1 tablespoon fennel seeds in a small, dry skillet over medium-low heat until fragrant, then pour onto a plate and let cool. In a spice grinder or a mortar, grind the fennel seeds until finely ground. Mix the ground fennel with 3 tablespoons fine sea salt.

wassail bowl

"Here we come a-wassailing among the leaves so green." Wassail-themed songs were once sung by winter carolers, walking from house to house, singing joyfully to their neighbors in exchange for small gifts, food, or a drink—in particular, wassail, a traditional English beverage that dates to the thirteenth century. It blends aromatic spices with honey or sugar, a touch of citrus, and cider, ale, or wine. There are a multitude of variations, including wassail with sherry, Madeira, or brandy. Some recipes include roasted apples, others do not. I like to float delicate-flavored roasted Lady apples on top. I prefer my wassail a bit sweeter and less bitter, so I include pale ale and apple cider and leave out the sherry.

12 TO 14 LADY APPLES, UNPEELED AND LEFT WHOLE

1 TEASPOON GROUND ALLSPICE

1 TEASPOON GROUND CINNAMON

1/2 TEASPOON GROUND CLOVES

1/2 TEASPOON GROUND GINGER

1/4 TEASPOON FRESHLY GRATED NUTMEG

1/2 CUP PACKED GOLDEN BROWN SUGAR

JUICE AND SPIRAL PEEL OF 1 ORANGE

JUICE AND SPIRAL PEEL OF 1 LEMON

1/2 CUP HOT WATER

4 BOTTLES (12 OUNCES EACH) PALE ALE

4 CUPS APPLE CIDER

Position a rack in the center of the oven. Preheat the oven to 375°F. Place the apples in a shallow pan and bake just until tender when pierced with a knife tip, about 12 minutes. Set aside.

In a large non-aluminum pot, combine the spices, brown sugar, orange and lemon juice, orange and lemon peels, and hot water. Bring to a simmer over medium heat and cook for 10 minutes to infuse the flavors. Add the ale and cider and cook until steaming hot, but do not boil.

Place the apples in a heatproof punch bowl or a slow cooker. Ladle the wassail over the top and serve hot.

Makes 2 1/2 quarts; serves 12 to 14

ginger and apple hot toddy

Frigid temperatures and cold hands require a restorative rush of warmth. Cupping a warm mug filled with a steaming, bourbon-laced drink of ginger-infused apple cider quickly comforts and satisfies. All you need are a glowing fire and good friends.

6 CUPS APPLE CIDER

3 TABLESPOONS PEELED AND MINCED FRESH GINGER

2/3 CUP BOURBON

6 CINNAMON STICKS, EACH ABOUT 4 INCHES LONG

1 CRISP APPLE, CORED AND CUT CROSSWISE INTO 6 SLICES

In a 2½-quart saucepan over medium-high heat, combine the cider and ginger. Bring to a boil and remove from the heat. Set aside to steep for 30 minutes. Strain through a fine-mesh sieve.

To serve, bring the infused cider to a simmer, add the bourbon, stir well, and divide among 6 warmed mugs. To garnish each mug, slide a cinnamon stick through the hole in the center of each apple slice, centering the slice on the stick. Balance the cinnamon stick across the rim of the mug, so part of the apple slice is immersed in the drink. Serve immediately.

Serves 6

pomegranate martini

A perfect balance of sweet and tart, and blushed with color. Bring out the seasonal joy of fresh pomegranates with a garnish of fresh ruby-red seeds.

SUPERFINE SUGAR

1 LEMON WEDGE

2 OUNCES (1/4 CUP) CITRUS VODKA

1 OUNCE (2 TABLESPOONS) POMEGRANATE JUICE

1/4 OUNCE (1 1/2 TEASPOONS) FRESH LEMON JUICE

1/2 TEASPOON GRENADINE

6 POMEGRANATE SEEDS

LEMON TWIST

Spread a little superfine sugar on a small saucer. Rub the rim of a martini glass with the lemon wedge, and then invert the glass onto the sugar to coat the rim. Discard the wedge.

Fill a cocktail shaker with ice and add the vodka, pomegranate juice, lemon juice, and grenadine. Cover, shake vigorously, and then strain into the prepared glass. Garnish with the pomegranate seeds and lemon twist.

Serves 1

blood orange mimosa

Bring together the juice of glorious blood oranges that arrive in the market in December with Champagne and a hint of orange liqueur and you can say, "Here's to Christmas brunch."

1 OUNCE (2 TABLESPOONS) FRESH
BLOOD ORANGE JUICE

1/4 OUNCE (1 1/2 TEASPOONS) MANDARINE
NAPOLÉON LIQUEUR OR TRIPLE SEC

5 OUNCES (2/3 CUP) CHILLED BRUT CHAMPAGNE

BLOOD ORANGE TWIST

Pour the blood orange juice and the liqueur into a Champagne flute. Tilt the flute and very carefully add the Champagne. Twist the blood orange peel over the drink, and then drop it in. Serve immediately.

Serves 1

2 soups, chowders + salads

Imagine a steaming bowl of soup—hale and hearty or light and delicate—accompanied by wintry greens ablaze with pomegranate seeds and satsuma tangerines. It's a picture-perfect meal for a holiday decorating party or a caroling get-together, or the ideal pick-me-up after hours of wrapping and of writing your annual Christmas letter! Many cultural traditions feature stews and soups for Christmas Eve supper, and the Saffron-Scented Fish Stew included here will transport you to Italy, I promise.

saffron-scented fish stew

This recipe comes from Domenica Marchetti, my friend, colleague, and author of the cookbook *The Glorious Soups and Stews of Italy*. I made this fish stew for my family for Christmas Eve dinner and everyone loved the full flavors, yet lightness, of the meal. I chopped the vegetables, peeled the shrimp, cut the lobster meat from the shells, and prepared the seafood broth early in the day. This advance preparation streamlined the work of finishing the stew at dinnertime.

1/2 CUP EXTRA-VIRGIN OLIVE OIL

5 CLOVES GARLIC, LIGHTLY CRUSHED WITH THE FLAT SIDE OF A KNIFE

1 CARROT, PEELED AND COARSELY CHOPPED

1 RIB CELERY, TRIMMED AND COARSELY CHOPPED

1 SMALL YELLOW ONION, COARSELY CHOPPED

1 CUP COARSELY CHOPPED FRESH FLAT-LEAF PARSLEY, INCLUDING STEMS, PLUS 2 TABLESPOONS FINELY MINCED, LEAVES ONLY

2 SMALL LOBSTER TAILS, REMOVED FROM THEIR SHELLS (SEE COOK'S NOTE, PAGE 58), CUT INTO 2-INCH CHUNKS, AND SHELLS WASHED AND RESERVED

16 LARGE (21/30 COUNT) UNCOOKED SHRIMP, PEELED AND DEVEINED, SHELLS WASHED AND RESERVED

1 3/4 CUPS DRY WHITE WINE

4 CUPS WATER

KOSHER OR SEA SALT

GENEROUS PINCH OF SAFFRON THREADS (ABOUT 1/2 TEASPOON)

1/4 TEASPOON RED PEPPER FLAKES, OR MORE TO TASTE

2 CUPS CANNED WHOLE TOMATOES, DRAINED AND COARSELY CHOPPED OR COARSELY CRUSHED WITH A POTATO MASHER OR FORK

2 POUNDS FIRM, MEATY WHITE FISH FILLETS OR STEAKS SUCH AS COD, HAKE, GROUPER, MONKFISH, OR RED SNAPPER, CUT INTO 2-INCH CHUNKS

18 LITTLENECK OR OTHER SMALL CLAMS, THOROUGHLY CLEANED

18 MUSSELS, THOROUGHLY CLEANED

6 OR 12 SLICES BRUSCHETTA (SEE COOK'S NOTE, PAGE 58)

To make the shellfish broth, in a saucepan, heat 1/4 cup of the olive oil over medium heat. Stir in 2 cloves of the garlic, the carrot, the celery, and the onion and sauté for 5 minutes, or until the vegetables have softened. Add the coarsely chopped parsley and the lobster and shrimp shells and cook, stirring occasionally, until the shells start to change color, about 2 minutes. Increase the heat to medium-high and pour in 1 cup of the wine. Boil until some of the wine evaporates, about 2 minutes. Pour in the water, add about 1 teaspoon salt, and bring to a boil. Reduce the heat to medium and let the stock simmer for 30 to 40 minutes to develop the flavor. Taste for salt and adjust the seasoning.

Drain the broth through a fine-mesh sieve lined with damp cheesecloth placed over a bowl. Discard the solids and return the broth to the saucepan. You should have 2 to 2 1/2 cups. Bring to a gentle boil over medium heat and reduce the broth further, to about 1 1/2 cups. Cover the broth to keep it hot while you prepare the stew (reheat on low if necessary).

To make the stew, put the saffron threads in a small bowl and stir in 3 tablespoons of the hot broth. Let the mixture sit, stirring once >>>

or twice, until the saffron threads have dissolved, 10 to 15 minutes.

In a large Dutch oven or other heavy-bottomed pot with a lid, heat the remaining 1/4 cup olive oil over medium heat. Add the remaining 3 garlic cloves and the red pepper flakes and sauté for a minute or two, or until the garlic releases its fragrance. Pour in the tomatoes, the remaining 3/4 cup wine, the remaining reduced shellfish broth, and the diluted saffron. Bring to a boil, adjust the heat so the mixture simmers, and simmer for a couple of minutes to allow the flavors to mingle.

Add all of the seafood to the pot except the mussels and shrimp. Cover and simmer until at least half of the clams have opened and the fish is opaque at the center when tested with a knife tip, 8 to 10 minutes. As the mixture cooks, carefully stir once or twice and reduce the heat to medium-low if it is simmering too hard. Add the mussels and shrimp to the pot, re-cover, and cook until all the clams have opened, the mussels have opened, and the shrimp are pink and opaque throughout, about 5 minutes longer. Sprinkle on the minced parsley and stir to incorporate. The more tender fin fish, such as hake, will have flaked apart, thickening the broth. Discard any clams or mussels that failed to open.

Place 1 or 2 slices of bruschetta in the bottom of each shallow bowl. Ladle the stew over the bread, making sure that each bowl contains a good mix of fish and shellfish.

Serves 6 as a main course

COOK'S NOTES

To remove the lobster meat from a tail shell, make a vertical cut through the softer underside of the shell from top to bottom and pry it open a little bit to loosen the meat. Use your fingers or a small fork to push the meat from the bottom through the top opening of the shell. ❋ *To make bruschetta, cut a 1-pound loaf of country-style bread crosswise into 3/4-inch-thick slices. In a small bowl, stir together 1/2 cup extra-virgin olive oil and 1 large clove garlic, finely minced. Arrange the bread slices in a single layer on a rimmed baking sheet and generously brush them on both sides with the garlic olive oil. Preheat a stove-top grill pan or a broiler. Grill or broil the bread slices, turning once, until they are slightly charred around the edges and are golden brown in the middle, about 4 minutes. Serve hot or warm.*

wild salmon chowder with leeks and celery root

I enjoy cooking with seasonal vegetables, which is why I chose celery root rather than potatoes for this recipe (see page 20 for more information on celery root). Serve this hearty chowder as the main course for a casual supper when hosting a holiday decorating party or gathering a crowd before an evening of Christmas caroling. I arrange big mugs of the steaming soup on a tray and put out a green salad or crudités and a dip and baskets filled with crusty bread and dinner rolls. To keep things simple, a week before the party, I bake a batch of Fudgy Chocolate Walnut Brownies (page 177) and freeze them. Pull them from the freezer a few hours before the party and arrange them on a tray for an instant bite-size dessert.

3 STRIPS BACON, CUT INTO 1/2-INCH DICE

3 LEEKS, WHITE AND LIGHT GREEN PART ONLY, HALVED LENGTHWISE AND CUT CROSSWISE INTO 1/4-INCH-THICK SLICES

1 LARGE CELERY ROOT (ABOUT 1 1/2 POUNDS), PEELED, HALVED, AND CUT INTO 1/4-INCH-THICK SLICES

3 CUPS BOTTLED CLAM JUICE

1 BAY LEAF

3 SPRIGS FRESH THYME

1 SALMON FILLET, 12 OUNCES, SKIN AND PIN BONES REMOVED AND CUT INTO BITE-SIZE PIECES

1 1/2 CUPS HALF-AND-HALF

1 TABLESPOON CHOPPED FRESH TARRAGON

2 TABLESPOONS CHOPPED FRESH FLAT-LEAF PARSLEY

2 TEASPOONS FRESH LEMON JUICE

KOSHER OR SEA SALT

FRESHLY GROUND PEPPER

In a heavy soup pot over medium-high heat, cook the bacon until crisp, about 5 minutes. Using a slotted spoon, transfer the bacon to a plate lined with paper towels to drain. Pour off all but 2 tablespoons of the fat from the pot.

Return the pot to medium-low heat, add the leeks, and sauté, stirring frequently, until softened but not brown, about 5 minutes. Add the celery root, clam juice, bay leaf, and thyme. Bring to a boil, reduce the heat to low, cover, and simmer until the celery root is tender, about 15 minutes.

Add the salmon, bacon, half-and-half, tarragon, and parsley to the soup pot. Cook just below a simmer until the salmon is cooked through, about 5 minutes. (The half-and-half will curdle if the soup comes to a boil.)

Remove and discard the bay leaf and thyme sprigs. Add the lemon juice, season to taste with salt and pepper, and stir gently to keep the salmon chunks intact. Serve immediately.

Serves 6 as a light supper

rustic butternut squash and cannellini bean soup

With all the heavy eating and entertaining around the holidays, I need to have a vegetable-packed soup on hand as a digestive break from the rich foods, meats, and sweets. This is the thick, rustic soup I make. If I'm organized, I make it before the holidays and freeze it. If I plan to serve it to company as a casual fireside supper, then I freeze it as one large batch. Otherwise, I divide the soup in half and freeze it in two containers, ready for a pair of quick weeknight meals. Serve a salad of spicy winter greens, such as the Radicchio Caesar Salad on page 63, and a crusty loaf of bread.

1/4 CUP EXTRA-VIRGIN OLIVE OIL

2 LARGE CLOVES GARLIC, MINCED

2 LEEKS, WHITE AND LIGHT GREEN PART ONLY, CUT INTO THIN SLICES

2 LARGE CARROTS, PEELED, HALVED LENGTHWISE, AND CUT CROSSWISE INTO 1/4-INCH-THICK SLICES

3 RIBS CELERY, TRIMMED, HALVED LENGTHWISE, AND CUT CROSSWISE INTO 1/4-INCH-THICK SLICES

6 CUPS HOMEMADE CHICKEN STOCK OR CANNED LOW-SODIUM CHICKEN BROTH

1 CAN (14 1/2 OUNCES) PEELED, DICED TOMATOES IN JUICE

1 1/2 CUPS PEELED, SEEDED, AND CHOPPED BUTTERNUT SQUASH

1 CAN (15 OUNCES) CANNELLINI BEANS, DRAINED AND RINSED

1/2 CUP SMALL DRIED MACARONI, SUCH AS ELBOWS OR SHELLS

2 SMALL ZUCCHINI, TRIMMED AND CUT INTO 1/2-INCH DICE

1 RED BELL PEPPER, SEEDED, DERIBBED, AND CUT INTO 1/2-INCH DICE

1 PACKAGE (9 OUNCES) FROZEN GREEN BEANS, THAWED

1/2 CUP MINCED FRESH FLAT-LEAF PARSLEY

3 TABLESPOONS BASIL PESTO, HOMEMADE OR STORE-BOUGHT, AT ROOM TEMPERATURE

KOSHER OR SEA SALT

FRESHLY GROUND PEPPER

3/4 CUP FRESHLY GRATED PARMESAN CHEESE, PREFERABLY PARMIGIANO-REGGIANO

In a 6-quart stockpot, heat the oil and garlic over medium heat, and allow the garlic to simmer in the oil until fragrant but not brown, about 1 minute. Add the leeks, carrots, and celery and cook, partially covered, stirring occasionally, until crisp-tender but not brown, about 5 minutes. Add the chicken stock and the tomatoes and their juice, bring to a boil, reduce the heat to low, cover, and simmer for 20 minutes.

Add the butternut squash, cannellini beans, and macaroni and continue to cook, partially covered, for 10 minutes longer. Add the zucchini, bell pepper, and green beans and continue to cook until the squash is fork-tender and the macaroni is al dente, about 10 minutes longer. (The soup can be made up to this point, cooled, covered, and refrigerated for up to 2 days or frozen for up to 2 weeks.)

Remove from the heat and add the parsley and pesto, stirring to distribute well. Season to taste with salt and pepper. Ladle into warmed bowls and pass the Parmesan cheese at the table.

Serves 8

radicchio caesar salad

I told dear friend and colleague Cathy Whims, co-owner of Portland's renowned Nostrana restaurant, that I was "borrowing her recipe" after I ate this salad there. What could be a more seasonal and colorful addition to Christmastime menus than a salad made with red-leaved, white-ribbed radicchio. Yes, radicchio has a slightly bitter flavor, but this dressing is creamy and rich and balances the salad greens perfectly. With the addition of crunchy herbed croutons and a showering of freshly grated Parmigiano-Reggiano, this salad is a welcome addition to a holiday meal. I especially like to serve it after a main course of prime rib or beef tenderloin, as it balances the richness of the meat, yet refreshes the palate before dessert.

3 HEADS RADICCHIO (ABOUT 1 1/2 POUNDS TOTAL WEIGHT), CORED

DRESSING
6 TABLESPOONS EXTRA-VIRGIN OLIVE OIL
2 TABLESPOONS RED WINE VINEGAR
1 TABLESPOON MAYONNAISE
1 VERY FRESH LARGE EGG YOLK (SEE COOK'S NOTE, PAGE 64)
2 TEASPOONS ANCHOVY PASTE
1 CLOVE GARLIC, FINELY MINCED
1/2 TEASPOON SUGAR
1/2 TEASPOON FRESHLY GROUND PEPPER

CROUTONS
2 CUPS (3/4-INCH) FRESH BREAD CUBES, CUT FROM AN ARTISANAL WHITE LOAF WITH THE CRUSTS REMOVED
2 TABLESPOONS UNSALTED BUTTER
1 TABLESPOON FINELY CHOPPED FRESH ROSEMARY
1 TABLESPOON FINELY CHOPPED FRESH SAGE

2 TABLESPOONS FRESHLY GRATED PARMESAN CHEESE, PREFERABLY PARMIGIANO-REGGIANO
FRESHLY GROUND PEPPER

Separate the leaves from the radicchio heads, tear them into large bite-size pieces, and soak in a bowl of cold water for 1 hour, so they become crisp. Drain and dry in a salad spinner. Spread the radicchio on a large cotton dish towel (not terry cloth) or on several sheets of paper towel. Roll up like a jelly roll and place in a large plastic bag. Refrigerate until ready to use. (This can be done up to 2 days in advance.)

To make the dressing, in a blender, combine the olive oil, vinegar, mayonnaise, egg yolk, anchovy paste, garlic, sugar, and pepper and process until emulsified. Alternatively, whisk together the ingredients in a medium bowl until emulsified. Transfer to a jar with a tight-fitting lid and refrigerate until ready to use. (The dressing can be made up to 1 day in advance.) >>>

radicchio caesar salad
CONTINUED

To make the croutons, position a rack in the center of the oven. Preheat the oven to 400°F. Arrange the bread cubes in a single layer on a rimmed baking sheet and bake until golden brown on all sides, about 8 minutes. Transfer to a large bowl and set aside. In a small sauté pan over medium heat, melt the butter. Add the rosemary and sage and sauté until the herbs are fragrant and lightly toasted, about 2 minutes. Pour the butter mixture over the croutons and toss to coat. Set aside until ready to use. (The croutons can be made up to 1 day in advance and stored in an airtight container at room temperature.)

When ready to serve, place the radicchio in a large salad bowl. Give the dressing a last-minute shake and pour over the salad. Toss gently until the leaves are well coated. Sprinkle with the Parmesan cheese and add the croutons and a few grinds of pepper. Toss gently to combine and serve immediately.

Serves 8

COOK'S NOTE
If you prefer not to use a raw egg yolk in the dressing, replace it with 1 additional tablespoon extra-virgin olive oil. Raw eggs in any form should not be served to young children, the elderly, pregnant women, or anyone with a compromised immune system.

blood orange salad with mâche and salt-cured black olives

With blood oranges in season and looking so dramatic on a plate, I developed this minty citrus salad as a refreshing accompaniment to a holiday dinner or buffet. Every component can be prepared well in advance of serving. Make the dressing several hours or even a day ahead. Buy washed and ready-to-use mâche in a cellophane bag. It takes time to peel and slice the blood oranges, so get that done ahead, too. Arrange the slices on a plate, cover with plastic wrap, and set aside at room temperature. The shallots can also be prepped early in the day. Although you could serve this salad at the start of a meal, I prefer to serve it after the main course as a palate cleanser before dessert. On a dinner or brunch buffet, arrange the salad on a large white oval or round platter for an impressive presentation.

DRESSING

3/4 CUP EXTRA-VIRGIN OLIVE OIL

1/4 CUP RICE VINEGAR

2 TEASPOONS DIJON MUSTARD

1/4 CUP FINELY MINCED FRESH MINT

1 TEASPOON SUGAR

1 1/4 TEASPOONS KOSHER OR SEA SALT

FRESHLY GROUND PEPPER

1/2 CUP THINLY SLICED SHALLOTS

4 OUNCES MÂCHE (SEE PAGE 23)

10 BLOOD ORANGES, PEELED, WHITE PITH REMOVED, AND CUT CROSSWISE INTO 1/4-INCH-THICK ROUNDS

40 SALT-CURED BLACK OLIVES

To make the dressing, in a small jar with a tight-fitting lid, combine the olive oil, vinegar, mustard, mint, sugar, salt, and lots of pepper. (Several good grinds of pepper make the vinaigrette taste robust, a perfect complement to the blood oranges.) Cover tightly and shake vigorously to blend. Taste and adjust the seasoning. Set aside. (The dressing can be made up to 1 day in advance and refrigerated. Remove from the refrigerator 2 hours before serving.)

Toss the shallots with 1 tablespoon of the dressing and set aside for 30 minutes.

To assemble the salad, divide the mâche evenly among 8 salad plates, leaving the center of the plate open. Overlap 5 or 6 orange slices in a circle at the center of each plate. Scatter the shallots evenly over tops of the salads. Randomly place 5 olives on each plate. Give the dressing a last-minute shake and drizzle over each salad, dividing evenly. Serve immediately.

Serves 8

butter lettuce salad with satsuma tangerines and pomegranate seeds

One of the jewels of winter fruits is the satsuma tangerine, and another is the pomegranate. I've combined them here to make a gorgeous union of taste, texture, and color. Satsumas are seedless, easy to peel, sweet, and succulent. Pomegranates look intimidating to work with, but are actually surprisingly easy when you know how. Paired with butter lettuce and a citrus vinaigrette, the tangerines and pomegranate seeds make a delightful and healthful addition to any holiday meal.

12 CUPS WHOLE BUTTER LETTUCE LEAVES
(FROM ABOUT 3 HEADS; SEE COOK'S NOTE)

4 SATSUMA TANGERINES

1 TABLESPOON EXTRA-VIRGIN OLIVE OIL

1 FIRM, SHINY, AND UNBLEMISHED POMEGRANATE

DRESSING

1/2 CUP EXTRA-VIRGIN OLIVE OIL

1/3 CUP FRESH ORANGE JUICE (FROM 1 ORANGE)

1 TABLESPOONS FRESH LEMON JUICE

3/4 TEASPOON KOSHER OR SEA SALT

2 TEASPOONS SUGAR

FRESHLY GROUND PEPPER

2 TABLESPOONS SNIPPED FRESH CHIVES

2 TABLESPOONS MINCED FRESH TARRAGON

Rinse the lettuce leaves, and dry them in a salad spinner or with paper towels. Place the lettuce in a large bowl, cover with a slightly damp cotton towel, and set aside until ready to serve.

Peel the tangerines and remove any white pith clinging to the flesh. Separate into sections, place in a medium bowl, add the 1 tablespoon olive oil, toss to coat evenly, and set aside. Extract the seeds from the pomegranate as directed on page 24.

To make the dressing, in a 2-cup glass measure, combine the 1/2 cup olive oil, the orange juice, lemon juice, salt, sugar, and a few grinds of pepper. Stir well to combine. Add the chives and tarragon, taste, and adjust with salt and pepper. Set aside until ready to serve.

To assemble the salad, add the tangerine sections to the lettuce. Stir the dressing to combine, pour over the salad, and toss well. Divide among individual salad plates and garnish each salad with as many pomegranate seeds as desired. (Save any remaining pomegranate seeds for another use.) Serve immediately.

Serves 10

COOK'S NOTE

I like to keep the butter lettuce leaves whole for an attractive presentation, but you can tear them into bite-size pieces if you prefer. If butter lettuce is unavailable, use a leaf lettuce such as green leaf, red leaf, or a mixture of the two. No matter what type you use, be sure you dry the lettuce well, as the dressing won't adhere to wet lettuce.

spinach salad with oven-dried portabella slices, hazelnuts, and shaved parmesan

A spinach salad, especially one with toasted hazelnuts and oven-dried mushrooms, is a welcome addition to the Christmas table. The salad can be served in a large bowl as part of a buffet, or on individual salad plates alongside the main course. With all the cooking you'll be doing, save yourself some time and buy the packaged, prewashed and trimmed baby spinach. The greens stay fresh for several days in the refrigerator.

3 TABLESPOONS EXTRA-VIRGIN OLIVE OIL

4 LARGE PORTABELLA MUSHROOMS, WIPED OR BRUSHED CLEAN, STEMMED, BLACK GILLS REMOVED, AND CUT INTO 1/8-INCH-THICK SLICES

1/2 TEASPOON KOSHER OR SEA SALT

FRESHLY GROUND PEPPER

DRESSING

1/2 CUP EXTRA-VIRGIN OLIVE OIL

2 TABLESPOONS BALSAMIC VINEGAR

2 TEASPOONS WHOLE-GRAIN MUSTARD

1 TEASPOON SUGAR

1 TEASPOON KOSHER OR SEA SALT

FRESHLY GROUND PEPPER

8 CUPS LIGHTLY PACKED BABY SPINACH LEAVES, STEMMED IF NEEDED

2/3 CUP (ABOUT 3 OUNCES) FRESH COARSELY GRATED PARMESAN CHEESE (SEE COOK'S NOTE, FACING PAGE)

2/3 CUP HAZELNUTS, TOASTED AND CHOPPED (SEE COOK'S NOTE, FACING PAGE)

Position one rack in the center and another rack in the lower third of the oven. Preheat the oven to 200°F. Lightly brush 2 large rimmed baking sheets with some of the olive oil.

Arrange the mushroom slices in a single layer, though slightly overlapping to save space, on the prepared baking sheets. Brush the slices lightly with the remaining olive oil. They should be just barely coated with oil. Season with the salt and a few grinds of pepper. Bake until browned and almost all of the moisture is removed, about 1 hour. They will be dried but still quite pliable. Remove from the oven and set aside until cool. (The mushrooms can be prepared up to 1 day in advance and stored in an airtight container at room temperature.)

Meanwhile, make the dressing. In a small jar with a tight-fitting lid, combine the olive oil, vinegar, mustard, sugar, salt, and pepper to taste. Cover tightly and shake vigorously to blend the ingredients. Taste and adjust the seasoning. Set aside until ready to serve. (The dressing can be made

up to 1 day in advance and refrigerated.
Remove from the refrigerator 2 hours
before serving.)

To assemble the salad, place the spinach
and mushrooms in a large serving bowl.
Scatter the cheese on top. Give the dressing
a last-minute shake and pour over the salad.
Toss gently to keep the mushroom slices
intact. Divide among individual salad plates
and garnish each salad with the nuts.
Serve immediately.

Serves 8

COOK'S NOTES

*I prefer the taste of Parmigiano-Reggiano cheese and recommend using it for this salad. To coarsely grate
the cheese, use either the large holes on a box grater or the medium shredding disk of a food processor. For
shavings, use a serrated vegetable peeler.* ❋ *Try to buy shelled hazelnuts (also known as filberts) with the skins
removed. To toast, spread the nuts on a rimmed baking sheet and place on the center rack of a preheated 375°F
oven until they take on color and are fragrant, about 12 minutes. If you are not using already-skinned nuts,
transfer the hot nuts to a clean terry kitchen towel. (The skins tend to discolor the towel, so use a clean towel that
is old or you don't mind washing with bleach.) Rub the nuts vigorously between your palms to remove most of the
skins (stubborn flecks inevitably remain). If you are using skinned nuts, pour them on to a plate to cool before
chopping. You can substitute unsalted cashews if you can't find hazelnuts. Toast them the same way; they will be
ready in 8 to 10 minutes.*

3 main courses

Christmas is both a culinary and a literary feast. One of the most famous Christmas tables is in Charles Dickens's *A Christmas Carol: "At last the dishes were set on, and grace was said. . . . Mrs. Cratchit, looking slowly all along the carving-knife, prepared to plunge it in the breast; but when she did, and when the long expected gush of stuffing issued forth, one murmur of delight arose all round the board, and even Tiny Tim, excited by the two young Cratchits, beat on the table with the handle of his knife and feebly cried Hurrah! . . ."There never was such a goose. . . . Its tenderness and flavour, size and cheapness, were the themes of universal admiration."* ❋ In Victorian England, a goose was far more affordable to the Cratchits and other working-class families than the luxury-item New World turkey. But in America, the wild and plentiful turkey reigned supreme. Other noble Christmas main dishes are included here.

juniper-brined roast turkey

This picture-perfect turkey will make a beautiful centerpiece for your Christmas table. The skin will be crisp and golden, the meat will be succulent (yes, even the breast meat), and the flavor will be knockout delicious because you took care every step of the way. Brining is the answer to a moist turkey, and basting and turning it ensures a fully browned bird. Giving the turkey time to rest after roasting (not you, just the bird) sets and seals in the juices. Your guests will be impressed. ❋ If you take the easy first step of brining your turkey, you will never again complain, nor hear complaints, about the dry breast meat of your holiday bird. After nearly twenty years of cooking a holiday turkey, I am convinced that brining produces the moistest, most flavorful turkey I have ever tasted. Brining requires nothing more than boiling water with salt, sugar, and spices; cooling the mixture; and then soaking the bird in the brine for 12 to 24 hours.

2 TURKEY-SIZE PLASTIC OVEN BAGS
(SEE COOK'S NOTE, PAGE 75)

1 FRESH OR THAWED FROZEN TURKEY
(12 TO 25 POUNDS)

JUNIPER BRINE
2/3 CUP DIAMOND CRYSTAL KOSHER SALT
(SEE COOK'S NOTE, PAGE 75)

2/3 CUP SUGAR

5 FRESH SAGE LEAVES

4 SPRIGS FRESH THYME

2 BAY LEAVES

6 WHOLE CLOVES

2 TEASPOONS ALLSPICE BERRIES, CRUSHED
(SEE COOK'S NOTE, PAGE 75)

1 TEASPOON JUNIPER BERRIES, CRUSHED
(SEE COOK'S NOTE, PAGE 75)

1/2 TEASPOON PEPPERCORNS, CRUSHED
(SEE COOK'S NOTE, PAGE 75)

10 CUPS COOL WATER

4 CUPS ICE WATER

2 LARGE YELLOW ONIONS
(ABOUT 12 OUNCES EACH), DICED

2 LARGE CARROTS, PEELED AND DICED

3 LARGE RIBS CELERY, TRIMMED AND DICED

4 CLOVES GARLIC, MINCED

7 FRESH SAGE LEAVES, CHOPPED

1 TABLESPOON FRESH THYME LEAVES

1 TEASPOON KOSHER OR SEA SALT

FRESHLY GROUND PEPPER

2 CUPS COOL WATER

1/2 CUP (1 STICK) UNSALTED BUTTER, MELTED

GRAVY
2 SPRIGS FRESH THYME

4 SPRIGS FRESH PARSLEY

1 BAY LEAF

6 PEPPERCORNS

2 TABLESPOONS ALL-PURPOSE FLOUR, IF NEEDED

KOSHER OR SEA SALT

FRESHLY GROUND PEPPER

>>>

juniper-brined roast turkey
CONTINUED

You need to prepare the juniper brine and start brining the turkey 12 to 24 hours before you plan to put it in the oven. Have ready a heavy roasting pan large enough to hold the turkey. Place one plastic oven bag inside the second bag to create a double thickness; then place these bags, open wide, in the roasting pan. Remove the turkey from its wrapping. Remove the neck and bag of giblets from the chest and neck cavities and store them in the refrigerator for making gravy. Fold back the top one-third of the bags, making a collar (this helps to keep the bags open). Place the turkey inside the double-thick bags, breast side down, and unfold the collar.

To make the brine, combine the salt, sugar, sage, thyme, bay leaves, cloves, allspice and juniper berries, peppercorns, and 8 cups of the cool water in a 4-quart saucepan. Bring to a boil over high heat, stirring to dissolve the salt and sugar. Boil for 3 minutes. Remove from the heat. Add the 4 cups ice water, stir, and set aside to cool completely.

Pour the cooled brine over the bird. Add the remaining 2 cups cool water. Draw up the top of the inner bag, squeezing out as much air as possible, and secure it closed with a twist tie. Do the same for the outer bag. Place the turkey, breast side down, in the roasting pan and refrigerate for 12 to 24 hours. Turn the turkey 3 or 4 times while it is brining.

To roast the turkey, remove the turkey from the refrigerator 1 1/2 hours before you plan to roast it. Set the roasting pan aside and place the brined turkey, still in its bags, in the sink. Open and discard the bags, brine, and any herbs or spices remaining on the bird. Rinse the turkey under cold water and pat thoroughly dry with paper towels.

Combine the onions, carrots, celery, garlic, sage, thyme, salt, and a few grinds of pepper in a medium mixing bowl. Mix well and set aside.

Position a rack on the second-lowest level in the oven. Preheat the oven to 500°F. Wash the roasting pan, if necessary, and place a roasting rack, preferably V-shaped, in the pan.

Put 1/2 cup of the vegetable mixture inside the neck cavity, and then put 1 1/2 cups of it inside the chest cavity. Scatter the remainder on the bottom of the roasting pan and add the 2 cups water to the pan.

To truss the turkey, have ready a 4-foot length of kitchen twine. Place the turkey on a work surface with the legs facing you. Center the twine across the back (under the shoulders) of the bird. Make sure the flap of neck skin covers the neck cavity and is secured by the twine. With an end in each hand, pull the twine up and over the top of the breast, tightening it so the wings are drawn in close to the body, then cross over the two ends and tie. Now bring the twine down to the legs, bring the legs together, wrap the twine around the ends (knobs) of the legs, and tie a knot. Trim any extra length of twine.

Use a pastry brush to brush the turkey with half of the butter. Place the turkey, breast side down, on the rack in the pan. Roast for 30 minutes. Lower the oven temperature to 350°F. Baste the turkey with the pan juices, and roast an additional 30 minutes. Remove the turkey from the oven. Wearing washable silicone oven mitts, or using wads of paper towels in each hand, turn the turkey breast side up. Baste with the pan juices, and then return the turkey to the oven.

Continue to roast, basting with the pan juices after 45 minutes. After another 45 minutes, baste with the remaining butter. Check the temperature of the turkey. The turkey is done when an instant-read thermometer inserted into the thickest part of the thigh not touching bone registers 165°F. When the internal temperature of the turkey reaches 125°F, the turkey is about 1 hour away from being done. (Roasting times will vary, depending on the size of the bird, its temperature when it went

into the oven, and your particular oven and the accuracy of the thermostat.) Typically, a brined 14- to 16-pound turkey will take about 2 to 2 1/2 hours to reach an internal temperature of 165°F. Plan on approximately 3 1/2 hours for a 25-pound bird.

While the turkey is roasting, begin the gravy by first making a turkey stock. Put the turkey neck, tail, gizzard, and heart in a medium saucepan. Add the thyme, parsley, bay leaf, peppercorns, and water to cover. Bring to a boil over medium-high heat, and then turn the heat to low. Skim off any brown foam that rises to the top. Simmer the stock, partially covered, for 1 hour. Pour the stock through a fine-mesh sieve set over a bowl or 4-cup glass measure. Discard the herbs and turkey parts. Set the stock aside, and when the fat rises to the top, skim it off with a large spoon.

When the turkey is done, transfer it to a carving board or serving platter, and cover the breast loosely with aluminum foil. Allow the turkey to rest for 25 to 45 minutes before carving to let the juices set.   >>>

COOK'S NOTES

Plastic oven bags made by Reynolds are found with other food storage bags at supermarkets. Buy the turkey-size bags. They are food-safe, plus they are big, strong, tear-resistant, and come with twist ties. I do not recommend using plastic garbage bags because they are not intended for food storage. I slip one bag inside the other to guard against leakage. For the same reason, I place the bagged turkey in a roasting pan. Brining the turkey by this method requires only one refrigerator shelf, while brining in a large stockpot means taking out at least one refrigerator shelf, if not two shelves, to make room for the pot. ✳ *I prefer Diamond brand kosher salt. It has a pleasant taste and is free of chemicals.* ✳ *The easiest way to crush whole spices is to use a mortar and pestle or a spice grinder. If you have neither of these kitchen tools, place the whole spices in a heavy lock-top plastic bag; seal the bag, pressing out all the air; and pound the spices with the bottom of a small, heavy saucepan.*

While the turkey rests, make the gravy: Pour the vegetables and pan drippings through a sieve set over a medium saucepan. Scoop the vegetables from the cavities of the turkey and place in the sieve. Use the back of a spoon to press down on the softened vegetables, extracting as much liquid as possible, and pressing the solids through the sieve. Bring the strained mixture to a boil, skimming any fat that comes to the surface. Add enough reserved turkey stock to make about 2 cups gravy. Boil until reduced slightly. If the gravy needs to be thickened, put the flour in a 1-cup measure, add a small amount of the simmering gravy, and blend until smooth. Slowly pour this mixture into the gravy in the sauce-pan and whisk until thickened, about 2 minutes. Season to taste with salt and pepper. Transfer to a warmed small bowl or sauceboat and keep warm.

To carve the turkey, place the turkey on a carving board, ideally one that has a moat and well to catch the delicious poultry juices. Untie the bird. Using a sharp carving knife and a meat fork, cut down between the thigh and body until you reach bone. Twist the leg and thigh a little until you see the thigh joint. Now cut through the joint to separate the thigh from the body. Cut the joint where the leg meets the thigh. Repeat on the other side. Now you have legs and thighs ready for a warmed platter.

To carve breast meat, start at the keel bone that runs along the top of the breast. Angle the knife and cut thin slices of breast meat from one side of the bird. Continue until you reach the rib cage; then carve the other breast. At this point you should have plenty of meat for serving. Lay slices of breast meat in an overlapping fashion down the center of the platter. Place the legs and thighs along the side. If a guest wants to have a wing, pull back the wing until you see the joint between the wing and the body, cut through that joint, and add the wing to the platter. Cover the rest of the turkey loosely with aluminum foil, and remove the remainder of the meat from the carcass later for some fine leftovers. Serve, accompanied by the gravy, and enjoy the results of your hard work!

Serves 12 to 20, depending on the size of the turkey

garlic and herb—rubbed crown roast of pork

A crown roast of pork makes a spectacular presentation on a holiday buffet or dining table. Traditionally, the center of the roast is filled with either a bread or rice stuffing. I prefer to roast the pork without stuffing for the same reason I don't stuff a turkey: the meat will be overcooked by the time the stuffing is cooked through. I also recommend you brine the pork. When I was developing this recipe, I first roasted the pork without brining it and was sorely disappointed in the blandness of the meat. Brining improves the texture of the pork, making it tender and juicy throughout, plus the flavors of the herbs and spices in the brine penetrate to the center of the roast. Plan ahead because you will need to special-order the roast from a butcher. Let the butcher know how many guests you will be serving to determine what size crown roast you will need. Plan on serving 1 or 2 chops per person. My favorite accompaniment to this roast is Wild Rice with Roasted Chestnuts and Cranberries.

2 TURKEY-SIZED PLASTIC OVEN BAGS
(SEE COOK'S NOTE, PAGE 75)

1 CROWN ROAST OF PORK (8 TO 10 POUNDS AND
ABOUT 14 TO 22 RIBS)

JUNIPER BRINE
1/2 CUP DIAMOND CRYSTAL KOSHER SALT
(SEE COOK'S NOTE, PAGE 75)

1/2 CUP SUGAR

3 FRESH SAGE LEAVES

3 SPRIGS FRESH THYME

1 BAY LEAF

4 WHOLE CLOVES

1 TEASPOON JUNIPER BERRIES, CRUSHED
(SEE COOK'S NOTE, PAGE 75)

1 TEASPOON ALLSPICE BERRIES, CRUSHED
(SEE COOK'S NOTE, PAGE 75)

1/2 TEASPOON PEPPERCORNS, CRUSHED
(SEE COOK'S NOTE, PAGE 75)

4 CUPS COOL WATER

4 CUPS ICE WATER

HERB AND GARLIC PASTE
4 LARGE CLOVES GARLIC, MINCED

1 TABLESPOON FINELY CHOPPED FRESH SAGE

1 TABLESPOON FINELY CHOPPED FRESH THYME

1/4 CUP EXTRA-VIRGIN OLIVE OIL

2 TEASPOONS KOSHER OR SEA SALT

1/2 TEASPOON FRESHLY GROUND PEPPER

WILD RICE WITH ROASTED CHESTNUTS AND
CRANBERRIES (PAGE 108), BREAD STUFFING WITH
SAUSAGE, APPLES, AND CARAMELIZED ONIONS
(PAGE 104), OR FRESH SAGE AND THYME SPRIGS

You need to prepare the juniper brine and start brining the crown roast 24 hours before you plan to start roasting it. Have ready a bowl large enough to hold the roast. Place one plastic oven bag inside the second bag to create a double thickness; then place these bags, open wide, in the bowl. Fold back the top one-third of the bags, making a collar (this helps to keep the top of the bag open). Remove the pork from its wrapping. Place the pork inside the double-thick bags, with the rib bones pointing upward, and unfold the collar. ▸▸▸

garlic and herb—rubbed crown roast of pork
CONTINUED

To make the brine, combine the salt, sugar, sage, thyme, bay leaf, cloves, juniper and allspice berries, peppercorns, and cool water in a 3-quart saucepan. Bring to a boil over high heat, stirring to dissolve the salt and sugar.

Boil for 3 minutes. Remove from the heat. Add the ice water, stir, and set aside to cool completely.

Pour the cooled brine over the pork. Draw up the top of the inner bag, squeezing out as much air as possible, and secure it closed with a twist tie. Do the same for the outer bag. The pork should be completely submerged in the brine. Place the pork in the refrigerator to brine for 24 hours.

To roast the pork, remove the pork from the refrigerator 1 1/2 hours before you plan to roast it. Set the bowl aside, and place the brined pork, still in its bags, in the sink. Open and discard the bags, brine, and any herbs or spices remaining on the pork. Rinse the pork under cold water and pat thoroughly dry with paper towels. Transfer the pork to a shallow roasting pan.

To make the herb and garlic paste, combine the garlic, sage, thyme, olive oil, salt, and pepper in a small bowl. Rub the herb paste generously over all the pork, including inside the cavity and between the bones. Set the pork, rib bones down (upside down), in the roasting pan. Set aside to marinate at room temperature for up to 1 hour.

Thirty minutes before you plan to roast the pork, position a rack in the lower third of the oven. Preheat the oven to 450°F.

Roast the pork for 15 minutes. Lower the oven temperature to 325°F and continue roasting the meat for 1 hour. Check the temperature of the pork. The pork is done when an instant-read thermometer inserted into the thickest part not touching bone registers 145° to 150°F. (A 9-pound roast should take about 1 3/4 hours to reach 145°F.) Keep in mind that the temperature of the meat will increase another 5° to 10°F as the meat rests before carving. Let the meat rest, tented with foil, for 20 minutes to allow the juices to set.

To serve, place the pork on a warmed platter so the rib bones face upward. Fill the cavity with the wild rice and scatter the remaining wild rice around the base of the roast. Alternatively, serve the wild rice or the bread stuffing on the side, or place the roast on a bed of herbs and fill the cavity with a bouquet of the same herbs. To carve the roast, use a carving fork to steady the roast and cut between the rib bones to separate the chops. Serve 1 or 2 chops per person.

Serves 8 to 12

salt and garlic–crusted prime rib of beef with horseradish cream

Serving a prime rib for Christmas dinner makes a spectacular presentation. You may quiver at the price, but you'll be confident in the kitchen because a prime rib is remarkably easy to cook. All you have to do is season the meat and roast it. Aside from a sturdy roasting pan, the only other critical piece of equipment you'll need is an accurate meat thermometer. ✳ Here are a few key points to know when selecting a prime rib: First, you can buy a 3-rib, 4-rib, 5-rib, or even a 7-rib standing rib roast. The seasoning and preparation stays the same, but the cooking time will vary depending on the size of the roast. (Of course, proportionately cut down on the quantity of the garlic-salt mixture if you are serving a smaller roast.) Because leftovers are so terrific, the smallest roast I ever buy is a 3-rib roast. The full 7-bone prime rib is cut from the back of the upper rib section of the steer. Prime rib can be cut from either the loin end or the chuck end of the rib section. I prefer roasts cut from the loin end, which is the back section closest to the short loin (toward the center of the animal and away from the shoulder). The meat in this section is tender, more flavorful, and has fewer fat pockets between the lean meat areas, so ask your butcher to cut your roast starting at the small end of the ribs or the loin end. Second, if a butcher shop dry-ages its beef, so much the better, as the meat will have a deeper flavor and texture. ✳ As to the cooking method, there are plenty of opinions. Some chefs prefer a slow-roasting method in a moderate oven for a uniformly rare roast, while others recommend searing in a hot oven for a short time and then finishing the roast in a moderate oven. I prefer the latter technique because I like my prime rib with a crusty, highly seasoned exterior and a uniformly rosy pink interior. To my taste, the best prime rib is a roast cooked rare and served with a full-bodied, creamy horseradish sauce.

PRIME RIB

5-BONE PRIME RIB ROAST OF BEEF
(10 TO 12 POUNDS), BONES REMOVED AND
TIED BACK ONTO THE ROAST (SEE COOK'S NOTE)

1/2 CUP DIAMOND CRYSTAL KOSHER SALT
(SEE COOK'S NOTE, PAGE 75) OR FLAKY SEA SALT

1/4 CUP FINELY CHOPPED GARLIC (ABOUT 12 CLOVES)

2 TEASPOONS FRESHLY COARSE-GROUND PEPPER

HORSERADISH CREAM

1 CUP SOUR CREAM

1/4 TO 1/2 CUP EXTRA-HOT PREPARED HORSERADISH

1 TEASPOON FRESH LEMON JUICE

1 TEASPOON DIJON MUSTARD

1/4 TEASPOON KOSHER OR SEA SALT

Remove the prime rib from the refrigerator 2 hours before you plan to roast it. Trim all but 1/2 inch of fat from the roast. (A thin layer of fat protects and bastes the beef while it roasts.) In a small bowl, combine the salt, garlic, and pepper. Rub the salt mixture all over the roast, especially in any spaces between the meat and the bones, covering it with a thick layer of the garlic salt. Lay the roast, bone side down, in a shallow roasting pan just large enough to hold it without crowding. The rib bones act as a natural rack, eliminating the need for wire rack. Let the roast sit at room temperature, loosely covered with plastic wrap, until ready to cook.

Meanwhile, make the horseradish cream. In a small bowl, combine the sour cream, horseradish (adding it according to your taste), lemon juice, mustard, and salt and mix well. Cover and refrigerate until ready to serve.

About 30 minutes before roasting the beef, position a rack in the center of the oven. Preheat the oven to 450°F.

Roast the beef, uncovered, for 30 minutes. Reduce the heat to 300°F but do not open the door to the oven. After about 1 1/2 hours of cooking, begin checking the roast for doneness with an instant-read thermometer. Insert the thermometer into the center of the roast, away from any bone or fat pockets. It is ready when the thermometer registers 115° to 120°F for rare, 125° to 130°F for medium-rare, or 130° to 140°F for medium. Keep in mind that the temperature will increase another 5° to 10°F while the meat rests before carving, which is why I like to pull my roast when it reaches 115°F. The prime rib may be done in 2 1/4 to 2 1/2 hours (which was the case for an 11-pound prime rib roast cooked to 115°F), or it may take a little longer, depending on your oven, the exact weight of the meat, and your desired level of doneness.

Transfer the meat to a carving board and tent with aluminum foil. Let the meat rest for at least 20 minutes to allow the juices to set. (If you are making the Yorkshire pudding on page 107 to accompany the prime rib, pour all of the drippings and the fat from the pan into a glass measure. Increase the oven temperature to 450°F and place a metal 12-cup standard muffin pan in the oven to heat for 10 minutes. Follow the directions for preparing and baking the pudding while the roast rests.)

To carve the roast, remove the twine that held the rib bones to the roast. Using a carving fork to hold the roast in place, slice the meat across the grain into whatever thickness you prefer. Cut between the rib bones to separate them and offer them to any bone-loving guests. Accompany the roast with the horseradish cream.

Serves 10 to 12

COOK'S NOTE

Make friends with a skilled, caring butcher and you will be rewarded with a rich, beefy-flavored, well-marbled prime rib. These roasts are expensive, so knowing what you are buying and how it is cut is important. In addition, a good butcher will be happy to remove the rib bones and tie them back on the roast for you. My husband grew up in Kansas City, Missouri, and his family loyally bought all their meat from McGonigle's Market on West 79th Street. They have skilled, friendly butchers and some of the best meat I have ever tasted. Even though we live in Oregon, we continue the tradition by ordering our standing rib roasts and steaks from McGonigle's. You can order from them, too. Visit their Web site, www.mcgonigles.com, or call the store toll-free at 888-783-2450.

christmas goose

When it came time to plan and roast my Christmas goose, I called my friend and game cookery expert, Janie Hibler. Janie is the author of several cookbooks, including *Wild About Game,* the bible of game cookbooks. Buying a plump, farm-raised goose is a delicious yet expensive choice for a holiday main course, and I wanted to make a perfect roast goose for my family. Here is Janie's recipe for an exceptional goose: crisp and golden on the outside and perfectly moist within. She calls it a gustatory delight and I agree completely. Serve the goose with either Wild Rice with Roasted Chestnuts and Cranberries (page 108) or Bread Stuffing with Sausage, Apples, and Caramelized Onions (page 104). ❄ Save the rendered goose fat and freeze it for a completely cholesterol-packed but decadent side dish of new potatoes sautéed in goose fat: Boil new potatoes in lightly salted water for 10 minutes; they should be only partially cooked. Drain the potatoes, cut them in half, and sauté them in goose fat in a heavy skillet until crisp on all sides and fork tender. Season with a finishing salt and freshly ground pepper.

1 FARM-RAISED GOOSE (ABOUT 12 POUNDS)

KOSHER OR SEA SALT

FRESHLY GROUND PEPPER

1 BUNCH FRESH THYME

1 LEMON, QUARTERED

3 CUPS HOMEMADE CHICKEN STOCK
OR CANNED LOW-SODIUM CHICKEN BROTH

1/2 CUP MADEIRA

1 TABLESPOON UNSALTED BUTTER,
AT ROOM TEMPERATURE

1 TABLESPOON ALL-PURPOSE FLOUR

Position a rack on the second-lowest level in the oven. Preheat the oven to 500°F. Have ready a roasting pan outfitted with a roasting rack, preferably V-shaped.

Remove the neck and giblets from the chest cavity, and save the liver to make liver pâté or another use, if desired. Discard the neck and other giblets Remove any visible fat from the bird and cut off the wing tips. Using paper towels, pat the goose dry inside and out. Sprinkle the cavity with salt and pepper. Put the thyme and lemon wedges in the cavity. Prick the breast of the bird with a two-pronged carving fork to release any fat as it cooks. Arrange the bird, breast side up, on the rack. Stick an ovenproof meat thermometer in the thickest part of the

COOK'S NOTE
A remote probe thermometer is the ideal thermometer to use in this instance where heat loss will result if the oven door is opened before the bird is done. See page 29 for how it works.

thigh without touching bone. Orient the thermometer so it is facing you as you put the bird in the oven. (Alternatively, and ideally, use a remote probe thermometer; see Cook's Note.)

Roast the goose for 45 minutes, and then turn the oven off. Do not open the door. Leave the bird in the oven until the thermometer reaches 165°F, 35 to 45 minutes longer. Keep in mind that the temperature will rise to 170°F while the bird rests before carving. Remove the goose from the oven and transfer to a carving board or warmed serving platter. Tent with foil and let the bird rest for 15 to 20 minutes to allow the juices to set.

Spoon the fat off the top of the pan juices, and save the fat for another use. Put the roasting pan with the pan juices on the stove top over medium-high heat. Add the stock and Madeira and deglaze the pan, using a wooden spoon to scrape the bottom to release any caramelized bits that have stuck to it. Simmer the liquid until it is reduced to 2 cups, about 15 minutes. While the liquid is reducing, use a small fork to work together the butter and flour to make a paste. When the liquid is reduced, whisk the butter paste, a little at a time, into the gravy to thicken it slightly. Taste and adjust the seasoning with salt and pepper. Keep warm.

Carve the goose as you would a turkey; see page 76 for carving details. Arrange the meat on a warmed platter and serve. Pour the gravy into a warmed gravy boat and pass at the table.

Serves 6

herb and garlic—stuffed roast leg of lamb

For lamb lovers, there is nothing more festive for Christmas dinner than a roast leg of lamb. Roasting a bone-in whole leg provides a dramatic presentation. However, I prefer to serve a boned, butterflied, and rolled roast for three reasons: first, for maximum flavor, a boned-out roast allows the cook to season the meat from within; second, I can utilize the chopped leg bones to make a sauce; and third, it is much easier to carve a boned roast. If you do decide to roast the leg with the bone intact, then combine the garlic mixture with the mustard mixture and smear all of it thickly on the outside of the leg to maximize flavor. Accompany the roast with Potatoes au Gratin with Fresh Thyme and a Parmesan Crust (page 116) or Purée of Celery Root (page 117).

LAMB ROAST

1 BONE-IN LEG OF LAMB (5 TO 6 POUNDS), BONED, BUTTERFLIED, AND BONES RESERVED (SEE COOK'S NOTE, FACING PAGE)

3 TABLESPOONS EXTRA-VIRGIN OLIVE OIL

1 TABLESPOON FINELY MINCED GARLIC

2 TABLESPOONS MINCED FRESH FLAT-LEAF PARLEY

2 TEASPOONS MINCED FRESH OREGANO

1 TEASPOON KOSHER OR SEA SALT

3/4 TEASPOON FRESHLY GROUND PEPPER

1/4 CUP DIJON MUSTARD

1 TABLESPOON MINCED FRESH ROSEMARY

SAUCE

2 TABLESPOONS EXTRA-VIRGIN OLIVE OIL

1 SMALL YELLOW ONION, COARSELY CHOPPED

4 LARGE CLOVES GARLIC, UNPEELED, SMASHED WITH THE SIDE OF A CHEF'S KNIFE

1/2 CUP DRY WHITE WINE

1 SPRIG FRESH OREGANO

3 CUPS HOMEMADE CHICKEN STOCK OR CANNED LOW-SODIUM CHICKEN BROTH

1 TABLESPOON UNSALTED BUTTER, AT ROOM TEMPERATURE

1 TABLESPOON ALL-PURPOSE FLOUR

Have ready a shallow roasting pan just large enough to hold the roast without crowding. Place a flat roasting rack in the pan. Have kitchen twine ready.

To prepare the lamb, remove it from the refrigerator 1 1/2 hours before you plan to roast it. Trim any layers of fat on the skin side of the meat to a 1/4-inch thickness. (Some fat helps keep the lamb moist while roasting.) Open the lamb on a cutting board, skin side down. Trim any internal pockets of fat, if needed.

In a small bowl, combine the olive oil, garlic, parsley, oregano, salt, and 1/2 teaspoon of the pepper. In another small bowl, combine the mustard, rosemary, and the remaining 1/4 teaspoon pepper.

Spread the garlic mixture over the lamb. Starting from a long side, roll up the lamb firmly and securely to form a rolled roast. Using kitchen twine, secure the roast by tying it in 5 or 6 places at regular intervals. The twine should be snug without creating ridges in the meat. Rub the outside of the roast with the mustard mixture, coating it completely. Place the lamb on the rack in the pan and set aside at room temperature until ready to cook.

Meanwhile, begin making the sauce. In a medium sauté pan, heat the olive oil over medium-high heat and swirl to coat the pan. Add the lamb bones and sear on all sides until well browned, 5 to 7 minutes. Add the onion and garlic cloves and cook, stirring occasionally, until nicely browned, about 5 minutes. Add the wine and deglaze the pan, using a wooden spoon to scrape the bottom to release any caramelized bits that have stuck to it. Simmer the wine until reduced to 2 tablespoons, about 2 minutes. Add the oregano and chicken stock and simmer until reduced to 1½ cups, about 25 minutes. Meanwhile, use a small fork to work together the butter and flour to make a paste and set aside. When the sauce is ready, strain it through a fine-mesh sieve into a small, clean saucepan. Discard the solids. Set the sauce aside to finish later.

Position a rack in the center of the oven. Preheat the oven to 400°F.

Roast the lamb for 1 hour and then check for doneness. The lamb is ready when an instant-read thermometer inserted into the thickest part registers 120° to 125°F for rosy rare lamb, 125° to 130°F for medium-rare, or 130° to 140°F for medium. Keep in mind that the temperature of the meat will increase another 5° to 10°F while the meat rests before carving. The lamb may be done in 1 to 1¼ hours (which was the case for a 5½-pound lamb roast cooked to 120°F), or it may take longer depending on your oven, the exact weight of the meat, and your desired level of doneness. Transfer the meat to a carving board and tent with aluminum foil. Let the meat rest for 20 minutes to allow the juices to set.

While the meat is resting, finish the sauce. Pour the drippings from the roasting pan into a 1-cup glass measure and set aside for 5 minutes to allow the fat to rise to the top. Spoon off and discard the fat. Pour the defatted pan drippings into the sauce and whisk to incorporate. Place the sauce over medium heat and bring to a simmer. Whisk the butter paste, a little at a time, into the sauce to thicken it slightly. Keep warm.

Remove the twine and carve the roast crosswise into ½-inch-thick slices. Arrange the lamb on a warmed platter. Pour the sauce into a warmed sauceboat and pass at the table.

Serves 6 to 8

COOK'S NOTE

Ask your butcher to bone and butterfly the leg of lamb and chop the lamb bones into several smaller chunks for easy browning. Don't bother to have the butcher tie the roast, as you need to season the inside of the meat with the herb paste before roasting.

roast loin of pork stuffed with apricots and dried plums

This roast is simple enough for a Sunday supper with the family, yet elegant enough for holiday entertaining. In both cases, it is a snap to prepare. The dried fruit creates a colorful, flavorful channel down the center of the roast, while the mustard coating seals in the moisture, creating a delectable crust. Serve with Wild Rice with Roasted Chestnuts and Cranberries (page 108) or Whipped Garnet Yams with a Pecan Praline Crust (page 120) and a seasonal vegetable.

1 BONELESS TOP LOIN PORK ROAST
(ABOUT 2 1/2 POUNDS)

5 OUNCES (ABOUT 16) DRIED PITTED PLUMS (PRUNES)

3 OUNCES (ABOUT 14) DRIED APRICOTS

1/4 CUP DIJON MUSTARD

1/4 TEASPOON GARLIC POWDER

1/4 TEASPOON FRESHLY GROUND PEPPER

2 CARROTS, PEELED AND CUT INTO 1-INCH CHUNKS

2 RIBS CELERY, TRIMMED AND CUT INTO 1-INCH CHUNKS

1 YELLOW ONION, CUT INTO 1-INCH CHUNKS

1 CUP DRY WHITE WINE

ABOUT 1/2 CUP WATER

Remove the roast from the refrigerator 45 minutes before you plan to bake it. Position a rack in the lower third of the oven. Preheat the oven to 350° F.

Stand the roast on one end and insert a thin-bladed knife down the center of the roast lengthwise, creating a tubelike opening. Stuff the length of the roast with the dried fruits, alternating the plums and apricots. (If necessary, cut a slit at the other end of the roast, and stuff half of the fruit from one side of the roast and half of the fruit from the other side.)

In a small bowl, combine the mustard, garlic powder, and pepper and mix well. Rub the roast all over with the mustard mixture.

Arrange the carrots, celery, and onion in the bottom of a 9-by-13-inch baking pan. Place the roast on top of the vegetables. Pour the wine over the top of the roast and then pour the water into the bottom of the pan, adding just enough to come up the sides of the vegetables but not touch the bottom of the roast.

Roast the pork for 45 minutes, or until an instant-read thermometer inserted into the meat but away from the fruit registers 155°F.

Transfer the roast to a carving board, tent with aluminum foil, and let rest for 10 minutes before carving to allow the juices to set. Discard the vegetables and liquid in the pan.

To serve, cut the roast into 1/2-inch-thick slices and arrange them, slightly overlapping, on a warmed platter.

Serves 6

roast tenderloin of beef with bordelaise sauce

Elegance is the word for this main course, especially when accompanied with Bordelaise sauce. The tenderloin of beef is the cut from which filet mignon steaks are portioned, so you and your lucky guests will be eating a tender, great-flavored cut. Armed with an instant-read thermometer and an accurately calibrated oven, any cook can succeed with this recipe—even a novice. The same is true for making the Bordelaise sauce. If you can slice a few vegetables and simmer liquid with a watchful eye, the sauce is a snap to make.

1 WHOLE BEEF TENDERLOIN (5 TO 7 POUNDS), PEELED AND ROAST READY (SEE COOK'S NOTE)

3 TABLESPOONS EXTRA-VIRGIN OLIVE OIL

1 1/2 TABLESPOONS MINCED FRESH THYME

1 TABLESPOON MINCED GARLIC

1 1/2 TEASPOONS KOSHER OR SEA SALT

1 TEASPOON FRESHLY GROUND PEPPER

BORDELAISE SAUCE (PAGE 91)

Remove the tenderloin from the refrigerator 1 hour before you plan to roast it. Position a rack in the center of the oven. Preheat the oven to 400°F. Line a large rimmed baking sheet with aluminum foil to make cleanup easier. Place a flat roasting rack on the baking sheet.

Rub the olive oil all over the meat. In a small bowl, combine the thyme, garlic, salt, and pepper and mix well. Rub the meat all over with the garlic mixture. Place the roast on the rack in the pan. >>>

COOK'S NOTE

The tenderloin you buy should be about 15 inches long and 4 inches thick at one end, tapering to a thin piece at the other end. Ask your butcher to provide you with a peeled and roast-ready tenderloin of beef, which means the silver skin has been removed. You don't need to have the tenderloin larded or marinated. However, if the butcher is willing, have the tapered end tucked under by about 3 inches and tied so it is about the same thickness as the other end. This way the roast will cook evenly. (It's easy enough to tie the meat yourself, but given how expensive a whole tenderloin of beef is, you might as well have it fully readied at the butcher shop.)

roast tenderloin of beef with bordelaise sauce
CONTINUED

Roast the meat for 25 minutes and then check for doneness. The beef is ready when an instant-read thermometer inserted into the thickest part registers 115° to 120°F for rare, 125° to 130°F for medium-rare, or 130° to 140°F for medium. Keep in mind that the temperature of the meat will increase another 5° to 10°F while the meat rests before carving. The beef may be done in 35 minutes (which was the case for a 5 1/2-pound tenderloin cooked to 115°F), or it may take 45 to 50 minutes, depending on your oven, the exact weight of the meat, and your desired level of doneness.

Transfer the meat to a carving board and tent with aluminum foil. Let the meat rest for 10 minutes to allow the juices to set. Carve across the grain into 1/2-inch-thick slices. Pour the sauce into a warmed sauceboat and pass at the table.

Serves 10 to 12

bordelaise sauce

This is one of the least complicated sauces you will ever make. Basically, you throw the vegetables and herbs into a saucepan, add the wine, and simmer until the wine is almost evaporated. You then add the veal stock, reduce it by half, strain and season the sauce, and finally swirl in a chunk of butter—voilà, the sauce is made. The best part is that it can be made up to 3 days ahead, covered, and refrigerated. Now, that's what I call entertaining with ease and style.

$1/2$ CUP THINLY SLICED CARROTS

$1/2$ CUP THINLY SLICED BUTTON MUSHROOMS

$1/3$ CUP THINLY SLICED SHALLOTS

2 LARGE CLOVES GARLIC, THINLY SLICED

1 BAY LEAF

2 SPRIGS FRESH THYME

8 SPRIGS FRESH FLAT-LEAF PARSLEY

10 PEPPERCORNS

$1 1/2$ CUPS HEARTY RED WINE

2 CUPS VEAL STOCK, VEAL DEMI-GLACE, OR BEEF STOCK (SEE COOK'S NOTE)

LARGE PINCH OF KOSHER OR SEA SALT

LARGE PINCH OF GRANULATED SUGAR

2 TABLESPOONS UNSALTED BUTTER, AT ROOM TEMPERATURE

In a medium saucepan over medium-high heat, combine the carrots, mushrooms, shallots, garlic, bay leaf, thyme, parsley, peppercorns, and wine and bring to a simmer. Simmer until the liquid is almost evaporated, about 15 minutes. Add the veal stock and simmer until reduced by half, 8 to 10 minutes longer.

Strain the sauce through a fine-mesh sieve into a small, clean saucepan. Season with the salt and sugar. Whisk in the butter, a tablespoon at a time. Keep the sauce warm in a double boiler until ready to serve, or, if made ahead, rewarm in a small saucepan over low heat.

Makes about 1 cup

COOK'S NOTE

Specialty stocks, such as veal stock, and demi-glace are increasingly available in natural-foods stores, gourmet markets, and online. Look for them in the freezer section, or in a concentrated form on the grocery shelf where canned broth is sold. I am a huge fan of the frozen stocks and demi-glace products made by Stock Options, a company based in Portland, Oregon. The products are available online at www.stockoptionsonline.com.

bourbon and brown sugar–crusted ham

A holiday ham is a traditional centerpiece of Christmas dinner. Since hams are sold fully cooked, the only task for the cook is to glaze the ham and warm it up. If you are serving a large crowd, say, 16 to 20 guests, then you might consider buying a whole ham that includes both the shank half and the butt half, and weighs 14 to 18 pounds. Otherwise, for a gathering of ten or so, I prefer to buy a half ham, preferably the butt or upper part because it is tastier and more tender than the shank half. Read the label on the ham or ask your butcher for a slow-dry-cured and natural wood–smoked ham with no water added. Adding water in the curing process dilutes the natural taste of the ham. Whipped Garnet Yams with a Pecan Praline Crust (page 120) would be a knockout accompaniment to the succulent meat and crunchy, sweet glaze.

1 BONE-IN SMOKED HAM, PREFERABLY THE BUTT OR UPPER HALF (7 TO 9 POUNDS)

24 TO 30 WHOLE CLOVES

1 1/2 CUPS PACKED GOLDEN BROWN SUGAR

1 1/2 TABLESPOONS DRY MUSTARD

5 TABLESPOONS BOURBON WHISKEY, PLUS 1 TABLESPOON FOR THE SAUCE (OPTIONAL)

3 1/2 CUPS APPLE CIDER

2 TABLESPOONS PURE MAPLE SYRUP

PINCH OF CAYENNE PEPPER

1 TABLESPOON CORNSTARCH MIXED WITH 2 TABLESPOONS WATER

Have ready a roasting pan just large enough to hold the ham without crowding. Place a flat roasting rack in the pan.

Remove the ham from the refrigerator 2 hours before you plan to bake it. Using a sharp boning knife, trim away any skin and all but 1/4 inch of the external fat from the ham. Set the ham fat-side up, and make parallel cuts 1/2 inch deep and 1 1/2 inches apart all over the ham. Give the ham a quarter turn and repeat to produce a cross-hatched diamondlike pattern. Stick a clove in the center of each diamond.

In a small bowl, combine the sugar, mustard, and bourbon and mix to form a paste. Rub the paste all over the ham. Set the ham, fat side up, on the rack in the pan, cover loosely with plastic wrap, and set aside until ready to bake.

About 30 minutes before baking the ham, position a rack in the lower third of the oven. Preheat the oven to 350°F.

Pour about 2 1/2 cups of the apple cider into the pan to a depth of 1/4 inch. Bake the ham uncovered, basting it at least twice and adding the remaining apple cider as needed to maintain a 1/4-inch depth, until an instant-read thermometer inserted into the center of the ham, not touching bone, registers 120°F, 1 3/4 to 2 hours. (It should take about 15 minutes per pound for the ham to reach an internal temperature between 120° and 125°F.)

Transfer the ham to a carving board or warmed platter and tent with aluminum foil. Let the ham rest for 20 minutes before carving to allow the juices to set. >>>

bourbon and brown sugar—crusted ham
CONTINUED

Meanwhile, pour the pan juices into a 4-cup heatproof measuring cup. Set aside for 5 minutes to allow the fat to rise to the top, and then spoon off the fat and discard. Pour the defatted pan juices into a small saucepan and bring to a simmer over medium-high heat. Whisk in the maple syrup and cayenne pepper. Taste the sauce. If the flavor is concentrated and tasty, then whisk in the cornstarch mixture to thicken the sauce. If the sauce tastes thin, then simmer the sauce for a few minutes to reduce the pan juices and concentrate the flavors before adding the cornstarch mixture. Add the 1 tablespoon bourbon, if desired, and keep warm.

Use a sharp carving knife to cut the ham into thin slices. Pour the sauce into a warmed sauceboat and pass at the table.

Serves 10 to 12

diane cohen's brisket

I grew up eating either chicken or brisket for Friday night dinner, and always ate brisket for one of the nights of Chanukah. I thought my mother made the best brisket until I made this recipe. (Sorry, Mom, I love you all the same.) Diane Cohen is the mother of Lisa Ekus-Saffer, cookbook publicist and literary agent. Lisa says, "It's wonderful the night it is cooked, but gets better the second or third day. And it freezes well." The wine-braised onions and sauce are deeply flavored and wondrous. It's hard to get enough. In fact, I increased the amount of onions and wine from the original recipe Lisa sent. I asked Lisa about the change and she said, "Oh, yes, I add more wine and onions all the time; they're the best."

1 TEASPOON SWEET HUNGARIAN PAPRIKA

1 TEASPOON KOSHER OR SEA SALT

1 TEASPOON FRESHLY GROUND PEPPER

1 FLAT CUT BEEF BRISKET (4 TO 5 POUNDS), WITH 1/4 INCH OF FAT CAP ATTACHED (SEE COOK'S NOTE, FACING PAGE)

2 LARGE YELLOW ONIONS, HALVED AND THINLY SLICED

1/4 CUP WATER

1 CUP HEARTY RED WINE

2 OR 3 CLOVES GARLIC, FINELY MINCED

1 TABLESPOON MINCED FRESH FLAT-LEAF PARSLEY

1 TABLESPOON MINCED FRESH BASIL

Position a rack in the center of the oven. Preheat the oven to 450°F.

In a small bowl, stir together the paprika, salt, and pepper. Rub the brisket on both sides with the spice mixture. Using some of the onions, arrange a thin layer on the bottom of a Dutch oven or small roasting pan. Place the brisket, fat side down, on top of the onions. Brown the meat, uncovered, in the oven for 20 minutes. Turn the brisket over, scatter the remaining onions over the meat, and brown the second side for 20 minutes longer.

While the brisket is browning, in a 2-cup glass measure, combine the water, wine, garlic, parsley, and basil. Remove the brisket from the oven and lower the oven temperature to 350°F. Pour the wine mixture over the meat, cover the pot, and continue to roast until the brisket is fork-tender, about 2 hours longer.

Transfer the brisket to a carving board, tent with aluminum foil, and let rest for 10 to 15 minutes before carving to allow the juices to set. Keep the onions and juices in the pot warm.

Cut the brisket crosswise into thin slices and arrange on a warmed platter. Pour the juices and onions from the pot over the top and serve immediately.

Serves 8

COOK'S NOTE

A whole beef brisket can weigh over 10 pounds. Butchers often cut the brisket into two parts, the flat cut and the point cut. The flat cut used in this recipe is the one you'll see most often. It is leaner and thinner than the point cut and has a rectangular shape with a thick cap of fat on one side. (The point cut has an irregular shape and pockets of fat. It is terrific for slow barbecuing because the interior fat keeps the brisket moist.) You'll want to leave a 1/4-inch-thick layer of fat on the brisket to give it moisture. Either trim the brisket yourself or ask your butcher to trim it.

whole roast salmon with farro-herb stuffing

Another memorable presentation when you are entertaining is to serve a whole roast salmon stuffed with a *farro* pilaf. The stuffing can be cooked several hours or even a day ahead, then cooled and set aside or refrigerated until it is time to stuff the salmon. This will ease last-minute preparations for the cook. Although *farro* looks a lot like spelt, and many cooks consider them interchangeable, they are not. Look for imported Italian *farro*, primarily from Abruzzo and Tuscany. It has a sweet, nutty flavor and a more tender texture. Although the *farro* package calls for soaking the grain, it is not necessary for this recipe. Accompany the salmon with a steamed or sautéed green vegetable—green beans, Brussels sprouts, broccolini—and an easy and satisfying holiday dinner will be at hand. Have drinks and nibbles while the salmon bakes, or start with a soup or salad course.

FARRO PILAF

4 CUPS CANNED LOW-SODIUM VEGETABLE BROTH

2 CUPS WATER

2 CUPS *FARRO*

3 TABLESPOONS EXTRA-VIRGIN OLIVE OIL

1 LARGE CLOVE GARLIC, MINCED

1 YELLOW ONION, CUT INTO 1/4-INCH DICE

1 YELLOW BELL PEPPER, SEEDED, DERIBBED, AND CUT INTO 1/4-INCH DICE

1 TEASPOON KOSHER OR SEA SALT

1/2 TEASPOON FRESHLY GROUND PEPPER

1/2 CUP PINE NUTS, TOASTED (SEE COOK'S NOTE, PAGE 45)

3 TABLESPOONS SMALL CAPERS, RINSED AND BLOTTED DRY

FRESHLY GRATED ZEST OF 1 LEMON

1/3 CUP CHOPPED FRESH FLAT-LEAF PARSLEY

1 TABLESPOON CHOPPED FRESH OREGANO

VEGETABLE-OIL COOKING SPRAY FOR PREPARING THE ALUMINUM FOIL

1 WHOLE SALMON (5 TO 7 POUNDS), CLEANED AND SCALED, WITH HEAD AND TAIL LEFT ON

JUICE OF 1 LEMON

1/2 CUP DRY WHITE WINE

CHOPPED FRESH FLAT-LEAF PARSLEY FOR GARNISH

To make the *farro* pilaf, in a 6-quart saucepan, bring the vegetable broth and water to a boil over high heat. Add the *farro*, reduce the heat so the liquid just simmers, and cook the *farro* until soft but still with a bit of firmness at the center, 20 to 25 minutes. Drain the *farro* in a sieve placed over a heatproof bowl, reserving the liquid. Place the *farro* in a bowl and set aside.

In a 12-inch sauté pan over medium heat, heat the oil and swirl to coat the pan. Add the garlic and onion and sauté, stirring frequently, until soft but not brown, about 3 minutes. Add the bell pepper and sauté until well coated with the oil and the pepper softens slightly, about 2 minutes longer. Add the *farro*, 2/3 cup of the reserved liquid, and the salt and pepper. Stir to combine. Add the pine nuts, capers, lemon zest, parsley, and oregano, stir to combine, and cook for 1 minute longer. Remove from the heat and set aside.

Meanwhile, preheat the oven to 400°F. Line a large rimmed baking sheet (11 by 17 inches) with aluminum foil. Spray the foil with vegetable-oil cooking spray. Place the salmon on the pan, positioning diagonally if necessary to make it fit. If the fish is still too large, use a sharp chef's knife to cut off the head. Squeeze the lemon juice all over the fish, and then tilt the fish on its back, open the cavity, and squeeze lemon juice inside. Lay the fish back on its side and spoon the cooled *farro* pilaf along the length of the cavity, mounding it and allowing some to tumble out. Place any remaining pilaf in a buttered baking dish and heat separately. Pour the wine evenly over the fish. Spray a second sheet of foil large enough to cover the fish with nonstick spray and place it, sprayed side down, over the fish to cover completely.

Place the pan in the oven and bake the fish for 30 minutes. Remove the foil covering the salmon and bake the fish for 10 minutes longer. Insert an instant-read thermometer into the thickest part of the fish, avoiding the spine; when it registers 125° to 130°F, the fish is done. My preference is for the fish to be closer to 125°F, when it is moist and just beginning to flake.

Remove the pan from the oven and let the fish rest for 5 minutes. Using 2 large spatulas, transfer the fish to a large, warmed platter. Scatter the chopped parsley around the sides of the platter for garnish. (Alternatively, if you would rather carve the fish and plate the servings in the kitchen, instead of presenting the salmon whole at the table, leave the fish in the pan.)

To serve the fish whole, peel off the top skin or leave it on. (This decision is up to the chef—you either like salmon skin or you don't.) Using a carving knife, cut along the seam running lengthwise down the middle of the side of the fish, then make cuts crosswise into serving-size portions. Using a knife and serving spatula, loosen the pieces of fish. This will make it easier for your guests to serve themselves. When the top fillet has been served with generous spoonfuls of the *farro* pilaf, spoon the remaining stuffing to the side so you can lift off the backbone and ribs. Cut the bottom fillet into crosswise portions and serve with the pilaf.

If you are plating individual servings in the kitchen, follow the same procedure, portioning the salmon and pilaf onto each warmed plate. Garnish with the parsley.

Serves 8

short ribs bourguignonne

Years ago, my husband and I lived in Chicago while he attended graduate school. He was busy studying mathematics and I was busy working and studying cooking with Alma Lach, the local doyenne of French cooking. Alma had been food editor of the *Chicago Sun-Times* for twenty years and decided to retire and start a cooking school. I was her assistant for five years. Under her tutelage, I learned French cooking in all its glory, precision, and detail. She was a patient but exacting teacher, teaching me the importance of balancing flavors and textures. Although I have substituted short ribs for beef cubes in this recipe, the succulent, deep, rich flavors of the Bourguignonne are a credit to her palate. It would be a mistake to skip the addition of Madeira and Cognac at the end of the recipe—it takes the recipe from wonderful to amazing, and that was always Alma's style. Serve with Purée of Celery Root (page 117).

2 TABLESPOONS UNSALTED BUTTER

2 TABLESPOONS EXTRA-VIRGIN OLIVE OIL

2/3 CUP ALL-PURPOSE FLOUR FOR DREDGING

6 POUNDS INDIVIDUAL BEEF SHORT RIBS (NOT CROSS-CUT FLANKEN), ABOUT 3 INCHES LONG, TRIMMED OF EXCESS FAT

2 TEASPOONS KOSHER OR SEA SALT

1 TEASPOON FRESHLY GROUND PEPPER

3 CLOVES GARLIC, MINCED

2 TABLESPOONS TOMATO PASTE

1 TEASPOON MINCED FRESH THYME, PLUS 4 SPRIGS FRESH THYME

1 BOTTLE (750-MILLILITER) RED BURGUNDY

4 SPRIGS FRESH FLAT-LEAF PARSLEY, PLUS 1/4 CUP MINCED PARSLEY FOR GARNISH

1 BAY LEAF

1 1/2 CUPS WATER, OR AS NEEDED

1 1/2 POUNDS SMALL WHITE BOILING ONIONS

1 POUND BABY CARROTS

1 POUND BUTTON MUSHROOMS, WIPED OR BRUSHED CLEAN, ENDS TRIMMED

1/4 CUP MADEIRA

2 TABLESPOONS COGNAC OR OTHER BRANDY

Position a rack on the second-lowest level in the oven. Preheat the oven to 325°F.

In a large (at least 6-quart) Dutch oven or other heavy-bottomed ovenproof pot with a lid, heat the butter and oil over medium-high heat. Spread the flour on a plate. Working in batches, roll the short ribs in the flour, tapping off the excess, and add to the pan, without crowding. Cook, turning occasionally, until browned on all sides, 6 to 8 minutes per batch. Using tongs, transfer the browned meat to a rimmed baking sheet. Continue until all the meat is browned. Season the browned short ribs with the salt and pepper.

Pour off all but 2 tablespoons of the fat from the pan and return the pan to medium-low. Add the garlic, tomato paste, and minced thyme and sauté until fragrant, about 1 minute. Add the Burgundy and stir to loosen the browned bits on the bottom of the pan. Bring the wine to a simmer.

While the wine is heating, make a bouquet garni by laying the sprigs of thyme and then parsley on top of the bay leaf. Bend the stems and leaves of the parsley around the bay leaf and thyme to form a bundle, and tie the bundle together with kitchen string. Add the bouquet garni to the pot.

Return the browned meat to the pot, and any accumulated juices from the baking sheet. Pour in the water, adding just enough so the meat is barely covered with liquid, and bring to a boil over medium-high heat. Cover with a tight-fitting lid, transfer to the oven, and braise for 2 hours, stirring the meat once after 1 hour. After 2 hours, add the onions and carrots to the pot, stir to submerge them in the liquid, and cook until barely tender, about 30 minutes. Add the mushrooms and cook until tender and cooked through, about 15 minutes. At this point the meat should be falling-off-the-bone tender and all the vegetables should be tender. (The recipe can be made up to this point 1 day in advance. Let cool, cover, and refrigerate.)

Remove the pot from the oven and set it over a burner turned to medium-low. Skim off any fat from the surface of the cooking liquid and discard the bouquet garni. Add the Madeira and Cognac and simmer for 5 minutes, stirring occasionally.

Taste and adjust the seasoning. Use tongs to transfer the short ribs to a warmed platter. Spoon the sauce along with the carrots, onions, and mushrooms over the meat. Garnish with the minced parsley and serve immediately.

Serves 6

4 festive side dishes

I love accessories and consider side dishes the mix-and-match accents of a menu. They bring important visual and cultural cues, as well as gastronomic treasures, to your holiday table. Looking good enough to eat really does matter, but food can do much more: it can express personal history, affections, and style (adventuresome, playful, or play-it-safe!). Christmas Kugel and Fa-La-La-La Latkes pay homage to my Jewish heritage; Whipped Garnet Yams with a Pecan Praline Crust and Puree of Celery Root reflect my fondness for root vegetables. And if you're uncertain about Brussels sprouts or parsnips, just try them on for size—they're eye-catching and palate-pleasing on any holiday plate.

roasted carrots and parsnips with fresh dill

Here's one vegetable dish that doesn't need any last-minute attention from the busy Christmas cook—and I consider that a gift. These orange and ivory root vegetables, flecked with dill, are a colorful addition to the holiday buffet and complement beef, turkey, goose, lamb, and even ham. Parsnips are woefully underused, and once most people try them, they are surprised by how sweet and complex they taste. They will keep, wrapped in paper towels and slipped into a plastic bag, in the refrigerator for up to 2 weeks. They are also terrific combined with potatoes for a puréed winter soup.

7 PARSNIPS (ABOUT 2$^{1}/_{2}$ POUNDS), PEELED AND CUT INTO 3-BY-$^{1}/_{2}$-INCH STICKS

1$^{1}/_{2}$ POUNDS TENDER CARROTS, PEELED AND CUT INTO 3-BY-$^{1}/_{2}$-INCH STICKS

$^{1}/_{3}$ CUP EXTRA-VIRGIN OLIVE OIL

2 TABLESPOONS CHOPPED FRESH DILL

1 TEASPOON FRESHLY GROUND PEPPER

2 TEASPOONS KOSHER OR SEA SALT

Position a rack in the center of the oven. Preheat the oven to 400°F.

In a large roasting pan or 9-by-13-inch baking dish, toss the parsnips and carrots with the olive oil, dill, pepper, and salt. Roast, stirring once or twice, until the vegetables are tender when pierced with a knife and lightly caramelized in spots, about 45 minutes. Serve immediately, or cover and keep warm for up to 1 hour before serving.

Serves 8 to 10

bread stuffing with sausage, apples, and caramelized onions

Who can resist Italian sausage slices, sautéed apples, and the slightly blackened edges of caramelized onions? The addition of savory herbs makes this the perfect combination for stuffing. Children, especially those who don't like mushrooms (like mine!), really gobble this up. This stuffing pairs deliciously with Juniper-Brined Roast Turkey (page 72) or with Garlic and Herb—Rubbed Crown Roast of Pork (page 77). If you have room in your oven, bake the stuffing while the turkey or pork is roasting. Otherwise, bake it beforehand and reheat it once the turkey or pork is out of the oven.

1 TABLESPOON UNSALTED BUTTER, AT ROOM TEMPERATURE

10 CUPS UNSEASONED DRY BREAD CUBES (SEE PAGE 19)

1 TABLESPOON OLIVE OIL

12 OUNCES MILD ITALIAN SAUSAGES

1 BAG (14 OUNCES) FROZEN PEARL ONIONS, THAWED AND BLOTTED DRY WITH PAPER TOWELS

1 TABLESPOON SUGAR

2 GRANNY SMITH APPLES (ABOUT 6 OUNCES EACH), PEELED, CORED, AND CUT INTO 1/2-INCH DICE

3 LARGE RIBS CELERY, TRIMMED AND CHOPPED

2/3 CUP MINCED FRESH FLAT-LEAF PARSLEY

1 TABLESPOON FRESH THYME LEAVES

2 TABLESPOONS MINCED FRESH SAGE

1 TEASPOON KOSHER OR SEA SALT

FRESHLY GROUND PEPPER

3 LARGE EGGS, LIGHTLY BEATEN

4 CUPS HOMEMADE CHICKEN STOCK OR CANNED LOW-SODIUM CHICKEN BROTH

Position a rack in the center of the oven. Preheat the oven to 350°F. Coat a deep, 9-by-13-inch oven-to-table baking pan with the butter. Place the bread cubes in a very large bowl.

In a 10-inch sauté pan, heat the oil over medium-high heat and swirl to coat the pan. Cook the sausages until nicely browned on all sides, about 10 minutes. Transfer to a plate and let cool. Remove all but 2 tablespoons of the fat from the pan, reserving the extra. Add the onions to the fat in the pan, place over medium-high heat, and saute, stirring frequently, until softened and lightly browned, about 3 minutes. Sprinkle the sugar over the onions and sauté, stirring constantly, until the onions turn golden and the edges caramelize, 3 to 5 minutes. Add the onions to the bread in the bowl.

Return the pan to medium heat, add the reserved fat, and swirl to coat the pan. Add the apples and celery and sauté, stirring frequently, until softened, 5 to 7 minutes. Add the parsley, thyme, sage, salt, and a few grinds of pepper and sauté for 1 minute longer. Add this mixture to the bread cubes, and stir to combine. Add the eggs and stock to the bowl, and mix well.

Transfer the stuffing to the prepared pan. Bake, uncovered, until the top is lightly browned and crusty, 50 minutes to 1 hour. Serve directly from the pan.

Serves 12

christmas kugel

How did noodle kugel end up in *The Christmas Table*? It's a funny story. For years, our family has shared many Thanksgivings and Christmases with our closest friends, Harriet and Peter Watson, and their children. Harriet always makes a noodle kugel for the holidays, so that tradition has become a part of the Morgan family tradition, too. The question is, which noodle kugel do we make? My mother's recipe for noodle kugel, which I grew up eating and loving, is made with eggs, sugar, cottage cheese, sour cream, and crushed pineapple. My daughter, Molly, loved mine until she tasted Harriet's and declared hers far superior. So, this is Harriet's winning recipe, which owes a big nod to one of her sister's friends.

8 OUNCES EXTRA-WIDE DRIED EGG NOODLES

7 TABLESPOONS BUTTER, MELTED

6 LARGE EGGS

1 TEASPOON KOSHER OR SEA SALT

1 CUP SUGAR

1 PINT (16 OUNCES) SMALL-CURD COTTAGE CHEESE

1 1/2 CUPS SOUR CREAM

1 CONTAINER (15 OUNCES) WHOLE-MILK RICOTTA CHEESE

1 PACKAGE (3 OUNCES) CREAM CHEESE, AT ROOM TEMPERATURE

2 CUPS MILK

1 CUP GOLDEN RAISINS

2 TABLESPOONS GROUND CINNAMON

Position a rack in the center of the oven. Preheat the oven to 350°F.

Fill a medium saucepan two-thirds full of water, cover, and bring to a boil over high heat. Add the egg noodles, stir, and cook, uncovered, until al dente (cooked through but still slightly chewy), about 8 minutes. Drain in a colander and then transfer to a medium bowl. Toss the noodles with 6 tablespoons of the butter and set aside. Butter a 9-by-13-inch glass or porcelain baking dish with the remaining 1 tablespoon butter.

In a large bowl, whisk the eggs until blended and then whisk in the salt and sugar. Using a rubber spatula or large spoon, add the cottage cheese, 1 cup of the sour cream, the ricotta cheese, and the cream cheese and mix until combined. Add the milk, raisins, and noodles and mix gently until thoroughly combined.

Pour the mixture into the prepared baking dish. Sprinkle the top with the cinnamon. Bake, uncovered, until the kugel is set and the sides are lightly browned, about 1 1/2 hours. (The kugel can be baked up to 2 days in advance, allowed to cool, covered, and refrigerated. Bring to room temperature and then cover and reheat in a preheated 250°F oven until hot, about 40 minutes.)

To serve, cut the noodle kugel into 2-inch squares and transfer to a warmed serving platter, or serve directly from the baking dish. Alternatively, cover and keep warm for up to 1 hour before serving. Put the remaining 1/2 cup sour cream in a small bowl and pass at the table for diners to add a dollop to their serving.

Serves 12

yorkshire pudding with chives

At Christmas, it's hard to imagine a slice of rare prime rib or leg of lamb without Yorkshire pudding to accompany it. These festive puddings, a cross between a popover and a puffy Dutch baby, are delightful, especially with the colorful addition of fresh herbs and the savory drippings from the roast. The key to making these puddings puffy and crisp is to have the pan very hot, the drippings or butter very hot, and the batter at room temperature. ❋ Timing is important. The puddings must be served straight from the oven because they deflate when cool. Here's how I do it: When the roast is done, I transfer it to a carving board and tent it with aluminum foil to rest for 20 minutes. I pour the drippings from the pan into a ½-cup heatproof measure. I heat the muffin pan for 10 minutes until hot and then bake the puddings for about 15 minutes. While they bake, I set out all the other hot food and accompaniments, and then begin carving the roast a few minutes before the puddings are done. As soon as they are ready, I transfer them to a warmed bowl and gather all my guests to begin the celebration feast.

1¼ CUPS ALL-PURPOSE FLOUR

¼ TEASPOON FRESHLY GROUND PEPPER

1¼ CUPS MILK

3 LARGE EGGS, BEATEN

1 TABLESPOON SNIPPED FRESH CHIVES

2 TABLESPOONS MINCED FRESH
FLAT-LEAF PARSLEY

½ CUP HOT RESERVED BEEF OR
LAMB DRIPPINGS OR MELTED BUTTER

In a medium bowl, or preferably a 4-cup glass measuring cup, combine the flour and pepper. Slowly whisk in the milk until smooth. Whisk in the eggs and then add the chives and parsley. Let the batter stand at room temperature for 1 hour. Whisk before using.

Position a rack in the center of the oven. Preheat the oven to 450°F.

Place a 12-cup standard muffin pan in the oven until hot, about 10 minutes. Place 2 teaspoons of the meat drippings in each muffin cup. Immediately divide the batter among the muffin cups. Bake the puddings until puffy and golden brown, about 15 minutes. Serve immediately.

Makes 12 puddings; serves 6 to 12

wild rice with roasted chestnuts and cranberries

In my cooking classes, the students are always asking what recipes can be made in advance to simplify entertaining. This is a terrific do-ahead recipe for the busy holiday host. The chestnuts and the dried cranberries and apricots bring a seasonal sweetness to this savory side dish. I especially like wild rice paired with pork, goose, game birds, and a holiday turkey. See my notes on wild rice in the Foods of the Season section (page 27).

1 1/4 POUNDS FRESH CHESTNUTS (ABOUT 1 1/2 CUPS PEELED, SEE COOK'S NOTE, PAGE 110)

2 CUPS WILD RICE

2 CUPS HOMEMADE CHICKEN STOCK OR CANNED LOW-SODIUM CHICKEN BROTH

2 CUPS WATER

1/2 TEASPOON KOSHER OR SEA SALT

1/2 CUP SWEETENED DRIED CRANBERRIES

3/4 CUP DRIED APRICOTS, QUARTERED

5 TABLESPOONS UNSALTED BUTTER

2 LARGE RIBS CELERY, TRIMMED AND FINELY CHOPPED

2 LARGE CARROTS, PEELED AND FINELY CHOPPED

1 YELLOW ONION, FINELY CHOPPED

1 TABLESPOON FRESH THYME LEAVES

2 TABLESPOONS MINCED FRESH SAGE

1/2 CUP MINCED FRESH FLAT-LEAF PARSLEY

FRESHLY GROUND PEPPER

Position a rack in the center of the oven. Preheat the oven to 400°F.

Using a sharp paring knife, score the flat side of each chestnut with a big X, cutting through the outer shell and inner brown skin. Place the chestnuts on a rimmed baking sheet and roast until tender when pierced with a fork, about 20 minutes. While the chestnuts are still quite warm but cool enough to handle, peel them with a sharp paring knife, removing both the outer shell and the inner brown skin. Discard any chestnuts that look rotten. Set aside the chestnuts that are hard to peel and rewarm them in a 400°F oven; or place them on a paper towel and rewarm in a microwave for 45 seconds on High, repeating if necessary. Cut the roasted chestnuts in half and set aside. Lower the oven temperature to 350°F.

Meanwhile, in a medium saucepan, combine the rice, chicken stock, water, and 1/4 teaspoon of the salt. Bring to a boil over medium-high heat. Reduce the heat to a simmer, cover partially, and cook, stirring occasionally, until the rice is tender, about 40 minutes. (Not all of the liquid will be absorbed.)

In a small bowl, combine the cranberries and apricots, add hot water to cover, and allow to plump for 20 minutes. Drain and reserve. >>>

wild rice with roasted chestnuts and cranberries
CONTINUED

In a 12-inch sauté pan, melt 4 tablespoons of the butter and swirl to coat the bottom. Add the celery, carrots, and onion and sauté until soft and lightly browned, about 5 minutes. Add the thyme, sage, and parsley and sauté for 1 minute longer. Remove from the heat.

When the rice is tender, drain it in a sieve and add it to the sautéed vegetables. Add the reserved chestnuts, cranberries, and apricots and stir to combine. Add the remaining 1/4 teaspoon salt and a few grinds of pepper. Taste and adjust the seasoning.

Use the remaining 1 tablespoon butter to grease an oven-to-table casserole. Spoon the rice into the casserole and cover with aluminum foil. (The wild rice can be made up to this point 1 day in advance, cooled, covered, and refrigerated. Remove from the refrigerator 1 hour before baking, and increase the baking time from 20 minutes to 40 minutes to ensure it is heated through.)

Twenty minutes before serving, bake the rice until heated through, then serve directly from the casserole.

Serves 8 to 10

COOK'S NOTE
If you prefer not to roast your own chestnuts, you can buy peeled chestnuts in vacuum-sealed packages, cans, or jars at specialty-foods stores. If they are packed in liquid, drain it off. Prepared chestnuts are usually boiled rather than roasted, resulting in some flavor loss. To improve their flavor before using, place them on a rimmed baking sheet and roast them in the center of a 350°F oven for 12 to 14 minutes.

creamed spinach

It's hard to find exciting wintertime green vegetables that are also easy to prepare. I get bored with broccoli, and it takes a mountain of kale or chard to produce a last-minute sauté to feed a crowd. As much as I love green beans, they can be stringy and tough in winter, and the always-tender slim French haricots verts are expensive when serving a crowd. I'm including a recipe for creamed spinach because it's a crowd-pleaser, a cinch to sauté, and doesn't require oven space. Baked vegetable casseroles and gratins make wonderful cold-weather fare, but juggling the oven space for a holiday meal that typically includes roasted meat or poultry can be challenging. A traditionalist would serve creamed spinach with roast beef, but this side dish goes with any of the main courses in Chapter 3.

5 TABLESPOONS UNSALTED BUTTER

2 TABLESPOONS ALL-PURPOSE FLOUR

1 CUP HEAVY (WHIPPING) CREAM

1/8 TEASPOON FRESHLY GRATED NUTMEG

3/4 TEASPOON KOSHER OR SEA SALT

1/2 TEASPOON FRESHLY GROUND PEPPER

2 SHALLOTS, FINELY MINCED

1 1/2 POUNDS FRESH BABY SPINACH LEAVES, CHOPPED

In a 2 1/2-quart saucepan over medium-low heat, melt 2 tablespoons of the butter. Add the flour and whisk until well blended with the butter. Continue to cook, stirring constantly, until the flour is cooked through and the roux turns a light tan, about 1 minute. Add the cream and whisk briskly until smooth, thickened, and creamy, about 1 minute. Remove from the heat and stir in the nutmeg, salt, and pepper. Set the béchamel sauce aside. (The sauce can be made up to 2 hours before serving. Arrange and press the plastic wrap directly on the surface of the sauce so a skin doesn't form on the top of the sauce.)

In a large sauté pan over medium-low heat, melt the remaining 3 tablespoons butter. Add the shallots and sauté until soft but not brown, about 1 minute. Add the spinach a handful at a time, stirring constantly and adding more as soon as there is room in the pan. Cook just until the spinach is wilted and heated through, about 5 minutes. Add the béchamel sauce and stir until creamy and heated through.

Serve immediately in a warmed serving bowl.

Serves 6 to 8

sautéed brussels sprouts with garlic and parmesan

As cute as Brussels sprouts look at the farmers' market still attached to their branches, or in the produce aisle piled high in a vegetable basket, they are one of the most maligned winter vegetables because they are so often cooked poorly. They are usually served whole, overcooked and underflavored. But simply trimming and halving the Brussels sprouts— or, better yet, shredding them—makes all the difference in a successful dish. ❄ In my book *The Thanksgiving Table*, I have a favorite recipe for Brussels sprouts. I shred them, sauté them in fat saved from crisply cooking bacon, and then add the bacon and some chopped toasted hazelnuts at the end for savory flavor and crunch. My friend and esteemed cookbook author Joyce Goldstein suggested a terrific recipe that she makes for her family at Christmastime. This is my adaptation of her method and seasonings. Add more garlic if you like. Joyce loves garlic and uses a dozen cloves.

2 1/2 POUNDS BRUSSELS SPROUTS

3 TABLESPOONS UNSALTED BUTTER

3 TABLESPOONS EXTRA-VIRGIN OLIVE OIL

6 LARGE CLOVES GARLIC, FINELY MINCED

1 CUP HOMEMADE CHICKEN STOCK OR CANNED LOW-SODIUM CHICKEN BROTH

KOSHER OR SEA SALT

FRESHLY GROUND PEPPER

3/4 CUP FRESHLY GRATED PARMESAN CHEESE, PREFERABLY PARMIGIANO-REGGIANO

Trim the stem end of the Brussels sprouts and remove any yellow or spotted outer leaves. Cut the Brussels sprouts lengthwise into 1/16-inch-thick slices, and use your fingertips to separate the slices into shreds. Alternatively, shred the Brussels sprouts using a food processor fitted with the coarse shredding disk. Place in a medium bowl and set aside until ready to sauté.

In a 14-inch sauté pan, melt the butter with the oil over medium heat and swirl to coat the pan. Add the garlic and sauté until soft but not brown, about 2 minutes. Add the Brussels sprouts and sauté until bright green and barely crisp-tender, about 3 minutes. Increase the heat to high and add the chicken stock. Stir to blend, cover, and cook until crisp-tender, about 2 minutes. Season to taste with salt and pepper.

Transfer to a warmed serving bowl and top with the Parmesan cheese. Serve immediately.

Serves 8 to 10

fa-la-la-la latkes

Here's the best part about hybrid holidays: the fabulous foods from one tradition can merge with the favorite holiday foods from another tradition. These latkes, or potato pancakes, fried in a very hot skillet, are crisp, thin, with wavy shreds of delicately browned potato at the edges. It is hard to resist breaking off the crunchy edge pieces as the pancakes are moved from the oil to the wire rack. I consider those fabulous shards a treat for the cook (me!), though I do share generously with my favorite dishwasher, my husband. ❋ Latkes are served with brisket (page 94) for a Chanukah meal. At Christmastime, I serve latkes with either prime rib (page 80) or beef tenderloin (page 89). If you have the patience, you can also make miniature latkes, about 1½ inches in diameter, and serve them as hors d'oeuvres topped with a small slice of lox, a tiny dollop of sour cream or crème fraîche, and minced chives.

3 POUNDS IDAHO OR RUSSET POTATOES, PEELED
AND RINSED UNDER COLD WATER

1 YELLOW ONION, HALVED

1 LARGE EGG, LIGHTLY BEATEN

2 TABLESPOONS ALL-PURPOSE FLOUR

½ TEASPOON BAKING POWDER

1 TEASPOON KOSHER OR SEA SALT

FRESHLY GROUND PEPPER

PEANUT OR GRAPESEED OIL FOR FRYING

1 CUP SOUR CREAM FOR SERVING

1 CUP APPLESAUCE FOR SERVING

Have a colander and a large bowl of cold water ready. Using the large holes on a box grater or a food processor fitted with the coarse grating disk, coarsely grate the potatoes. Place in the cold water for 1 minute and then drain the potatoes in the colander. Rinse the potatoes under cold water once or twice until the water runs clear. This removes the starch and keeps the potatoes from turning reddish. Use your hands or the back of a broad spoon to squeeze out as much liquid as possible. Dry the bowl and transfer the potatoes to the bowl.

Using the box grater or the food processor, coarsely grate the onion. Add the onion to the potatoes and mix to combine. Add the egg, flour, baking powder, salt, and a few grinds of pepper, and mix to combine. (Use immediately or cover and set aside at room temperature for up to 1 hour.)

Position a rack in the center of the oven. Preheat the oven to 250°F. Have ready a large wire rack set in a rimmed baking sheet.

Pour oil to a depth of 1/2 inch into 1 or 2 large, heavy frying pans, preferably cast iron. Heat the oil over medium-high heat until hot but not smoking. Scoop up about 1/4 cup of the potato mixture and gently drop it in the pan. Use a spatula to flatten it lightly, forming a pancake. Form as many additional pancakes as will comfortably fit in the pan without crowding. Fry on one side until golden brown, about 3 minutes. Turn and brown the other side, about 3 minutes longer. Adjust the heat and add more oil as needed to fry additional batches. Transfer the latkes to the wire rack and keep warm, uncovered, in the oven while frying additional batches. (The potato latkes can be made up to this point 1 day ahead if refrigerating or 2 weeks ahead if freezing. Let cool, layer between sheets of waxed paper in a covered container, and refrigerate or freeze. Arrange them, straight from the refrigerator or freezer, in a single layer on a wire rack set in a rimmed baking sheet, and reheat in a preheated 350°F oven until hot and crisp, 15 to 20 minutes.)

Arrange the latkes on a warmed platter and serve immediately, or keep warm for up to 10 minutes before serving. Pass bowls of sour cream and applesauce at the table.

Makes about twenty 2-inch-diameter latkes; serves 8 to 10

potatoes au gratin with fresh thyme and a parmesan crust

Creamy, Parmesan-topped potato gratin has graced my holiday buffet for years. The crisp cheese-baked crust, browned and crunchy at the edges, is an ideal foil for multiple layers of paper-thin potato slices scented with garden-picked thyme, nutmeg, and white pepper. The Parmesan sprinkled on each layer adds just the right amount of saltiness, and the garlic-infused cream brings a rustic earthiness to the gratin. For one casual holiday dinner party with only eight guests, I cut the recipe by one-third and made individual portions in five-inch round white porcelain gratin dishes. It's a fun way to serve the gratin for a relaxed, sit-down dinner.

3 CUPS HEAVY (WHIPPING) CREAM

1 LARGE CLOVE GARLIC, FINELY MINCED

2 TABLESPOONS UNSALTED BUTTER, AT ROOM TEMPERATURE

6 LARGE RED POTATOES (ABOUT 4 POUNDS), PEELED AND CUT INTO PAPER-THIN SLICES

1 CUP FRESHLY GRATED PARMESAN CHEESE, PREFERABLY PARMIGIANO-REGGIANO

2 TABLESPOONS MINCED FRESH THYME

FRESHLY GRATED NUTMEG

FRESHLY GROUND WHITE PEPPER

In a small saucepan over medium heat, simmer the cream with the garlic for 5 minutes. Remove from the heat and let the cream steep while you prepare the potatoes.

Position a rack in the center of the oven. Preheat the oven to 325°F. Generously butter a 12- to 14-cup shallow flameproof baking dish or gratin dish. Set aside.

Arrange a layer of potato slices in the bottom of the dish, creating rows of overlapping slices. Sprinkle the potatoes with 2 tablespoons of the Parmesan cheese, a big pinch of thyme, and a smidgen of nutmeg and pepper. Stir the cream and gently pour about 1/4 cup over the top. Repeat, layering the potatoes and

adding the cheese, seasonings, and cream, until all of the potatoes are used. (Depending on the shape of the dish, you should have about 3 layers of potatoes.) Pour the remaining cream over the top. Sprinkle the remaining Parmesan evenly over the gratin. Cover with foil. (The gratin can be made up to this point and set aside for up to 2 hours before baking.)

Bake the gratin until the potatoes are almost tender and the liquid is mostly absorbed, about 1 1/2 hours. Uncover the gratin and continue to bake until the liquid is completely absorbed and the potatoes are browned and moist, about 30 minutes longer. If desired, place the gratin under the broiler to crisp and brown the top. Set aside to rest for 10 minutes before serving.

Cut into wedges or squares and serve directly from the casserole.

Serves 12

purée of celery root

As a change of pace from classic mashed potatoes, I like to serve a combination of puréed celery root and potatoes because they pair well together and the sweet, mild celery flavor complements roasted meats, turkey, or game. Celery root, also called celeriac or knob celery, is in season from November until April. Its delicate flavor more than makes up for its ugly looks! Look for large, hard, relatively smooth-skinned knobs to minimize waste when peeling. A sharp knife, rather than a vegetable peeler, is the best tool for removing the skin. There is a certain amount of waste because the skin is bumpy and grooved, which is why I prefer to buy larger knobs. Store celery root in the refrigerator until needed; it keeps for a week or so.

2 LARGE CELERY ROOTS (ABOUT 3 POUNDS TOTAL)

2 RUSSET POTATOES (ABOUT 1$^1/_4$ POUNDS TOTAL)

1 TEASPOON KOSHER OR SEA SALT, PLUS MORE TO TASTE

$^1/_2$ CUP (1 STICK) UNSALTED BUTTER, AT ROOM TEMPERATURE, CUT INTO CHUNKS

$^1/_2$ TO $^3/_4$ CUP HEAVY (WHIPPING) CREAM, WARMED

FRESHLY GROUND WHITE PEPPER

Fill a 6-quart saucepan two-thirds full of water and set aside. Working with 1 celery root at a time, use a sharp knife to cut off the top and a thin slice from the base of the root. Pare away the tough outer skin and then cut the root into 1-inch chunks. Immediately add the chunks to the water in the pan to keep them from browning. Repeat with the second celery root. Using a vegetable peeler, peel the potatoes, cut them into 1-inch chunks, and add them to the pan with the celery root. Add 1 teaspoon salt. Partially cover the pot and bring the water to a boil over high heat. Reduce the heat so the water simmers and cook until the vegetables are tender when pierced with a knife, about 15 minutes.

Drain the vegetables in a colander and return them to the pot. Place the pot over low heat for 1 minute to evaporate any excess moisture.

In a food processor fitted with the metal blade, process half of the vegetables just until puréed and then transfer to a large warmed bowl. Repeat to purée the remaining vegetables. Whisk in the butter, a chunk at a time, until incorporated. Gradually add the cream and whisk until the mixture is smooth.

Season the purée to taste with salt and pepper and serve immediately. Or, if not serving right away, keep warm in the top of a double boiler, or cover and rewarm in a microwave oven.

Serves 8

lisa morrison's cranbeer-y relish

Once a year, I teach a six-week food-writing course in Portland, Oregon, where I live. I was teaching the course while writing this book, and Lisa Morrison was one of my talented students. When she heard about the book, she offered to give me her favorite recipe for cranberry relish, which calls for a twelve-ounce bottle of framboise Lambic, a raspberry-flavored Belgian beer. Not surprisingly, I was skeptical, but Lisa writes extensively about beer for many publications and is known locally as "the beer goddess," so it was worth a try. The recipe worked beautifully and the relish tastes terrific. An obvious side dish to serve with turkey or goose, it also pairs well with Salt and Garlic–Crusted Prime Rib of Beef (page 80).

1 BOTTLE (12 OUNCES) LINDEMAN'S FRAMBOISE LAMBIC BEER

1 PACKAGE (12 OUNCES) FRESH OR FROZEN CRANBERRIES, PICKED OVER AND STEMS REMOVED

1/4 CUP FINELY DICED CRYSTALLIZED GINGER (SEE COOK'S NOTE)

1/4 CUP SUGAR

In a deep, 4-quart saucepan over medium-high heat, bring the beer to a boil. Add the cranberries, ginger, and sugar. Adjust the heat so the mixture simmers and stir to dissolve the sugar. Cook, stirring occasionally, until the cranberries begin to pop open, about 10 minutes. Remove from the heat and let cool to room temperature. (The relish will keep, tightly covered, in the refrigerator for up to 10 days.)

Transfer the cooled relish to a bowl, cover, and refrigerate until serving.

Makes 2 1/4 cups

COOK'S NOTE
Crystallized ginger slices are typically packaged in 4-ounce boxes and are available in the Asian-foods section of well-stocked supermarkets. I've also seen diced ginger sold in vacuum-sealed cans in the baking section of grocery stores.

whipped garnet yams with a pecan praline crust

Candied yams are traditional on the Thanksgiving table, but this winter root vegetable is a colorful and welcome addition to the Christmas table, too. For years, I have taught Thanksgiving classes around the country, and every time I demonstrate this recipe and the students sample the dish, they tell me these yams are the best they have ever tasted. They are lightened with eggs and enriched with butter and brown sugar. But the praline crust is what makes this casserole divine. Hot from the oven, the meltingly lush topping is bubbly in the center and browned to a caramelized sugary-crisp at the edges. ✳ If time permits, you can make the whipped yams and the topping a day in advance. Cover and refrigerate them separately. Remove the yams and topping an hour before you plan to bake the casserole. Warm the topping and spread it over the yams just before baking.

6 LARGE GARNET YAMS (ABOUT 5^1/2 POUNDS TOTAL), SCRUBBED

^{3}/4 CUP MILK

^{1}/2 CUP (1 STICK) UNSALTED BUTTER

3 LARGE EGGS, LIGHTLY BEATEN

^{3}/4 CUP PACKED DARK BROWN SUGAR

PRALINE TOPPING
4 TABLESPOONS (^{1}/2 STICK) UNSALTED BUTTER

^{3}/4 CUP PACKED DARK BROWN SUGAR

^{1}/2 TEASPOON KOSHER OR SEA SALT

^{1}/2 TEASPOON GROUND CINNAMON

^{1}/2 TEASPOON FRESHLY GRATED NUTMEG

^{3}/4 CUP HEAVY (WHIPPING) CREAM

1^1/2 CUPS COARSELY CHOPPED PECANS

2 TEASPOONS PURE VANILLA EXTRACT

Position a rack in the center of the oven. Preheat the oven to 350°F. Pierce each yam several times with a fork and place them in a baking pan. Bake the yams until very tender when pierced with a fork, 1^1/4 to 1^1/2 hours. Set aside until cool enough to handle.

In a small saucepan over medium heat, heat the milk and butter until the butter has melted and the mixture is hot but not boiling. Cut the yams in half, scoop the flesh into a large bowl, and discard the skins. Pass the yams through a ricer or food mill held over a bowl, or mash with a potato masher. Stir the milk mixture into the yams. Whisk in the eggs and continue whisking until well combined with the yam mixture. Add the brown sugar and stir until thoroughly blended.

Butter a 9-by-13-inch baking pan, or an 11-inch round oven-to-table casserole. Spread the sweet potato mixture evenly in the casserole. Set aside while making the topping. Increase the oven temperature to 375°F.

To make the praline topping, melt the butter in a 2-quart saucepan over low heat. Stir in the brown sugar, salt, cinnamon, nutmeg, cream, and pecans. Bring to a simmer and cook, stirring constantly, until the sugar has dissolved and the mixture is thick, about 5 minutes. If the mixture begins to boil and splatter, turn down the heat to maintain a simmer. Remove from the heat and stir in the vanilla. Pour the topping over the sweet potatoes and spread in an even layer with a rubber spatula.

Bake until the topping is slightly crusty and set, about 30 minutes. Serve immediately directly from the dish.

Serves 8 to 10

5 holiday desserts

Hundreds of years ago, when sugar was a costly and exotic commodity, only the wealthy enjoyed it regularly. For everyone else, it was a special treat reserved for holidays and other celebrations. No wonder the enchanted forest in *The Nutcracker* so delights Clara, with trees laden with sugarplums and lemon drops and leaves of spun sugar. A sugary nebula hovers over Christmas to this day. You'll find my favorite holiday desserts here, including custards and puddings, a seasonal trifle, Eggnog Cheesecake and Candied Kumquats, and a scene-stealing French Bûche de Noël.

eggnog cheesecake with candied kumquats

"Decadent" and "scrumptious" come to mind when I think about this cheesecake. In the tradition of New York–style cheesecakes, this eggnog version is rich, dense but still light, and creamy beyond belief. The eggnog adds a sweet, sophisticated flavor to the cheesecake, and the booze will be noticed, but splendidly so.

CRUST

5 TABLESPOONS UNSALTED BUTTER, MELTED

1 1/4 CUPS POST GRAPE-NUTS CEREAL

1/4 CUP PLUS 1 TABLESPOON GRANULATED SUGAR

1/4 TEASPOON GROUND CINNAMON

PINCH OF KOSHER OR SEA SALT

FILLING

3 PACKAGES (8 OUNCES EACH) CREAM CHEESE, SOFTENED

1 CUP GRANULATED SUGAR

4 LARGE EGGS, LIGHTLY BEATEN

1 TABLESPOON PURE VANILLA EXTRACT

1 CUP EGGNOG

1 TABLESPOON BOURBON

1 TABLESPOON DARK RUM

1 TABLESPOON BRANDY

GARNISH

1/2 CUP HEAVY (WHIPPING) CREAM, VERY COLD

1 TABLESPOON CONFECTIONERS' SUGAR, SIFTED

CANDIED KUMQUATS (PAGE 126), OPTIONAL

Position a rack in the center of the oven. Preheat the oven to 375°F. Butter a 9- or 10-inch springform pan with 1 tablespoon of the melted butter. Set aside.

To make the crust, in a food processor fitted with the metal blade, process the Grape-Nuts until fine crumbs form, allowing the processor to run for 2 minutes. Add the granulated sugar, cinnamon, and salt and process to combine. Pour the remaining 4 tablespoons butter through the feed tube and process just until

incorporated, about 30 seconds. Turn the crumbs out into the prepared pan and press evenly onto the bottom and about 1 inch up the sides. (I use a flat-bottomed, stainless-steel 1/2-cup measuring cup to help press the crumbs, which prevents the corners from being thicker than the sides.)

Bake the crust until crisp and lightly colored, 10 to 12 minutes. Transfer to a wire rack to cool while you prepare the filling. When the crust is hot out of the oven, press the bottom crust with the measuring cup again to smooth it. Reduce the oven temperature to 350°F.

To make the filling, in a food processor fitted with the metal blade, process the cream cheese until smooth. Add the granulated sugar and then the eggs, processing after each addition and then continuing to process until the mixture is thoroughly combined and creamy, stopping to scrape down the sides of the bowl once or twice. Add the vanilla, eggnog, bourbon, rum, and brandy and process until completely smooth and all ingredients are thoroughly combined. (Alternatively, beat the ingredients in a large bowl using an electric mixer.)

Gently pour the cheesecake filling into the prebaked crust. The filling will likely rise above the crust. Bake until the sides are slightly puffed, about 40 minutes. The center will still be very soft and will jiggle when you shake the >>>

eggnog cheesecake with candied kumquats
CONTINUED

pan gently. Turn off the oven, set the oven door ajar, and leave the cheesecake, undisturbed, in the oven for 40 minutes. Then transfer the cheesecake to a wire rack and let cool completely in the pan. Cover and refrigerate for at least 6 hours, but preferably overnight.

To decorate the cheesecake, unlatch the sides of the pan and remove. In a medium bowl, combine the cream and confectioners' sugar and beat with a whisk or electric mixer until stiff peaks form. Transfer the cream to a pastry bag fitted with a medium star tip and pipe rosettes around the edge of the cheesecake, spacing them 1 inch apart. Place a candied kumquat in the spaces between the rosettes.

To serve, dip a sharp knife in hot water, wipe it dry, and cut the cake into slices, dipping the knife and wiping it dry before each cut. Serve with 2 kumquats placed alongside each slice.

Serves 10 to 12

candied kumquats

These petite orange gems are a seasonal favorite of mine. They look wonderful on the cheesecake, but are also a good accompaniment to almost any holiday dessert and make a delightful food gift.

12 OUNCES (ABOUT 45) FRESH KUMQUATS, STEMS REMOVED
2 1/2 CUPS GRANULATED SUGAR
3/4 CUP WATER

Using a paring knife, and piercing only the skin, cut 4 evenly spaced lengthwise slits in each kumquat. Place the fruits in a medium saucepan with cold water to cover, bring to a simmer over medium heat, and poach the fruit for 5 minutes. Drain in a colander.

Using the same pan, combine 1 1/2 cups of the sugar with the water. Stir to dissolve the sugar, add the kumquats, place over medium heat, and bring to a simmer. Reduce the heat to low, so the liquid barely simmers, and cook, uncovered, for 30 minutes. The fruit will look glazed and still be whole. Using a slotted spoon, transfer the kumquats to a wire rack set over a rimmed baking sheet and separate them. Let cool for 10 minutes.

Place the remaining 1 cup sugar in a small bowl. One at a time, roll the kumquats in the sugar and return them to the rack, again not touching. Allow the fruits to dry at room temperature overnight. Transfer to individual paper candy cups to prevent them from sticking together, and store an airtight container in a cool, dry place. The candied kumquats will keep for up to 3 months.

Makes about 45

persimmon pudding

Family friends from North Carolina told me their holidays weren't complete without persimmon pudding. This tradition was new to me, but once I made the pudding for our Christmas celebration, my family was hooked. In fact, I caught my husband and children rewarming the leftover pudding for breakfast the day after Christmas. It is plenty rich as is, yet it's customary to serve a dollop of whipped cream on the side, even at breakfast! ❊ In the South and Midwest, the American persimmon (*Diospyros virginiana*) is readily found in markets in the fall. On the East Coast and West Coast, two varieties of the Japanese persimmon (*D. kaki*), one with a pointed base and the other smaller and more spherical, are more common. Any of these will work just fine as long as the fruit is exceedingly ripe— so soft to the touch that it would land with a splat if dropped on the ground.

1 TABLESPOON UNSALTED BUTTER, AT ROOM TEMPERATURE, FOR PREPARING THE PAN

ABOUT 3 POUNDS PERSIMMONS

2 CUPS GRANULATED SUGAR

2 LARGE EGGS, LIGHTLY BEATEN

1 TEASPOON PURE VANILLA EXTRACT

1 3/4 CUPS UNBLEACHED ALL-PURPOSE FLOUR

1 TEASPOON BAKING SODA

1 TEASPOON BAKING POWDER

1 TEASPOON KOSHER OR SEA SALT

1 TEASPOON GROUND CINNAMON

1 1/2 CUPS BUTTERMILK

1/2 CUP HEAVY (WHIPPING) CREAM

2 TABLESPOONS UNSALTED BUTTER, MELTED

CONFECTIONERS' SUGAR FOR DUSTING

Position a rack in the center of the oven. Preheat the oven to 350°F. Butter a 9-by-13-inch baking pan.

Cut the persimmons in half crosswise and use a spoon to scoop out the flesh into a small bowl, picking out the seeds and discarding the stem and skins. Use the back of a spoon to press the flesh into a soft pulp. Measure 2 cups and add to a medium bowl (reserve the remainder for another use; it can be frozen for up to 6 months). Add the granulated sugar, eggs, and vanilla to the pulp and mix together until well combined.

In a large bowl, sift together the flour, baking soda, baking powder, salt, and cinnamon. Add the persimmon mixture one-third at a time, beating well after each addition until incorporated. Stir in the buttermilk, cream, and melted butter.

Pour into the prepared pan. Bake until nicely browned and slightly puffed at the edges, about 45 minutes. Let cool on a wire rack for 20 minutes. Using a small fine-mesh sieve, dust the top of the pudding with the confectioners' sugar. Cut into squares and serve warm directly from the pan. (The pudding can be baked up to 8 hours in advance, cooled, covered, and stored at room temperature. To serve, rewarm in a preheated 350°F oven for 15 minutes and dust with confectioners' sugar.)

Serves 12 to 16

individual anjou pear tarts with caramel ice cream

Frozen puff pastry streamlines the making of these fanciful fruit tarts. A typical package holds two pastry sheets, each of which can be cut into quarters, and then the edges of each quarter are turned in to create a lovely 5-inch square tart with a shallow rim. The recipe can be completed in stages a day ahead and baked the day of the party. The puff pastry will stay crisp at room temperature, but these tarts will hit the sweet spot if given a five-minute blast in the oven right before you serve them. There is nothing like warm glistening fruit, crunchy layers of pastry, and a scoop of ice cream melting into a pool of richness on the side.

2 LARGE EGGS

1^1/2 TABLESPOONS WATER

14 CRISP GINGERSNAP COOKIES
(EACH ABOUT 1^1/2 INCHES IN DIAMETER)

^{1}/4 CUP GRANULATED SUGAR

1 TEASPOON GROUND CINNAMON

2 SHEETS FROZEN PUFF PASTRY DOUGH,
FROM A 17.3-OUNCE PACKAGE, THAWED AT
ROOM TEMPERATURE FOR 30 MINUTES

2 TO 3 TABLESPOONS APRICOT JAM
OR PRESERVES (WITHOUT CHUNKS)

4 FIRM BUT RIPE ANJOU PEARS, PEELED,
HALVED LENGTHWISE, CORED, AND CUT
LENGTHWISE INTO THIN SLICES

ABOUT ^{1}/4 CUP CONFECTIONERS' SUGAR
FOR DUSTING

1 PINT CARAMEL ICE CREAM FOR SERVING

In a small bowl, beat together the eggs and water until blended and set aside. Place the cookies in a heavy lock-top plastic bag and, using a rolling pin, crush the cookies to make fine crumbs. (Alternatively, crush the cookies in a food processor.) Set aside. Combine the granulated sugar and cinnamon in a small bowl and set aside.

Have ready 2 rimmed baking sheets, preferably nonstick. For pans without a nonstick finish, line the pans with parchment paper or nonstick baking liners.

Unfold the pastry sheets and lay them flat on a large cutting board. Using a sharp knife, cut each pastry sheet into quarters, creating eight 5-inch squares. Place 4 squares on each prepared baking sheet, spacing them about 2 inches apart. Fold in the 4 sides of each pastry square about ^{1}/2 inch toward the center, so the edges will be a double thickness. Use your little finger to make indentations about ^{1}/2 inch apart around the edge of each pastry, creating a fluted effect. Place the pastry in the refrigerator for 15 minutes. (The pastry can be prepared up to this point, covered lightly with plastic wrap, and refrigerated overnight.) **>>>**

individual anjou pear tarts with caramel ice cream
CONTINUED

Position 1 rack in the center and another rack in the lower third of the oven. Preheat the oven to 400°F. Place the apricot jam in a small bowl and microwave just until melted, about 10 seconds. Alternatively, heat in a small saucepan over low heat until melted. Set aside. Prepare the pears.

Remove the pastry from the refrigerator. Using a pastry brush, brush the pastry with the beaten egg mixture. Place a rounded tablespoonful of the cookie crumbs in the center of each pastry shell and use your finger to spread it around evenly, keeping the crumbs off the edges. Lay the pear slices in a tight overlapping pattern over the cookie crumbs. Sprinkle the pears with the cinnamon-sugar mixture. Lightly brush the pears with the melted preserves.

Bake the tarts for 15 minutes, switch the position of the baking sheets and rotate the sheets 180 degrees, and continue to bake until the crusts are beautifully browned, 30 to 35 minutes longer. Let cool slightly on the pans on wire racks. (The tarts can be baked up to 8 hours ahead, allowed to cool completely, and then reheated in a 400°F oven for 10 minutes just before serving.)

Using a small fine-mesh sieve, dust the top of each tart with the confectioners' sugar. Serve warm on individual plates with a scoop of ice cream on the side.

Serves 8

bûche de noël

A bûche de Noël is the ultimate, fanciful, whimsical Christmas dessert. Yes, it takes patience and time, but breaking it into separate steps makes it completely doable for the enthusiastic home baker. The cute little meringue mushrooms can be completed a month in advance. The sponge cake and mocha buttercream can be made on the same day, rolled up jelly-roll fashion, and frozen for up to 2 weeks. That leaves only the chocolate glaze to make, and that's a cinch. Dipping cranberries and small rosemary branches in egg white and sugar makes them look frosty.

SPONGE CAKE

1 TABLESPOON UNSALTED BUTTER, MELTED

3/4 CUP SIFTED CAKE FLOUR, PLUS MORE FOR PREPARING THE PAN

9 TABLESPOONS GRANULATED SUGAR

3 LARGE EGGS, AT ROOM TEMPERATURE, SEPARATED

PINCH OF KOSHER OR SEA SALT

1/2 TEASPOON PURE VANILLA EXTRACT

CONFECTIONERS' SUGAR FOR DUSTING

2 TABLESPOONS COGNAC OR OTHER BRANDY

MOCHA BUTTERCREAM

1 CUP PLUS 2 TABLESPOONS GRANULATED SUGAR

1/2 CUP EGG WHITES (ABOUT 3 1/2 LARGE EGG WHITES)

1/4 TEASPOON KOSHER OR SEA SALT

1 1/4 CUPS (2 1/2 STICKS) UNSALTED BUTTER, AT ROOM TEMPERATURE, CUT INTO 1-TABLESPOON PIECES

1/4 CUP ESPRESSO OR DOUBLE-STRENGTH BREWED COFFEE

CHOCOLATE GLAZE

11 OUNCES DARK BITTERSWEET CHOCOLATE (AT LEAST 64% CACAO), CHOPPED (SEE COOK'S NOTE, PAGE 136)

1 1/4 CUPS HEAVY (WHIPPING) CREAM

GARNISHES

MERINGUE MUSHROOMS (PAGE 135)

SUGARED CRANBERRIES AND ROSEMARY BRANCHES (PAGE 136)

UNSWEETENED COCOA POWDER FOR DUSTING

CONFECTIONERS' SUGAR FOR DUSTING

To make the sponge cake, position a rack in the center of the oven. Preheat the oven to 325°F. Brush some of the melted butter over the bottom and sides of a 10-by-15-inch rimmed baking sheet. Line the bottom of the pan and the two short sides with waxed paper. Then turn the paper over, so it is buttered-side up. Brush the waxed paper again with butter.

Sprinkle the waxed paper and the sides of the pan with flour, tap the pan to distribute the flour evenly, and then shake off the excess flour.

In a stand mixer fitted with the whip attachment, combine 6 tablespoons of the granulated sugar, the egg yolks, and salt and beat on medium speed until light, fluffy, and very thick, about 10 minutes. Using a rubber spatula, gradually and gently fold in the 3/4 cup flour and the vanilla.

In a clean bowl, with the cleaned whip attachment, beat the egg whites at medium speed until big bubbles give way to tiny ones, and then start adding the remaining 3 tablespoons sugar. Turn the mixer to high speed once all the sugar is added, and continue beating until very stiff peaks form, 1 to 2 minutes longer. Using a rubber spatula, stir a "gob" of whites into the yolk mixture **>>>**

bûche de noël

to lighten it, and then carefully fold in the remaining whites.

Pour the batter into the prepared pan, and spread it evenly to the edges using a rubber spatula or, preferably, an offset metal spatula. Bake the cake until the top is light golden brown and springs back when lightly touched, about 15 minutes.

While the cake is baking, spread a large linen, regular cotton, or cotton-flour-sack towel on a counter and sprinkle it generously with confectioners' sugar. When the cake is done, remove it from the oven and immediately invert the pan onto the towel. Lift off the pan and then carefully peel the waxed paper from the cake. Cut all 4 crisp sides (edges) off the cake. Using a small fine-mesh sieve, lightly dust the top of the cake with confectioners' sugar. Starting from a long side, roll the cake with the towel jelly-roll fashion. (The towel will be rolled inside the cake.) Let the cake cool completely in this rolled position.

While the cake is cooling, make the mocha buttercream. In a clean metal bowl of the stand mixer, beat together the sugar, egg whites, and salt with a wire whisk until well blended. If using a handheld mixer, whisk the ingredients together in a deep, medium heatproof bowl. Select a saucepan that will hold the mixer bowl securely in its rim, with the base of the bowl about 3 inches above the bottom of the pan. Pour water to a depth of 2 inches into the saucepan. (The base of the bowl must not touch the water.) Place the saucepan over medium heat and bring the water

to a simmer. Turn the heat to low. Rest the bowl holding the sugar mixture in the rim of the saucepan and continue to whisk until the egg whites are hot and register 120°F on an instant-read thermometer, about 5 minutes.

Remove the bowl from the water and place on the stand mixer. (If using a handheld mixer, set the bowl on a damp kitchen towel to steady it.) Using the whip attachment, beat the egg mixture on high speed until thick, glossy, stiff peaks form when you lift the beater, about 6 minutes. Add the butter 1 tablespoon at a time, beating in each addition until completely incorporated before adding the next piece. When all the butter has been incorporated, the buttercream will look fluffy, satiny, and smooth. Add the coffee and mix on low speed at first and then on medium speed until the coffee is incorporated and the buttercream is again satiny smooth.

To assemble the cake, unroll the cooled cake with the aid of the towel. Replace the towel with a long sheet of plastic wrap and lightly sprinkle the plastic wrap with confectioners' sugar. Lay the cake on the plastic wrap. Using a pastry brush, moisten the top of the cake with the Cognac. Set aside about 1 cup of the buttercream in a small bowl. Using an offset metal spatula, spread the remaining buttercream evenly over the top of the cake to form a thick layer, leaving a 3/4-inch-wide strip of cake without buttercream on both long sides. Starting at the long side nearest you, roll up the cake tightly and evenly (without squishing out the buttercream) into a jelly roll. If needed, use **>>>**

bûche de noël

CONTINUED

the plastic wrap to aid in the rolling. Wrap the rolled cake in plastic wrap, twisting the ends to secure them. Place the cake on a rimmed baking sheet and freeze for 1 hour.

Remove the cake from the freezer, transfer it to a cutting board, and unwrap it. Using a sharp knife, cut a thick, angled slice off each end of the cake. Use some of the reserved buttercream to "glue" the 2 slices together to form a stump. Use a bit more buttercream to attach the stump to the top of the cake, positioning it about 2 inches in from one end. Transfer the cake back to the baking sheet. Spread the reserved buttercream thinly and evenly over the entire log, stump, and ends. Return the cake, uncovered, to the freezer for 30 minutes. At this point, proceed to finish the cake by making the glaze and garnishes, or cover the cake tightly with plastic wrap and refrigerate for up to 2 days, or freeze for up to 2 weeks. (If you have frozen the cake, thaw the cake in the refrigerator overnight before glazing and garnishing it.) Unwrap the cake carefully before proceeding.

To make the glaze, put the chocolate in a medium bowl. In a small saucepan over medium heat, bring the cream to a boil. Pour the cream over the chocolate and stir gently until the chocolate is completely melted and the glaze is shiny and smooth, about 2 minutes.

To finish the cake, place it on a wire rack set over a rimmed baking sheet. Pour the glaze evenly over the log, covering it completely. Use a small rubber spatula to touch up any spots that were missed along the base of the cake. Refrigerate the log on the rack for at least 1 hour to allow the glaze to set. (The cake can be glazed and refrigerated for up to 12 hours before garnishing and serving.) Scrape up the extra glaze that has dripped onto the baking sheet and save it for another use. (It can be warmed and used to drizzle over another dessert or onto dessert plates for a squiggly design. Or, it can be refrigerated until firm, rolled into balls, coated with cocoa and eaten as truffles or used to garnish the log.)

To garnish the log, carefully transfer the cake to a long, rectangular serving plate, preferably white. Whimsically arrange some of the meringue mushrooms around and on the log. Tuck some sugar-glazed rosemary branches and cranberries along the base of the log and near the stump, creating a woodsy scene. Dust the cake in places with a little cocoa powder to give it an earthy look. Sprinkle the plate and cake with confectioners' sugar to imitate freshly fallen snow. Present the cake whole and slice it at the dining table, or place it whole on the buffet table.

Serves 10 to 12

134 the christmas table

meringue mushrooms

Every traditional bûche de Noël is garnished with these mushrooms. They are as whimsical and fun to make as they are to look at and eat. You will need a pastry bag fitted with a 3/8-inch plain tip to make them. This recipe makes about 30 mushrooms; you'll only need about a dozen or so to decorate the cake, so indulge and let the family eat the rest as a treat. They're irresistible.

2 LARGE EGG WHITES, AT ROOM TEMPERATURE
2 TEASPOONS FRESH LEMON JUICE
2/3 CUP GRANULATED SUGAR
UNSWEETENED COCOA POWDER FOR DUSTING

Position a rack in the center of the oven. Preheat the oven to 225°F. Line a rimmed baking sheet with parchment paper.

In the bowl of a stand mixer fitted with the whip attachment, combine the egg whites and lemon juice and beat at medium-low speed until foamy. Increase the speec to medium and beat until soft peaks form, about 2 minutes. Add one-third of the sugar and beat on medium speed until combined. Add the remaining sugar and continue to beat on medium speed until combined. Increase the speed to high and beat until stiff peaks form, about 2 minutes.

Fit a pastry bag with a 3/8-inch plain tip. Fold back the top of the bag to form a collar. Using a rubber spatula, scoop the meringue into the bag. Twist the top of the bag closed, lightly squeezing the meringue down to the tip, forcing out any air pockets. To pipe the caps, hold the pastry bag upright with the tip slightly above the prepared baking sheet and pipe out 30 mounds, each 1 to 1½ inches in diameter, on one-half of the baking sheet. They can be spaced close together because they don't spread when baked. (I like to vary the size of the caps and stems, so the mushrooms differ in height and size when assembled.) To pipe the stems, hold the pastry bag upright with the tip touching the sheet, and squeeze and lift at the same time to form 30 cones each 3/4 to 1 inch high. Leave the remaining meringue in the pastry bag and set it aside at room temperature. Using a small fine-mesh sieve, lightly dust the caps with a little cocoa.

Bake the caps and stems until firm to the touch, about 45 minutes. Remove the pan from the oven. Leave the oven on.

Using a small paring knife, very carefully carve out a small hole in the center of the bottom of each cap. Fill the hole with a bit of the remaining meringue in the pastry bag. Attach a stem to the cap and set it upright on the baking sheet. Continue until you have made 30 mushrooms. Bake the mushrooms until set and thoroughly dry, about 30 minutes longer. Transfer the mushrooms to a wire rack and let cool completely. Store them in a single layer in an airtight container at room temperature for up to 1 month.

Makes 30 mushrooms

sugared cranberries and rosemary branches

2 LARGE EGG WHITES, AT ROOM TEMPERATURE

1/3 CUP GRANULATED SUGAR

5 OR 6 FRESH ROSEMARY BRANCHES,
3 TO 4 INCHES LONG

15 FRESH CRANBERRIES

In a shallow bowl or pie plate, beat the egg whites just until loosened and frothy. Put the sugar in another shallow bowl or in a pie plate. Have ready a small rimmed baking sheet.

Dip 1 rosemary branch in the egg whites and turn to coat on all sides. Gently shake to remove any excess egg white, and then dip the branch in the sugar and turn to coat all sides. Place the sugared branch on the baking sheet. Repeat to coat the remaining rosemary.

Dip the cranberries in the egg whites and turn to coat all sides. Using a slotted spoon, lift the cranberries from the egg whites, allowing the excess to drip off, and transfer the cranberries to the sugar. Roll in the sugar to coat all sides. Place on the baking sheet. Set aside until ready to garnish. (Keep the plate of sugar handy to dust the rosemary or cranberries again at the last minute.)

COOK'S NOTE

There is good chocolate and then there is great chocolate. It takes some serious tasting to find favorite brands. (I'm always up for the task.) Some of my favorites include Valrhona, Callebaut, and Scharffen Berger. I suggest you undertake this tasting task for yourself. See my notes on chocolate in the Foods of the Season section (page 20) for tips on decoding labels.

gingerbread bundt cake with crème anglaise

David Lebovitz, a friend and colleague, is the author of several dessert cookbooks, including *Room for Dessert*. The recipe for his famous fresh ginger cake is included in that book. In the introduction to his recipe he writes, "This is the most often requested recipe in my repertoire, and I've passed it on to many, many people." He mentions that it appears quite often on Bay Area menus, sometimes called "Dave's ginger cake." I asked David via e-mail (lucky guy, he now lives in Paris) if I could adapt his recipe for this book and he agreed. It is simply the most delectable, moist, and ginger-packed cake I have ever eaten. Friends who tasted samples of the cake when I was writing this book said, "How soon can I get the recipe?" Here it is. Thanks, David.

CAKE
1 TABLESPOON UNSALTED BUTTER, AT ROOM TEMPERATURE, FOR PAN

3 3/4 CUPS UNBLEACHED ALL-PURPOSE FLOUR, PLUS MORE FOR PREPARING THE PAN

1 1/2 TEASPOONS GROUND CINNAMON

3/4 TEASPOON GROUND CLOVES

3/4 TEASPOON FRESHLY GROUND PEPPER

1 1/2 CUPS UNSULPHURED DARK MOLASSES (NOT BLACKSTRAP)

1 1/2 CUPS GRANULATED SUGAR

1 1/2 CUPS CANOLA OR PEANUT OIL

1 1/2 CUPS WATER

1 TABLESPOON BAKING SODA

2/3 CUP PACKED, PEELED, AND MINCED FRESH GINGER (SEE COOK'S NOTE, PAGE 139)

3 LARGE EGGS, BEATEN

CRÈME ANGLAISE
1 CUP HEAVY (WHIPPING) CREAM

1 CUP MILK

4 LARGE EGG YOLKS

1/4 CUP GRANULATED SUGAR

1/4 TEASPOON KOSHER OR SEA SALT

1 1/2 TEASPOONS PURE VANILLA EXTRACT

CONFECTIONERS' SUGAR FOR DUSTING

Position a rack in the lower third of the oven. Preheat the oven to 350°F. Generously butter and flour a 12-cup nonstick Bundt pan, tapping the pan over the sink to remove the excess flour. (Make certain every interior surface is thoroughly coated or the cake will stick.)

In a large bowl, sift together the 3 3/4 cups flour, the cinnamon, cloves, and pepper. In another large bowl, whisk together the molasses, sugar, and oil.

In a 2 1/2-quart saucepan, bring the water to a boil. Remove from the heat and stir in the baking soda. Whisk this mixture into the molasses mixture, and then add the ginger.

Adding a generous cupful at a time, stir the flour mixture into the molasses mixture until the flour is absorbed. Whisk in the eggs until combined. Pour the batter into the prepared pan. **>>>**

gingerbread bundt cake with crème anglaise
CONTINUED

Bake the cake until a toothpick inserted into the center comes out clean, about 1 hour. If the cake appears to be browning too quickly, lay a piece of foil over the top of the pan. Let the cake cool in the pan on a wire rack for 1 hour. Invert the rack over the top of the pan, invert the pan and the rack together, and lift off the pan. Let the cake continue to cool on the rack until it is room temperature. (The cake can be covered and stored at room temperature for up to 3 days, or tightly wrapped and frozen for up to 1 month. Thaw overnight at room temperature.)

To make the crème anglaise, fill a large bowl three-fourths full with ice for cooling the sauce and set aside. In a 2½-quart saucepan over medium-low heat, combine the cream and milk. Bring to a simmer and remove from the heat. (Do not let the milk mixture boil.)

In a medium bowl, whisk together the egg yolks, granulated sugar, and salt. Slowly add ½ cup of the hot milk mixture while whisking to combine, and then pour the egg yolk mixture into the saucepan. Return the saucepan to low heat and whisk constantly until the mixture is as thick as whipping cream and coats the back of a spoon, 3 to 5 minutes. (The crème anglaise is done when it registers 160°F on an instant-read thermometer.) Remove from the heat and strain through a fine-mesh sieve into a clean bowl. Nest the bowl in the ice bath, stir in the vanilla, and let cool, stirring occasionally. Cover and refrigerate until ready to use. (The sauce can be made up to 2 days in advance.)

To serve, using a small fine-mesh sieve, dust the top of the cake with confectioners' sugar. Cut the cake into slices. Spoon 2 or more tablespoons of crème anglaise onto each dessert plate. Place a slice of cake in the center and serve immediately.

Serves 10 to 12

COOK'S NOTE
You'll need to buy 5 to 6 ounces of fresh ginger to yield ⅔ cup minced ginger. It can be minced by hand, but it takes a while. The quickest and easiest way to prepare it is to peel it, cut it into small chunks, and then mince it in a mini–food processor or a regular-size food processor using the metal blade.

almond torte with blood orange compote

I bake this tender, ambrosial cake year-round and serve it with seasonal fruit on the side. For Christmas, I make a citrus compote with ruby red, fragrant blood oranges. Not only does it create a dramatic color contrast on the plate, but the sweetness of the almond torte is nicely balanced by the tang of the oranges. The cake stays moist for three days, which makes it ideal for entertaining. Serve it with a strawberry-rhubarb sauce in the spring and with a pile of mixed berries in the summer.

ALMOND TORTE

3/4 CUP (1 1/2 STICKS) PLUS 1 TABLESPOON UNSALTED BUTTER, AT ROOM TEMPERATURE

3/4 CUP UNBLEACHED ALL-PURPOSE FLOUR

3/4 TEASPOON BAKING POWDER

1 CUP PLUS 3 TABLESPOONS (12 OUNCES) ALMOND PASTE (NOT MARZIPAN)

1 TABLESPOON WATER

1 CUP PLUS 2 TABLESPOONS GRANULATED SUGAR

5 LARGE EGGS

3 TABLESPOONS GRAND MARNIER OR OTHER ORANGE-FLAVORED LIQUEUR

CONFECTIONERS' SUGAR FOR DUSTING

BLOOD ORANGE COMPOTE

2 1/2 POUNDS (ABOUT 8) BLOOD ORANGES

1 CUP WATER

3/4 CUP GRANULATED SUGAR

To make the almond torte, position a rack in the lower third of the oven. Preheat the oven to 350°F. Line the bottom of a 9-inch springform pan with parchment paper. Generously butter the sides of the pan with 1 tablespoon of the butter.

In a bowl, sift together the flour and baking powder and set aside. Use your fingers to crumble the almond paste into the bowl of a stand mixer fitted with the whip attachment. Add the water and beat first on low speed and then on medium speed until the almond paste is smooth and the water is incorporated, about 2 minutes.

On medium speed, add the remaining butter 4 tablespoons at a time, beating after each addition for about 1 minute until incorporated and stopping to scrape down the sides of the bowl before adding more butter. Reduce the speed to low, add the granulated sugar, and beat until incorporated. Increase the speed to medium-high and beat until the mixture is light and fluffy, about 4 minutes.

Add the eggs one at a time, beating well after each addition. Add the liqueur and mix well.

Using a rubber spatula, fold half of the flour mixture into the creamed mixture just until combined. Then add the remaining flour, folding just until the flour disappears. Spread the batter in the prepared pan, smoothing the top.

Bake the cake for 40 minutes and then cover loosely with a piece of foil to prevent further browning. Continue to bake until a toothpick inserted in the center comes out clean, about 35 minutes longer. (Even if the cake looks well browned on top and has pulled away from the sides of the pan after baking for 1 hour, continue to bake it for the full 1 1/4 hours. If it is underdone, it will fall in the center as it cools.) Let cool completely in the pan on a wire rack.

Unlatch the sides of the pan and lift them off. Invert a cake plate over the top of the cake and invert the cake and the plate together. Carefully lift off the bottom of the pan and peel off the parchment paper. Using a small fine-mesh sieve, dust the top of the cake with the confectioners' sugar. (The cake can be made up to 3 days in advance. Cover and store at room temperature.)

To make the blood orange compote, using a sharp knife, cut a slice off the top and bottom of 1 orange to reveal the flesh. Stand the orange upright and, following the counter of the fruit, cut off the peel and pith in thick strips. Set a sieve over a bowl. Working over the sieve, and using a small serrated knife, cut along both sides of the membrane holding each segment. As the segments are freed, let them fall into the sieve, so all the juices drain into the bowl. Repeat with the remaining oranges.

In a 2 1/2-quart saucepan over medium heat, combine the water, sugar, and the captured juice from the bowl and bring to a boil, stirring only until the sugar has dissolved. Lower the heat to a steady simmer and simmer until the liquid is reduced and syrupy, 12 to 14 minutes. Remove from the heat and gently stir in the orange segments. Set aside to cool. Transfer to a serving bowl, cover, and set aside for up to 8 hours. (The compote can be made up to 1 day in advance. Remove from the refrigerator 2 hours before serving.)

To serve the dessert, cut the cake into slices and place upright in the center of each dessert plate. Spoon some orange segments and a small pool of the syrup onto each plate. If desired, dust the cake and the plate with confectioners' sugar and serve immediately.

Serves 12

mocha pots de crème

These individual custards make a sweet, pretty ending to a holiday meal. Use classic 6-ounce white ramekins or, for a little whimsy, use small porcelain coffee mugs. I developed and tested this recipe using Valrhona Le Noir Amer bittersweet chocolate with 71% cacao, and the custards were amazing.

1 1/2 CUPS MILK

1 1/2 CUPS HEAVY (WHIPPING) CREAM

1/2 CUP ESPRESSO-ROAST COFFEE BEANS, LIGHTLY CRUSHED (SEE COOK'S NOTE)

3 TABLESPOONS GRANULATED SUGAR

1 CINNAMON STICK, ABOUT 3 INCHES LONG, OR 1/4 TEASPOON GROUND CINNAMON

5 OUNCES DARK BITTERSWEET CHOCOLATE (AT LEAST 64% CACAO), CHOPPED (SEE COOK'S NOTE, PAGE 136)

4 LARGE EGG YOLKS

2 LARGE EGGS

GARNISH

1/2 CUP HEAVY (WHIPPING) CREAM

1 TABLESPOON CONFECTIONERS' SUGAR, SIFTED

In a heavy 2-quart saucepan, combine the milk, cream, coffee beans, granulated sugar, cinnamon, and chocolate. Place over medium heat and cook, stirring frequently, until the chocolate is melted, about 10 minutes. The mixture should remain just below a simmer. Remove from the heat; steep for 15 minutes.

Position a rack in the center of the oven. Preheat the oven to 350°F. Have ready eight 6-ounce ramekins and a roasting pan large enough to hold the ramekins without crowding.

In a medium bowl, whisk together the egg yolks and eggs. Pour the milk mixture through a fine-mesh sieve into the eggs and whisk until completely blended. Push through any remaining bits of chocolate in the sieve. Discard the solids.

Divide the mixture evenly among the ramekins. Set the ramekins in the roasting pan. Pour hot water into the pan to come about two-thirds of the way up the sides of the ramekins. Cover the pan loosely with aluminum foil. Bake the custards until just set in center, shaking a ramekin gently to see if the custard jiggles, 40 to 45 minutes. Transfer the ramekins to a wire rack and let cool for 30 minutes. Cover and refrigerate for at least 6 hours or up to overnight. (The pots de crème can be made up to 3 days in advance.)

Just before serving, make the garnish. Combine the cream and confectioners' sugar in a medium bowl and beat with a wire whisk or electric mixer until soft peaks form. Place a dollop of whipped cream in the center of each pot de crème and serve immediately.

Serves 8

COOK'S NOTE
The easiest way to crush coffee beans is to place them in a heavy lock-top plastic bag, and then press on them with a rolling pin or a heavy-bottomed pot.

banana and chocolate holiday trifle

If you have ever eaten bananas dipped in rich, dark chocolate and loved the flavor combination, you will love this dessert. A classic English trifle typically consists of layers of pound or sponge cake, fruit, pastry cream (known formally as crème pâtissière), and flavorings, preferably alcoholic. My version layers pound cake, thin banana slices, chocolate sauce, and pastry cream. The dessert is traditionally served in a straight-sided clear-glass pedestal bowl (in order to see the layers), but any straight-sided serving bowl will work. It tastes best when made a day or two before serving—and that's ideal for do-ahead holiday entertaining.

PASTRY CREAM

2 CUPS MILK

1 VANILLA BEAN, SPLIT LENGTHWISE
(SEE COOK'S NOTE, FACING PAGE)

1/2 CUP GRANULATED SUGAR

3 TABLESPOONS CORNSTARCH

1/4 TEASPOON KOSHER OR SEA SALT

4 LARGE EGG YOLKS

3 TABLESPOONS UNSALTED BUTTER, CUT INTO
SMALL CHUNKS

CHOCOLATE SAUCE

8 OUNCES DARK BITTERSWEET CHOCOLATE
(AT LEAST 64% CACAO), CHOPPED
(SEE COOK'S NOTE, PAGE 136)

1 CUP HEAVY (WHIPPING) CREAM

PINCH OF KOSHER OR SEA SALT

1 FROZEN POUND CAKE (10 3/4 OUNCES),
THAWED (SEE COOK'S NOTE, FACING PAGE)

6 BARELY RIPE BANANAS

1/4 TO 1/2 CUP BOURBON, COGNAC,
OR ORANGE-FLAVORED BRANDY

3 OUNCES DARK BITTERSWEET CHOCOLATE
(AT LEAST 64% CACAO), GRATED OR SHAVED,
FOR GARNISH (SEE COOK'S NOTE, FACING PAGE)

To make the pastry cream, pour the milk into a 2 1/2-quart saucepan. Use the tip of a paring knife to scrape the seeds from the vanilla bean into the pan, and then add the bean. Bring to a simmer over medium-low heat, and remove from the heat. Do not allow the milk to boil.

In a small bowl, whisk together the sugar, cornstarch, and salt. Add the egg yolks and whisk until the mixture is smooth, pale yellow, and thick, about 3 minutes. (This can be accomplished with a handheld mixer, too.) Slowly add 1/2 cup of the hot milk to the egg mixture while whisking to combine, and then pour the egg yolk mixture into the saucepan. Return the saucepan to low heat and whisk constantly until the mixture just barely comes to a boil and is as thick as lightly whipped cream, about 3 minutes. (The mixture needs to reach a boil in order for the cornstarch to cook and thicken the sauce; however, the pastry cream will curdle if it is cooked too long.)

Remove from the heat and strain through a fine-mesh sieve into a clean bowl. Let cool for 5 minutes and then add the butter 1 chunk at a time, stirring until it has melted before adding the next chunk. Cover the bowl with plastic wrap, pressing it directly onto the surface of the cream to prevent a skin from forming. Refrigerate until ready to use. (The sauce can be made up to 3 days in advance.)

To make the chocolate sauce, in a heavy 2-quart saucepan over medium heat, combine the chocolate, cream, and salt. Cook, stirring frequently with a wooden spoon, until the chocolate has melted. Use a whisk to thoroughly blend the mixture. Remove from the heat and set aside to cool.

To assemble the trifle, have ready a 2½- to 3-quart straight-sided clear-glass serving bowl. Cut the cake crosswise into ¼-inch-thick slices, and then cut each slice in half on the diagonal to form wedges. Peel the bananas and cut them into ¼-inch-thick rounds. Spoon just enough chocolate sauce into the bowl to cover the bottom, tilting the bowl to spread the sauce evenly. Lay cake wedges in a single layer on top of the chocolate, fitting them together tightly but not overlapping. The cake pieces should touch the sides of the bowl so they are visible through the glass. Drizzle or brush a bit of the bourbon over the cake to moisten it. Top with banana slices in a single layer, again making sure the slices touch the sides of the bowl. Spoon and spread just enough pastry cream over the bananas to cover them. Repeat the layering until all of the cake, sauce, bananas, and pastry cream are used, ending with a layer pastry cream. Cover and refrigerate for up to 2 days before serving.

Just before serving, garnish the trifle with grated chocolate.

Serves 8 to 10

COOK'S NOTE

If you don't have a vanilla bean for the pastry cream, whisk in 1 teaspoon pure vanilla extract when you add the butter. ❈ *I use a frozen all-butter pound cake from Sara Lee for this recipe and thaw it overnight in the refrigerator. You can, of course, make your own pound cake or use a high-quality bakery cake. You can even use a genoise or angel food cake.* ❈ *For the garnish, use a coarse Microplane grater or the large holes on a box grater to grate a block of chocolate, or use a small, sharp knife or a vegetable peeler to cut thin shavings from the edge of a chocolate bar. Reserve the grated chocolate or chocolate shavings at room temperature until you are ready to garnish the trifle.*

6 christmas breakfast

Christmas morning can be a magical time, especially if the children don't awaken at five and you weren't up too late the night before struggling with "some assembly required"! These days it is a cherished gift just to be with my family in the same time zone and place. Add a log burning in the fireplace and the fragrant aromas and delicious tastes of Panettone French Toast, Overnight Cinnamon Bread Custard, or Savory Bread Pudding with Sausage and Ham and I feel blessed indeed.

apple wood–smoked bacon benedicts

I think I could eat this recipe for brunch every Sunday and never get tired of it! I love the combination of apple wood–smoked bacon, cooked so it is still meaty and tender, set over a crisp and toasty English muffin, topped with a gently poached egg, and covered with a chive-and-lemon-infused hollandaise sauce. When you cut into the egg, the runny yolk soaks into the bacon and crusty muffin. Each bite is a savory delight. This makes a delectable brunch main course, especially during the holidays. ❋ It may seem intimidating to try to make eggs Benedict when you are entertaining, but if you break this recipe into steps, it is easy to pull off. Three key parts of the recipe can be done in advance: the butter can be clarified and refrigerated; the hollandaise sauce can be made and frozen; and the eggs can be poached a day ahead and reheated. See the Cook's Note on page 151 for detailed do-ahead preparations.

HOLLANDAISE SAUCE

4 LARGE EGG YOLKS, WITH THE THICK WHITE
PIECE CLINGING TO THE YOLK REMOVED

2 TABLESPOONS WATER

1 CUP (2 STICKS) UNSALTED BUTTER,
 CLARIFIED (SEE COOK'S NOTE, PAGE 151)

1/4 TEASPOON KOSHER OR SEA SALT

1/8 TEASPOON FRESHLY GROUND WHITE PEPPER

PINCH OF CAYENNE PEPPER

1 TABLESPOON FRESH LEMON JUICE

2 TEASPOONS FINELY SNIPPED FRESH CHIVES

1 POUND APPLE WOOD–SMOKED BACON

2 TEASPOONS DISTILLED WHITE VINEGAR
OR FRESH LEMON JUICE

1 TEASPOON KOSHER OR SEA SALT

12 LARGE EGGS (SEE COOK'S NOTE, PAGE 151)

6 ENGLISH MUFFINS, SPLIT AND TOASTED

2 TABLESPOONS FINELY SNIPPED CHIVES
FOR GARNISH

FRESHLY GROUND PEPPER FOR GARNISH

Position one rack in the center and another rack in the lower third of the oven. Preheat the oven to 425°F.

To make the hollandaise sauce, fill the bottom pan of a double boiler or a medium saucepan one-third full with water and bring to a simmer over medium heat. Place the egg yolks and water in the top of the double boiler or in a heatproof bowl that will fit snugly on top of the saucepan and place over the water. Reduce the heat to low and whisk the yolks and water continuously until the yolks start to thicken and form a custard, 2 to 3 minutes. (If the mixture is cooking too quickly, remove the top pan or the bowl from the heat and set the base in cold water to stop the cooking process.) **>>>**

Remove the bowl or top pan from the heat and set it on a damp towel on the counter. Whisking continuously, slowly pour the clarified butter into the yolks in a fine stream. The butter will emulsify into the yolks as if you were making mayonnaise. Whisk in the salt, white pepper, cayenne, lemon juice, and chives. If the sauce is too thick, thin it down with a few drops of warm water. Keep the sauce warm until ready to serve by placing the bowl or pan in a pan of warm water no hotter than the sauce. If it is too hot, the sauce will curdle.

Line 2 large rimmed baking sheets with a double thickness of paper towels. Arrange the bacon strips in a single layer, without crowding, on the baking sheets, dividing the strips evenly. (The paper towels keep the bacon from splattering and cooking directly in the rendered fat.) Bake until the bacon is cooked through but still meaty and pliable, about 12 minutes. (If the bacon is too crisp, it is hard to eat when layered on the Benedicts.) Cut the bacon strips in half crosswise. Keep the bacon warm while you poach the eggs. (Toast the English muffins while the eggs are poaching.)

To poach the eggs, have ready a dinner plate lined with a double thickness of paper towels. Pour water to a depth of about 2 inches in a large sauté pan. When the water boils, add the vinegar and salt, and then adjust the heat so the water is at a simmer, not a rolling boil. Poach 6 eggs at a time. Crack each egg into a separate small bowl and slip them one at a time into the water. After 2 to 3 minutes, use a slotted spoon to lift an egg to see whether the white has completely set. When it has, remove the eggs with a slotted spoon and carefully set them on the paper towel–lined dinner plate. Use kitchen shears or a paring knife to trim any ragged edges or "tails" from the whites. Keep warm in a low oven while you poach the remaining 6 eggs.

To assemble and serve, arrange 2 toasted English muffin halves on each warmed brunch plate. Place 3 pieces of bacon on top of each English muffin half. Place a poached egg on top of the bacon. Spoon the hollandaise sauce over the top of the eggs. Garnish each serving with a generous sprinkling of chives and a couple grinds of pepper. Serve immediately.

Serves 6

COOK'S NOTES

To clarify the butter, in a small saucepan over medium-low heat, melt the butter. Let it simmer, without stirring, until the foam comes to the top and the milk solids settle to the bottom, about 1 minute. Remove the pan from the heat. Skim off the foam with the side of a soup spoon. (This foam can be refrigerated and saved for seasoning vegetables.) Gently tilt the pan to make a well of butter. The milk solids will have settled to the bottom of the well. Spoon or pour the clear golden liquid into a glass measure, leaving the milk solids behind. The clarified butter will keep indefinitely when covered and refrigerated. Clarified butter has a higher smoking point than regular butter, which means that it doesn't burn as quickly at relatively high temperatures, so it is good to have on hand for sautéing.
✳ *Hollandaise sauce can be made ahead and frozen for up to 1 month. Store the sauce in a quart-size lock-top plastic freezer bag. When the sauce is needed, stand the bag of frozen sauce in a small pan and let warm (not hot) tap water run over it for about 15 minutes. Cut open the bag and serve.*
✳ *Some kitchen shops carry a little metal cup with feet and a vertical wire handle for poaching eggs. The little cup sits in the water and contains each egg in a perfect shape. If you have the forms, crack the eggs directly into them.* ✳ *Poached eggs can be made up to 1 day in advance and then reheated. As soon as the eggs are cooked, immediately slip them into a bowl filled with cold water. Cover the bowl and refrigerate. To reheat, slip the eggs back into a pan filled with simmering water to a depth of about 2 inches and heat until warmed through, about 1 minute. (This is a great trick for entertaining.)*

panettone french toast

This heavenly French toast is made with panettone, an Italian sweet yeast bread flavored with citron, raisins, anise, and sometimes pine nuts. A Christmastime tradition, panettone originated in Milan and is baked in a tall, straight-sided, cylindrical mold. It is often sold in bright, colorful boxes with ribbon handles and detailed descriptions and images of the bakery where it was made. Most Italian markets in the United States proudly stock imported panettone during the holidays, typically stacking the boxes for a grand display.

1 IMPORTED PANETTONE (ABOUT 2 POUNDS)

8 LARGE EGGS, LIGHTLY BEATEN

2/3 CUP HEAVY (WHIPPING) CREAM

1/2 TEASPOON PURE VANILLA EXTRACT

1/4 TEASPOON GROUND CINNAMON

1/2 TEASPOON KOSHER OR SEA SALT

CANOLA OIL FOR OILING GRIDDLE

CONFECTIONERS' SUGAR FOR DUSTING

PURE MAPLE SYRUP, WARMED, FOR SERVING

Trim off the bottom crust and the top rounded crust of the panettone. Pick off and discard any pieces of raisin or citron that might have overdarkened during baking. Set the panettone on its side and use a bread knife to cut the loaf crosswise into 6 even slices, each about 1 inch thick. Cut each slice in half to form 2 half-moons. Set aside.

In a 9-by-13-inch baking pan or dish, whisk together the eggs, cream, vanilla, cinnamon, and salt until thoroughly combined and the mixture feels airy. Dip a piece of panettone in the egg mixture, turning to coat both sides, until saturated. Place the piece at one end of the baking pan. Repeat with the remaining pieces one at a time, arranging them in stacks of 4 pieces each. You will need to tilt the pan slightly to dip the last few slices. Let the bread soak while you heat the griddle.

Heat a large griddle, preferably well-seasoned cast iron, or a large nonstick skillet over medium heat. Fold a paper towel into a thick square. When the griddle is hot, add a tablespoon or two of oil to it and wipe the oil over the surface with the paper towel, evenly coating it with the oil so no pools remain. Add as many panettone pieces as will fit without crowding and cook on the first side until nicely browned, about 2 minutes. (Check after 1 minute to see how the bread is browning. If it is browning too quickly, lower the heat, or it won't be cooked through in the middle.) Flip the bread and cook on the other side until nicely browned, about 2 minutes longer. Keep warm in a low oven while you cook the remaining pieces.

To serve, place 2 slices, slightly overlapping, on each warmed plate. Using a small fine-mesh sieve, dust the French toast with the confectioners' sugar. Pass the maple syrup at the table.

Serves 6

smoked salmon frittata

You don't need to master a quick flick-of-the-wrist technique or fret over last-minute timing when making frittatas, Italy's traditional open-faced omelets. They are fast and easy, cooked in a skillet and usually finished under the broiler. Making frittatas for a holiday brunch is a snap when you have a number of people to feed, but don't overlook them for an easy weeknight meal, especially when entertaining out-of-town guests. I like to serve this frittata with a green salad and some crusty bread. For brunch, add sliced fruit and a coffee cake, and you're set.

3 TABLESPOONS EXTRA-VIRGIN OLIVE OIL

1 YELLOW ONION, CUT INTO 1/2-INCH DICE

12 OUNCES RED-SKINNED POTATOES, PEELED AND CUT INTO 1/2-INCH DICE

12 LARGE EGGS

1/2 CUP MILK

1/4 CUP CHOPPED FRESH FLAT-LEAF PARSLEY

1/4 CUP CHOPPED FRESH DILL

1 TEASPOON KOSHER OR SEA SALT

FRESHLY GROUND PEPPER

8 OUNCES ALDER-SMOKED OR OTHER HOT-SMOKED SALMON, SKIN REMOVED AND FLAKED INTO BITE-SIZED PIECES

In a 12-inch ovenproof skillet, preferably nonstick, heat the oil over medium heat. Swirl to coat the pan, add the onion and potatoes, and sauté, stirring occasionally, until the onion softens, about 4 minutes. Turn the heat to medium-low, cover the pan, and cook the onion and potato mixture, stirring occasionally, until they are tender and beginning to brown, about 10 minutes longer. Reduce the heat to low if the onions begin to darken too much.

Meanwhile, position an oven rack about 3 inches below the heat source and preheat the broiler. In a large bowl, whisk together the eggs and milk until thoroughly combined.

Whisk in the parsley, dill, salt, and pepper. Set aside.

As soon as the potatoes are tender, add the egg mixture to the pan and stir in the salmon. Reduce the heat to medium-low and cook, without stirring, until the frittata is set on the bottom and around the edges, about 4 minutes. While the frittata is cooking, simultaneously lift one edge of the frittata with a spatula and tilt the pan a little so the uncooked egg flows under the set edge. Repeat this at regular intervals around the edge of the frittata.

When the eggs are mostly cooked, place the frittata under the broiler and broil until the top is golden brown and the eggs are set but still moist, about 3 minutes.

Allow the frittata to rest for 5 minutes, then slice it into wedges and serve immediately on warmed plates.

Serves 6

gravlax

One of the most delicate and least embellished salmon preparations is gravlax, a Scandinavian specialty in which the fish is cured with a salt and sugar rub. Typically, gravlax is seasoned with fresh dill, a brandy such as Cognac, and spruce sprigs. Not everyone has a spruce tree growing in the backyard, including me, so I've decided to re-create that woodsy flavor by adding gin. Its mild juniper berry flavor is a lovely partner to the dill. ❅ Gravlax is a terrific do-ahead recipe for the holidays because it needs to cure for a few days. Plus, it can do double duty as both a splendid brunch main course and appetizer. Serve the salmon for brunch with buttered pumpernickel or toasted bagels and a condiment tray than includes cucumber slices, chopped chives, green onions, capers, chopped dill, and minced shallots or sliced red onions. Don't forget the cream cheese. For an appetizer, serve thin gravlax slices over rye toast rounds spread with herbed cream cheese. A tiny dollop of sour cream and a little sprig of dill make a festive garnish.

1/2 CUP COARSE SEA SALT OR KOSHER SALT

1/2 CUP SUGAR

1 WHOLE SALMON FILLET (3 TO 4 POUNDS), SKIN ON, SCALED, AND PIN BONES REMOVED

10 SPRIGS FRESH DILL, COARSELY CHOPPED, PLUS MORE FOR GARNISH

1/4 CUP GIN

Select a 2-inch-deep glass or ceramic baking dish just large enough to accommodate the length of the fillet. In a small bowl, stir together the salt and sugar. Spread half of the mixture on the bottom of the baking dish. Lay the salmon, skin side down, in the dish. Gently rub the remaining salt mixture over the flesh side of the fillet. Spread the dill over the fillet. Slowly drizzle the gin evenly over the fish, being careful not to rinse off the salt cure.

Place a large sheet of plastic wrap directly on top of the fish. Select a slightly smaller baking dish, or other large, flat object, and place it on top of the fish. Put something that weighs about 2 pounds in the top dish. I use 3 to 4 full beer bottles, laying them on their sides. Place the weighted salmon in the refrigerator for at least 2 days or up to 5 days. Turn the salmon once a day, being sure to weight the salmon again after each turn.

To serve, remove the weight and plastic wrap and transfer the salmon to a cutting board, discarding the dill. Carefully remove the skin from the fillet and then cut the fillet crosswise into 1/8-inch-thick slices. Arrange the slices on a platter and garnish with fresh dill, if desired. (The uncut gravlax will keep for up to 1 week in the refrigerator. To freeze, wrap the uncut gravlax tightly in plastic wrap and then in a double layer of aluminum foil and store for up to 3 months.)

Serves 10 for brunch or 20 as an appetizer

spinach, cherry tomato, and feta frittata

Frittatas make ideal brunch food, especially during the holidays, because they are quick to assemble and can be kept warm or served at room temperature. I have included two in this chapter. For the vegetable lovers in the crowd—and everyone else—this is a nutrition-packed main course, with its iron-rich spinach and protein-rich eggs. But it's also a cheery seasonal dish perfectly colored for Christmastime, with bright green spinach and scarlet red tomatoes. If serving in a buffet, accompany the frittata with platters of fresh fruit and bacon or smoked ham and a basket of homemade or bakery-bought breakfast sweets. Or, you could continue the savory theme and serve corn muffins or even warmed focaccia.

12 LARGE EGGS

1/2 CUP HALF-AND-HALF

1 TEASPOON KOSHER OR SEA SALT

1/2 TEASPOON FRESHLY GROUND PEPPER

3 TABLESPOONS EXTRA-VIRGIN OLIVE OIL

1 SMALL YELLOW ONION, HALVED LENGTHWISE AND CUT INTO THIN WEDGES

6 OUNCES BABY SPINACH LEAVES, COARSELY CHOPPED (ABOUT 4 CUPS FIRMLY PACKED)

1 PINT CHERRY TOMATOES, STEMMED AND HALVED

1 1/2 TABLESPOONS CHOPPED FRESH OREGANO

1/2 CUP (ABOUT 3 OUNCES) CRUMBLED FETA CHEESE

In a large bowl, whisk together the eggs and half-and-half until thoroughly combined. Whisk in the salt and pepper. Set aside.

Position an oven rack about 3 inches below the heat source and preheat the broiler.

In a 12-inch ovenproof skillet, preferably nonstick, heat the olive oil over medium heat. Swirl to coat the pan, add the onion, and sauté, stirring occasionally, until the onion softens, about 2 minutes. Add the spinach a handful at a time, and sauté just until wilted and bright green, about 3 minutes. As soon as the spinach is wilted, add the tomatoes and oregano and sauté, stirring constantly, until the tomatoes are heated through, about 1 minute.

Add the egg mixture to the pan, reduce the heat to medium-low, and cook, without stirring, until the frittata is set on the bottom and around the edges, about 4 minutes. While the frittata is cooking, simultaneously lift one edge of the frittata with a spatula and tilt the pan a little so the uncooked egg flows under the set edge. Repeat this at regular intervals around the edge of the frittata.

When the eggs are mostly cooked, scatter the feta cheese over the top and place the frittata under the broiler. Broil until the top is golden brown and the eggs are set but still moist, about 3 minutes.

Allow the frittata to rest for 5 minutes, then slice it into wedges and serve immediately on warmed plates.

Serves 6

overnight cinnamon bread custard

Cinnamon bread custard has always been a holiday breakfast treat for my children. It's a pleasure for me, too, because I'm sitting down with the family instead of making hot-from-the-griddle French toast. Buy a wonderfully scrumptious loaf of cinnamon raisin bread from your local bakery or purchase the best-quality grocery-store loaf you can find. Because local berries (really the best) are out of season at Christmastime, I splurge and buy fresh berries imported from Chile or Mexico, so I can accompany this dish with a mixed-berry compote. I add just enough sugar to get the berries to release some of their juices and create a little sauce. You could also use frozen berries; just be sure to allow time for them to thaw.

1/2 CUP (1 STICK) UNSALTED BUTTER, AT ROOM TEMPERATURE

16 SLICES CINNAMON RAISIN BREAD

2 LARGE EGG YOLKS

4 LARGE EGGS

3/4 CUP PLUS 2 TABLESPOONS GRANULATED SUGAR

1 TABLESPOON PURE VANILLA EXTRACT

1 CUP MILK

3 CUPS HEAVY (WHIPPING) CREAM

1 1/2 CUPS BLUEBERRIES

1 1/2 CUPS RASPBERRIES

1 1/2 CUPS STRAWBERRIES, STEMMED AND HALVED

CONFECTIONERS' SUGAR FOR DUSTING

PURE MAPLE OR BERRY SYRUP, WARMED, FOR SERVING (OPTIONAL)

Use 1 tablespoon of the butter to butter a 9-by-13-inch baking dish, preferably attractive oven-to-table glass or porcelain. Set aside.

Lightly butter both sides of each bread slice with the remaining butter. Arrange the slices, overlapping them to create a snug fit, in the prepared baking dish.

In a medium bowl, whisk together the egg yolks, eggs, 3/4 cup of the granulated sugar, and the vanilla. Add the milk and cream and whisk until blended. Carefully pour the egg mixture over the bread. Gently press down on the slices to soak the bread thoroughly and distribute the liquid evenly. Cover and refrigerate overnight.

The next morning, remove the custard from the refrigerator about 1 1/2 hours before you plan to bake it, so it will warm a little before it goes into the oven. Position a rack in the center of the oven. Preheat the oven to 375°F.

In a medium bowl, combine the blueberries, raspberries, strawberries, and the remaining 2 tablespoons granulated sugar and stir gently to mix. Cover and set aside until ready to serve.

Bake the custard until it is set in the middle, puffed, and lightly browned on top, 45 to 50 minutes. Remove from the oven and let stand for about 10 minutes before serving.

Using a small fine-mesh sieve, generously dust the custard with the confectioners' sugar. Cut into rectangles and serve immediately on warmed plates, passing the mixed berries and syrup at the table.

Serves 8

cranberry muffins with brown sugar–almond streusel

Is it possible to have hot-from-the-oven muffins on Christmas morning without getting up at the crack of dawn? That was my goal, so I developed this recipe with do-ahead steps in mind. I make the streusel topping a day ahead and leave it in a covered bowl on the counter. I do the same for the dry ingredients in the muffin batter. I toast the almonds and set them aside. All the wet ingredients are measured and ready to add. The next morning, I preheat the oven and mix everything together. The sweet smell of almonds and bubbling brown sugar perfumes the house as we open our presents.

VEGETABLE-OIL COOKING SPRAY FOR
PREPARING THE PAN

STREUSEL TOPPING
1/3 CUP FINELY CHOPPED WHOLE ALMONDS
1/2 CUP UNBLEACHED ALL-PURPOSE FLOUR
1/4 CUP PACKED DARK BROWN SUGAR
1/4 TEASPOON SALT
3 TABLESPOONS UNSALTED BUTTER, MELTED

MUFFINS
2 CUPS PLUS 1 1/2 TABLESPOONS
UNBLEACHED ALL-PURPOSE FLOUR
1/2 CUP GRANULATED SUGAR
2 TEASPOONS BAKING POWDER
1/2 TEASPOON BAKING SODA
1 TABLESPOON FRESHLY GRATED ORANGE ZEST
1 LARGE EGG, BEATEN
1/2 TEASPOON PURE ALMOND EXTRACT
1 CUP BUTTERMILK
1/2 CUP (1 STICK) UNSALTED BUTTER, MELTED
1 1/2 CUPS FRESH OR FROZEN CRANBERRIES,
PICKED OVER AND STEMS REMOVED
1/2 CUP WHOLE ALMONDS, TOASTED AND FINELY
CHOPPED (SEE PAGE 23)

Position a rack in the center of the oven. Preheat the oven to 425°F. Generously grease the cups and top of a 12-cup standard muffin pan with vegetable-oil cooking spray.

To make the streusel topping, in a medium bowl, combine the almonds, flour, brown sugar, and salt. Stir in the butter. Use your fingers to pinch the streusel into small clumps. Set aside.

To make the muffins, in a large bowl, sift together 2 cups of the flour, the granulated sugar, baking powder, and baking soda. Add the orange zest and use your fingers to distribute the zest evenly in the flour mixture. In a medium bowl, whisk together the egg, almond extract, buttermilk, and butter. Using a rubber spatula, stir the wet ingredients into the dry ingredients, mixing only until no flour is visible. The batter will look lumpy. In a small bowl, toss the cranberries with the remaining 1 1/2 tablespoons flour. Fold the cranberries and toasted almonds into the batter with 1 or 2 swift strokes.

Spoon a generous 1/4 cup of the batter into each muffin cup. Cover the top of each muffin with 1 generous tablespoon of the streusel topping, pressing it lightly onto the batter so it adheres. Bake until a toothpick inserted in the center comes out clean, about 20 minutes. Let the muffins cool in the pan on a wire rack for 10 minutes. Carefully release the muffins and serve immediately, or transfer to the rack until ready to serve.

Makes 12 muffins

blueberry ricotta pancakes

Think "blintzes drizzled with maple syrup," and you've got the flavors for these pancakes. These are griddle-hot, cheesy-rich ricotta flapjacks, speckled with blueberries, that I made for my children when they were growing up. (Now, they are away at college and have the recipe so they can make them for themselves.) I'm almost always cooking from scratch, rather than using mixes of any sort, but during a wintertime family vacation in a rented cabin I decided to buy pancake mix for Sunday breakfast. I doctored it by adding ricotta cheese and frozen blueberries and the pancakes were splendid. Here's the quick recipe, perfect for Christmas morning, or any weekend morning when you are pressed for time. And if you don't have berries on hand, the pancakes are still delicious.

2 LARGE EGGS, LIGHTLY BEATEN

1 CONTAINER (15 OUNCES) RICOTTA CHEESE

1 CUP MILK

2 TABLESPOONS GRANULATED SUGAR

2 CUPS BISQUICK OR BETTY CROCKER PANCAKE MIX (SEE COOK'S NOTE)

1 CUP FRESH OR FROZEN BLUEBERRIES

CANOLA OIL FOR OILING GRIDDLE

CONFECTIONERS' SUGAR FOR DUSTING

PURE MAPLE OR BERRY SYRUP, WARMED, FOR SERVING

In a large bowl, combine the eggs, ricotta, milk, and granulated sugar. Beat with a wooden spoon until well blended. Add the pancake mix, stirring just until it disappears. Stir in the blueberries.

Heat a large griddle, preferably well-seasoned cast iron, or a large nonstick skillet over medium heat. Fold a paper towel into a thick square.

When the griddle is hot, add 1 or 2 tablespoons oil to it and wipe the oil over the surface with the paper towel, evenly coating it with the oil so no pools remain. Pour about $1/4$ cup of the batter for each pancake onto the hot surface, being careful not to crowd the surface. Cook until the pancakes have puffed and little holes have formed on top, about 2 minutes. Flip and cook until nicely browned on the second side, about 2 minutes longer. Repeat until all the batter is used. Serve as you cook the pancakes, or keep warm in a low oven, if necessary.

To serve, place 2 to 3 pancakes, slightly overlapping, on each warmed plate. Using a small fine-mesh sieve, dust the pancakes with the confectioners' sugar. Pass the syrup at the table.

Makes sixteen 4-inch pancakes

COOK'S NOTE
Bisquick and Betty Crocker pancake mixes call for the addition of eggs and milk. If you buy a pancake mix that requires only the addition of water, omit the eggs and milk. Instead, mix the ricotta with $1^{1}/_{2}$ cups water, mix in the sugar, and stir in the pancake mix. (That said, I think this recipe works best with Bisquick or Betty Crocker pancake mix, and I have tested many brands.)

savory bread pudding with sausage and ham

Savory bread pudding is one of my favorite Christmas brunch dishes, especially for company. You put it all together the night before, refrigerate it, and it's ready to bake in the morning. When everyone is caught up in the excitement of exchanging gifts, and kids are playing with their new toys, it's nice to have a dish that needs nothing more than to be slipped into the oven. For a buffet, I set out a pitcher of orange juice, a large platter of fresh fruit, and an assortment of breads and breakfast sweets in linen-lined baskets. The bread pudding is the main course. I have coffee and tea for the adults and hot chocolate or milk for the children. Depending on whom I am entertaining, I might serve mimosas or Bloody Marys. The Cranberry Muffins with Brown Sugar–Almond Streusel (page 160) would be a lovely accompaniment.

1 TABLESPOON UNSALTED BUTTER, AT ROOM TEMPERATURE

1 LOAF (1 1/2 TO 2 POUNDS) ARTISANAL OR COUNTRY-STYLE WHITE OR SOURDOUGH BREAD

12 OUNCES BREAKFAST PORK LINK SAUSAGES

1 YELLOW ONION, CUT INTO 1/2-INCH DICE

1 LARGE RED BELL PEPPER, SEEDED, DERIBBED, AND CUT INTO 1/2-INCH DICE

1 LARGE GREEN BELL PEPPER, SEEDED, DERIBBED, AND CUT INTO 1/2-INCH DICE

1 TABLESPOON CHOPPED FRESH SAGE

1 TEASPOON FRESHLY GROUND PEPPER

12 OUNCES BLACK FOREST HAM OR OTHER SMOKED BAKED HAM, CUT INTO 3/4-INCH CUBES

1/4 CUP CHOPPED FRESH FLAT-LEAF PARSLEY

2 LARGE EGG YOLKS

4 LARGE EGGS

1 CUP MILK

3 CUPS HEAVY (WHIPPING) CREAM

2 CUPS GRATED PEPPER JACK CHEESE

Butter a 9-by-13-inch flameproof baking dish, preferably attractive oven-to-table glass or porcelain. Set aside.

Trim the crusts from the bread. Cut the bread into 1-inch cubes. Measure 10 cups of cubes, pressing lightly—don't compress the bread— to get a level measure. Transfer the cubes to an extra-large bowl. Set aside.

In a 10-inch sauté pan with a tight-fitting lid, cook the sausages, uncovered, over medium heat until nicely browned on all sides, about 5 minutes. Cover and cook, turning occasionally, until the sausages are no longer pink at the center, about 3 minutes. Remove the pan from the heat, transfer the sausages to a plate to cool, and measure the fat in the pan. You should have about 2 tablespoons. If not, add a little olive oil to the pan.

Return the sauté pan to medium-high heat, add the onion and bell peppers, and sauté, stirring frequently, until the peppers are brightly colored and crisp-tender, about 3 minutes. Add the sage and ground pepper and stir for 1 minute longer. Remove from the heat.

Cut the reserved sausages into 3/4-inch lengths and add to the bread in the bowl. Add the ham, parsley, and sautéed vegetables.

In a medium bowl, whisk together the egg yolks and eggs. Add the milk and cream and whisk until blended. Pour the egg mixture over the bread in the bowl and stir gently to combine and thoroughly soak the bread. Transfer to the prepared baking dish. Cover and refrigerate overnight.

The next morning, remove the bread pudding from the refrigerator about 1 1/2 hours before you plan to bake it, so it will warm a little before it goes in the oven. Position a rack in the center of the oven. Preheat the oven to 350°F.

Bake the pudding until it is set in the middle, puffed, and lightly browned on top, 50 to 60 minutes. Remove from the oven. Position an oven rack about 4 inches below the heat source and preheat the broiler. Scatter the cheese evenly over the top. Broil until the cheese is melted, bubbly, and lightly browned in spots, about 3 minutes.

Remove from the broiler and let stand for 10 minutes before serving. Cut the bread pudding into rectangles and serve immediately on warmed plates.

Serves 8 to 10

7 the great cookie exchange

Mmmmmm. Christmas cookies. Food historians trace the tradition of these small, often crispy, sweet cakes to medieval Europe. English settlers brought sugar-cookie recipes with them to America, and Dutch and German settlers introduced the all-important cookie cutter and countless other cookies for holidays, including German Lebkuchen (gingerbread). It's even thought that animal crackers were originally edible ornaments! So turn the volume up on your favorite holiday music and settle in for some serious fun making Chocolate-Dipped Shortbread Stars, Grandma Rose's Sugar Cookies, and Coconut-Orange Snowballs. Everyone will understand if there's a little bit of confectioners' sugar in your smile at the end of the day.

grandma rose's sugar cookies

My first-ever published recipe appeared in *Kosher Kalories,* a cookbook produced by the sisterhood of Tree of Life synagogue in Pittsburgh, Pennsylvania. My mother, Irene LevKoy, and my aunt Barbara Trellis edited and assembled the recipe collection. Simply titled "Sugar Cookies," and attributed to me, this recipe was in fact my grandmother Rose's. She and I made the cookies together almost every time I had the opportunity to spend the day at my grandparent's house. Perhaps I'm biased, and why wouldn't I be, but I think these are the most perfect sugar cookies I have ever tasted. The touch of sour cream in the dough provides ideal balance, ensuring a fine-textured crumb and imparting a slight tang to the sweet and buttery flavor. Cut shapes using your favorite holiday cookie cutters, or drop the dough by teaspoonfuls onto the baking sheets and use the bottom of a juice glass to press out rounds—that's how I learned from my grandmother to shape my sugar cookies.

3 CUPS UNBLEACHED ALL-PURPOSE FLOUR, PLUS MORE FOR DUSTING

1 TEASPOON BAKING POWDER

1/4 TEASPOON KOSHER OR SEA SALT

1 CUP (2 STICKS) UNSALTED BUTTER, AT ROOM TEMPERATURE

1 CUP GRANULATED SUGAR, PLUS MORE FOR DUSTING

1 LARGE EGG, BEATEN

2 TABLESPOONS SOUR CREAM

1 TEASPOON PURE VANILLA EXTRACT

PEARL SUGAR, SPARKLING WHITE SUGAR, OR SPARKLING COLORED SUGAR FOR SPRINKLING (SEE COOK'S NOTE, PAGE 168)

In a medium bowl, sift together the flour, baking powder, and salt and set aside. In the bowl of a stand mixer fitted with the paddle attachment, beat together the butter and granulated sugar on medium speed until smooth and creamy, about 3 minutes. Add the egg, sour cream, and vanilla and beat on medium speed until well combined, about 1 minute. (The mixture will look grainy.) Add 1 cup of the flour mixture and mix on low speed just until the flour disappears. Mix in the remaining flour mixture 1 cup at a time, stopping to scrape down the sides of the bowl once or twice with a rubber spatula. Do not overmix.

Divide the dough in half. Shape each half into a thick disk about 6 inches in diameter. Tightly wrap each disk in plastic wrap and refrigerate until well chilled, at least 2 hours. (The dough can be made up to 2 days in advance.) **>>>**

grandma rose's sugar cookies

CONTINUED

Remove the dough from the refrigerator 20 minutes before rolling and shaping the cookies. Line 2 baking sheets with parchment paper or nonstick baking liners, or use nonstick baking sheets. Lightly dust a work surface with flour and granulated sugar. Place a dough disk on the work surface and dust the top of the dough with flour and granulated sugar. Roll out the dough 1/8 inch thick. Using your favorite cookie cutter, cut out as many cookies as possible. Arrange the cookies on the prepared baking sheets, spacing them about 1 inch apart. Gather up the dough scraps, lightly dust with flour and sugar if needed, reroll the dough, and cut out cookies until all the dough is used. (Alternatively, drop the dough by rounded teaspoonfuls onto the prepared baking sheets and flatten them by pressing with the bottom of a glass.) Sprinkle the cookies with decorating sugar. Refrigerate the baking sheets for 1 hour.

Position one rack in the center and another rack in the lower third of the oven. Preheat the oven to 350°F Bake the sugar cookies until firm but not brown, 10 to 12 minutes, switching the pans between the racks and rotating them 180 degrees at the midpoint if the cookies appear to be baking unevenly. The cookies should be lightly golden on the bottom but not have any browning at the edges. Let the cookies cool on the pans on wire racks for 5 minutes, then transfer to the racks and let cool completely. (The cookies can be made up to 1 week ahead. Layer them between sheets of waxed paper in an airtight container and store at room temperature. Or, they can be frozen for up to 1 month.)

Makes about 6 dozen 2-inch-round cookies

COOK'S NOTE
You can top your cookies simply with granulated sugar, or you can try a more exotic alternative. Pearl sugar has bright white, large, irregular grains that do not melt in baking. Sparkling white sugar has clear, large crystal grains that melt slowly. Sparkling colored sugar comes in either coarse or fine grain and in a myriad of colors. Of course, green and red are traditional for Christmas, but if you allow your children to choose, you might end up with a rainbow. Find these sugars in the baking section of well-stocked grocery stores or order them from The Baker's Catalogue (800-827-6836 or www.bakerscatalogue.com).

coconut-orange snowballs

These are good cookies to make with children. My mother taught me to how to make them when I was about eight years old. I called them snowballs because I enjoyed rolling them in confectioners' sugar—and I still do!

1 CUP (2 STICKS) UNSALTED BUTTER,
AT ROOM TEMPERATURE

2$^{1}/_{4}$ CUPS SIFTED CONFECTIONERS' SUGAR

1 TEASPOON PURE VANILLA EXTRACT

2$^{1}/_{4}$ CUPS UNBLEACHED ALL-PURPOSE FLOUR

$^{1}/_{4}$ TEASPOON KOSHER OR SEA SALT

1 CUP PACKED SWEETENED FLAKED COCONUT

1$^{1}/_{2}$ TABLESPOONS FRESHLY GRATED ORANGE ZEST

In the bowl of a stand mixer fitted with the paddle attachment, combine the butter, $^{1}/_{2}$ cup of the confectioners' sugar, and the vanilla and beat on medium speed until smooth and creamy, about 3 minutes. Add the flour, salt, coconut, and orange zest and beat on low speed just until combined, about 2 minutes. Cover the bowl and chill for 1 hour.

Position 1 rack in the center and another rack in the lower third of the oven. Preheat the oven to 350°F. Line 2 rimmed baking sheets with parchment paper or nonstick baking liners, or use nonstick baking sheets.

Roll the dough between your palms into 1-inch balls. Arrange them on the prepared baking sheets, spacing them about 1 inch apart.

Bake until light brown on the bottom, about 12 minutes.

While the cookies are baking, place the remaining 1$^{3}/_{4}$ cups confectioners' sugar in a medium bowl. When the cookies are done, remove them from the oven and roll them in the confectioners' sugar while they are still hot. Then transfer them to wire racks and let cool completely. Once cooled, roll them again in the remaining confectioners' sugar. (The cookies can be made up to 5 days ahead. Layer the cookies between sheets of waxed paper in an airtight container and store at room temperature. Or, they can be frozen for up to 2 weeks. Roll again in confectioners' sugar once thawed.)

Makes about 3 dozen cookies

cranberry-pistachio biscotti

With speckles of green pistachios and sweetened dried cranberries, these are my all-time favorite Christmas biscotti. For complete indulgence, I like to dip one end in melted white chocolate.

2 1/4 CUPS UNBLEACHED ALL-PURPOSE FLOUR, PLUS MORE FOR DUSTING

1 1/2 TEASPOONS BAKING POWDER

1/2 TEASPOON KOSHER OR SEA SALT

1/3 CUP (2/3 STICK) UNSALTED BUTTER, AT ROOM TEMPERATURE

3/4 CUP GRANULATED SUGAR

2 LARGE EGGS

2 TEASPOONS FRESHLY GRATED LEMON ZEST

1 TEASPOON PURE VANILLA EXTRACT

1 CUP SWEETENED DRIED CRANBERRIES

3/4 CUP SHELLED NATURAL PISTACHIO NUTS

6 OUNCES WHITE CHOCOLATE, CHOPPED

1 1/2 TEASPOONS CANOLA OIL

Position one rack in the center and another rack in the lower third of the oven. Preheat the oven to 325°F. Line 2 rimmed baking sheets with parchment paper or nonstick baking liners, or use nonstick baking sheets.

In a medium bowl, sift together the flour, baking powder, and salt and set aside. In the bowl of a stand mixer fitted with the paddle attachment, cream together the butter and sugar on medium speed until fluffy, about 3 minutes. Add the eggs one at a time, beating well after each addition. Mix in the lemon zest and vanilla. Add the flour mixture to the butter mixture and mix just until blended. Stir in the cranberries and nuts.

Turn the mixture out onto a lightly floured work surface. The dough will be a bit sticky.

Divide the dough in half. With lightly floured hands, roll each half into a log 1 1/2 inches in diameter and about 15 inches long. Place both logs on one of the prepared baking sheets, spacing them 3 inches apart. Bake on the center oven rack until lightly firm to the touch, about 25 minutes. Remove from the oven and let stand for 10 minutes.

Transfer the logs to a cutting board. With a sharp serrated knife, and using a sawing motion, carefully cut 1 log on a slight diagonal into 1/2-inch-thick slices. Lay the slices on their sides in a single layer on the baking sheet. Repeat with the second log, arranging the slices on the second baking sheet. Bake until dried out and lightly golden on top, about 7 minutes. Turn each slice over and bake until lightly golden on the second side, about 7 minutes longer. Transfer to wire racks and let cool completely.

Place the chocolate in the top of a double boiler over barely simmering water in the lower pan, or in a heatproof bowl set over barely simmering water in a saucepan. Slowly melt the chocolate, stirring occasionally. Stir in the canola oil and continue to stir until the chocolate is smooth. Remove the top of the double boiler or the bowl from over the water and wipe the bottom to prevent any water from coming in contact with the chocolate. **>>>**

cranberry-pistachio biscotti

CONTINUED

Line rimmed baking sheets with waxed paper or parchment paper. Holding it vertically, dip 1 cookie at a time into the chocolate, coating about one-third of the cookie and letting the excess chocolate drip back into the bowl. As the cookies are dipped, carefully place them on the prepared baking sheets.

Let dry and harden for about 1 hour. The cookies will release from the paper once they are dry. (The biscotti can be made up to 5 days ahead. Layer them between sheets of waxed paper in an airtight container and store at room temperature.)

Makes about 3 dozen biscotti

chocolate—dipped shortbread stars

I find these cookies impossible to resist. Buttery shortbread with a tender crumb is cut into eye-catching shapes—stars are my favorite—and dipped in silky, deeply rich chocolate. Make all the cookies a uniform size, or vary the size of the stars and have a plateful of big stars and tiny ones. Any fun cookie cutter will work. One year I even made these cookies in the shape of dog bones and dipped half of the "bone" in chocolate. You can also add sweet spices, nuts, or even ground espresso beans to enhance the flavor of the cookies. For example, add I teaspoon ground cinnamon to the flour for a cinnamony shortbread, or substitute ¼ cup finely ground pecans, hazelnuts, or walnuts for ¼ cup of the flour. Or, for a deliciously intense espresso shortbread, substitute ¼ cup extra finely ground espresso-roast coffee for ¼ cup of the flour. It's Christmas, so put on your baking apron and play.

1 CUP (2 STICKS) UNSALTED BUTTER, AT ROOM TEMPERATURE FOR 30 MINUTES, CUT INTO SMALL CUBES

2/3 CUP SIFTED CONFECTIONERS' SUGAR, PLUS MORE FOR DUSTING

¼ TEASPOON KOSHER OR SEA SALT

2 CUPS UNBLEACHED ALL-PURPOSE FLOUR, PLUS MORE FOR DUSTING

6 OUNCES DARK BITTERSWEET CHOCOLATE (AT LEAST 64% CACAO), CHOPPED (SEE COOK'S NOTE, PAGE 136)

2 TEASPOONS CANOLA OIL

In the bowl of a stand mixer fitted with the paddle attachment, beat together the butter and sugar on medium speed until smooth and creamy, about 2 minutes. Reduce the speed to low, add the salt and flour, and mix just until the flour disappears, stopping and scraping down the sides of the bowl once with a rubber spatula. Do not overmix. The dough should look dry. Form the dough into a disk about 3/4 inch thick and wrap tightly in plastic wrap. Chill the dough for 30 minutes.

Line 2 rimmed baking sheets with parchment paper or nonstick baking liners, or use nonstick baking sheets. Transfer the dough to a lightly floured work surface. Dust the top of the dough with flour. Using a lightly floured rolling pin, roll out the dough 1/4 inch thick. Using a star cookie cutter, cut out as many cookies as possible. (I have a nesting set of star cutters and make star cookies in various sizes.) Place the cookies close together but not touching (the cookies do not spread) on the prepared baking sheets. Gather up the dough scraps, lightly dust with flour and sugar if needed, reroll the dough, and cut out cookies until all the dough is used. Refrigerate the baking sheets for 1 hour.

Position one rack in the center and another rack in the lower third of the oven.

Preheat the oven to 300°F. Bake the cookies until firm but not brown, 25 to 30 minutes, switching the pans between the racks and rotating them 180 degrees at the midpoint if the cookies appear to be baking unevenly. The cookies should be lightly golden on the bottom but not have any browning at the edges. Transfer to wire racks and let cool completely.

To dip the cookies, place three-fourths of the chocolate in the top of a double boiler over barely simmering water in the lower pan, or in a heatproof bowl set over barely simmering water in a saucepan. Slowly melt the chocolate, stirring occasionally. Remove the top of the double boiler or the bowl from over the water and wipe the bottom to prevent any water from coming in contact with the chocolate. Stir in the remaining chocolate and the oil and continue to stir until all of the chocolate has melted. Use an instant-read thermometer to check the temperature of the chocolate. It will stay glossy without any white streaking if the temperature is between 86° and 90°F when the cookies are dipped.

Dip 1 cookie at a time into the chocolate, coating about one-third of the cookie and letting the excess chocolate drip back into the bowl. As the cookies are dipped, carefully place them on the prepared baking sheet. Let dry and harden for about 1 hour. (If your kitchen is warm and the chocolate isn't setting, place the cookies in the refrigerator for 20 minutes to set the chocolate.) The cookies will release from the paper once they are dry. (The dipped cookies can be made up to 1 week ahead. Layer them between sheets of waxed paper in an airtight container and store at room temperature. Undipped cookies can be frozen for up to 1 month. In order to keep the chocolate glossy and bright, I dip the cookies after they have been frozen and thawed.)

Makes about 3 1/2 dozen cookies

spiced puff pastry pinwheels with candied fruit

For these crisp pinwheel cookies, buy the mixed candied fruit that is sold for making fruitcakes. For beautiful color, make sure the fruitcake blend includes cherries, pineapple (colored green), orange peel, citron, and lemon peel.

2 SHEETS FROZEN PUFF PASTRY DOUGH, FROM A 17.3-OUNCE PACKAGE

1/2 CUP GRANULATED SUGAR, PLUS MORE FOR DUSTING

2 TEASPOONS GROUND CINNAMON

1/2 TEASPOON GROUND ALLSPICE

1/2 TEASPOON GROUND GINGER

1/2 TEASPOON FRESHLY GRATED NUTMEG

4 TABLESPOONS (1/2 STICK) UNSALTED BUTTER, MELTED

2 CUPS MIXED CANDIED FRUIT, INCLUDING CANDIED CHERRIES, DICED (SEE HEADNOTE)

1 LARGE EGG, BEATEN, FOR GLAZE

Remove the pastry sheets from the package and thaw the pastry at room temperature for 30 minutes.

In a small bowl, stir together the sugar, cinnamon, allspice, ginger, and nutmeg until well combined. Set aside.

Sprinkle a work surface generously with sugar. Working with 1 pastry sheet at a time, unfold the pastry sheet and place it on the prepared work surface. Cut it in half, forming two 9 1/2-inch-long rectangles. Brush each half generously with butter, leaving a 1/2-inch border uncovered on one long side. Sprinkle each rectangle generously with some of the spiced sugar mixture. Scatter 1/2 cup of the candied fruit on each rectangle. Brush the plain border with the egg glaze. Starting at the long side opposite the edge brushed with egg glaze, roll up each pastry rectangle tightly, jelly-roll style, pressing firmly to seal the long edges and the ends of the logs. Wrap each log separately in plastic wrap. Repeat with the second sheet of puff pastry to make 2 more logs. Chill the 4 logs until firm, about 3 hours or up to 8 hours.

Position one rack in the center and another rack in the upper third of the oven. Preheat the oven to 400°F. Line 2 rimmed baking sheets with parchment paper or nonstick baking liners. **>>>**

spiced puff pastry pinwheels with candied fruit
CONTINUED

Remove 2 logs from the refrigerator, unwrap, and cut into 1/2-inch-thick rounds. (Keep the other 2 logs refrigerated while these bake.) Arrange the rounds on the prepared baking sheets, spacing them 1 inch apart. Bake for 12 minutes and then switch the pans between the racks and rotate them 180 degrees. Continue baking until the cookies are golden brown, about 12 minutes longer.

Let the cookies cool on the pans on wire racks for 5 minutes. Using a spatula, transfer the cookies to the racks, turning them bottom-side up. (The beautifully bronzed sugared bottom of these cookies becomes the top.) Let cool completely and then carefully break off any excess sugar that has hardened around the edges. While the first batch cools, cut and bake the remaining 2 logs the same way. (The cookies can be made up to 2 days ahead. Layer them between sheets of waxed paper in an airtight container and store at room temperature.)

Makes about 5 dozen cookies

fudgy chocolate walnut brownies

These dense brownies are trufflelike gems with a nutty crunch and a subtle caffeine buzz. Brownie lovers typically fall into two camps: they either like cake-style brownies or fudge-style brownies. I'm definitely in the gooey, fudgy camp, and these wondrous nuggets of cocoa and chocolate are the best I've ever tasted. They are a guaranteed hit at any cookie exchange.

VEGETABLE-OIL COOKING SPRAY FOR PREPARING THE BAKING DISH

1 CUP CAKE FLOUR OR 3/4 CUP UNBLEACHED ALL-PURPOSE FLOUR

1/4 CUP UNSWEETENED NATURAL COCOA POWDER

1/4 TEASPOON KOSHER OR SEA SALT

3/4 TEASPOON BAKING POWDER

1 1/2 TABLESPOONS FINELY GROUND ESPRESSO-ROAST COFFEE BEANS

3 OUNCES UNSWEETENED CHOCOLATE, FINELY CHOPPED

3/4 CUP (1 1/2 STICKS) UNSALTED BUTTER, AT ROOM TEMPERATURE

1 1/2 CUPS GRANULATED SUGAR

3 LARGE EGGS, BEATEN

1 TEASPOON PURE VANILLA EXTRACT

3/4 CUP CHOPPED WALNUTS, TOASTED (SEE PAGE 23)

Preheat the oven to 350°F. Spray an 8-inch square baking pan with vegetable-oil cooking spray. Line the bottom and sides of the pan with aluminum foil, allowing the foil to overhang the sides of the pan slightly, and then spray the foil with the cooking spray.

In a small bowl, sift together the flour, cocoa powder, salt, and baking powder. Stir in the ground coffee and set aside.

Fill a medium saucepan one-third full with water and bring to a simmer. Place the chocolate and butter in a large heatproof bowl that will fit snugly on top of the pan without touching the water and place over the water. Turn the heat to low. Melt the chocolate and butter, stirring frequently, until completely smooth. Remove the bowl from the heat and stir in the sugar until combined. Whisk in the eggs and vanilla until fully incorporated. Stir in the flour mixture just until the flour is absorbed. Stir in the nuts.

Pour the batter evenly into the prepared pan. Bake until a crust forms on top and the center is still somewhat gooey, 30 to 35 minutes. Let cool completely in the pan on a wire rack, and then cover and refrigerate for 2 hours before serving.

Using the foil overhang, lift the uncut brownie out of the pan and place on a cutting board. Using a sharp knife, cut into 1-inch squares to serve. (The brownies can be made up to 3 days ahead. Layer them between sheets of waxed paper in an airtight container and store in the refrigerator. Remove them from the refrigerator 45 minutes before serving. The brownies can be frozen for up to 1 month. Leave the brownies uncut if you plan to freeze the whole pan.)

Makes about 5 dozen bite-size brownies

grandma becky's rugelach

Both of my grandmothers were amazing cooks and bakers, but my paternal grandmother, Rebecca LevKoy, was an especially talented baker in the old-world style of baking by feel rather than by measure. Every Friday night, Grandma joined us for dinner. She always arrived with a tin of pastries or cookies she had baked that day. I called her rugelach "Grandma cakes." She varied the filling, sometimes using apricot jam with chopped walnuts and currants (my favorite), and other times spreading plum jam on the filling and sprinkling chopped almonds and a different dried fruit on top. Her pastry was buttery, tender, and sweet. She died before I became passionate about cooking and baking, so I never watched her bake or thought to ask for a recipe. And even though my mother has my grandmother's hand-painted recipe box stuffed with grease-stained recipe cards, the rugelach recipe was never written down. Over the years, I have tried recipes and experimented hoping to duplicate her delicate pastries. This recipe, to the best of my recollection, is a match for my grandmother's rugelach.

PASTRY DOUGH

1 CUP (2 STICKS) UNSALTED BUTTER, AT ROOM TEMPERATURE

1 PACKAGE (8 OUNCES) CREAM CHEESE, AT ROOM TEMPERATURE

2 TABLESPOONS GRANULATED SUGAR

1/4 TEASPOON KOSHER OR SEA SALT

1/2 TEASPOON PURE VANILLA EXTRACT

2 CUPS UNBLEACHED ALL-PURPOSE FLOUR, PLUS MORE FOR DUSTING

FILLING

1/2 CUP GRANULATED SUGAR

2 TABLESPOONS GROUND CINNAMON

1/2 CUP APRICOT JAM

3/4 CUP FINELY CHOPPED WALNUTS

1/2 CUP DRIED CURRANTS

CONFECTIONERS' SUGAR FOR DUSTING

To make the pastry dough, in the bowl of a stand mixer fitted with the paddle attachment, beat together the butter and cream cheese on medium speed until smooth and creamy, about 2 minutes. Beat in the granulated sugar, salt, and vanilla. Add 1 cup of the flour and mix on low speed just until the flour disappears. Mix in the remaining flour, stopping and scraping down the sides of the bowl once with a rubber spatula. Do not overmix.

Transfer the dough to a lightly floured work surface. Flour your hands and form the dough into a rectangle. Divide it into thirds. Shape each piece into a thick disk about 5 inches in diameter. Tightly wrap each piece in plastic wrap and refrigerate until well chilled, at least 1 hour. (The dough can be made up to 2 days in advance.)

Position one rack in the center and another rack in the lower third of the oven. Preheat the oven to 350°F. Line 2 rimmed baking sheets with parchment paper or nonstick baking liner, or use nonstick baking sheets.

To make the filling, in a small bowl, stir together the granulated sugar and cinnamon and set aside. To make the jam easier to spread, place it in a small bowl and warm in a microwave on High for several seconds, or warm in a small saucepan over low heat.

Remove 1 dough disk from the refrigerator. Lightly flour a work surface and a rolling pin. Roll out the dough into a round about 14 inches in diameter. Using a pastry brush, spread the dough with one-third of the jam, leaving a 1-inch border uncovered. Evenly sprinkle with one-third of the sugar mixture, again leaving the border uncovered. Then scatter one-third of the walnuts and currants over the sugar mixture.

Using a knife, pastry cutter, or pizza wheel, cut the pastry round into quarters. Cut each quarter into 3 wedges. Starting at the outside edge and working toward the point, snuggly roll up each wedge to form a crescent. As the crescents are formed, arrange them on the prepared baking sheets, spacing them about 1 inch apart. Repeat with the remaining dough disks and filling ingredients.

Bake the cookies until lightly browned on the edges and bottom, 25 to 30 minutes. Transfer the cookies to wire racks and let cool completely. Just before serving, using a small fine-mesh sieve, generously dust the cookies. (The cookies can be made up to 3 days ahead. Layer them between sheets of waxed paper in an airtight container and store at room temperature. Or, they can be frozen for up to 2 weeks.)

Makes 3 dozen cookies

hazelnut butter and miniature chocolate chip buttons

This cousin of the traditional peanut butter cookie calls for rich-flavored hazelnut butter. Look for hazelnut butter at natural-foods stores. Kettle Foods makes a creamy, delicious version. Once you open the jar, use a table fork to stir the oil that is floating on top back into the butter. Because these cookies are petite, it is better to use miniature chocolate chips, rather than regular-sized chips.

1 1/2 CUPS UNBLEACHED ALL-PURPOSE FLOUR

3/4 TEASPOON BAKING SODA

1/2 TEASPOON BAKING POWDER

1/2 TEASPOON KOSHER OR SEA SALT

1/2 CUP (1 STICK) UNSALTED BUTTER, AT ROOM TEMPERATURE

1 CUP HAZELNUT BUTTER

1/2 CUP GRANULATED SUGAR

1/2 CUP PACKED GOLDEN BROWN SUGAR

1 TEASPOON PURE VANILLA EXTRACT

1 LARGE EGG, BEATEN

2 CUPS (12 OUNCES) MINIATURE SEMISWEET CHOCOLATE CHIPS

In a medium bowl, sift together the flour, baking soda, baking powder, and salt and set aside. In the bowl of a stand mixer fitted with the paddle attachment, combine the butter, hazelnut butter, and both sugars and beat on medium speed until light and fluffy, about 4 minutes. Add the vanilla and egg and beat for 1 minute, stopping and scraping down the sides of the bowl once or twice with a rubber spatula. Add the flour mixture to the butter mixture, beating on low speed just until the flour disappears. Using a rubber spatula, fold in the chocolate chips. Gather the dough into a ball, place in a bowl, cover, and chill for 2 hours. (The dough can be made up to 1 day ahead. Remove from the refrigerator about 20 minutes before shaping, so it softens slightly.)

Position one rack in the center and another rack in the lower third of the oven. Preheat the oven to 375°F. Line 2 rimmed baking sheets with parchment paper or nonstick baking liners, or use nonstick baking sheets.

For each cookie, measure 1 level tablespoon of dough and roll into a ball between your palms. Arrange the cookies on the prepared baking sheets, spacing them about 1 inch apart. Bake until the cookies are nicely browned, about 14 minutes. Remove the pans from the oven and, using a round skewer or the stem of an instant-read thermometer, immediately poke 4 equidistant buttonholes in the middle of each cookie, twirling the skewer to define each hole. Using a spatula, transfer the cookies to wire racks and let cool completely. (The cookies can be made up to 5 days ahead. Layer them between sheets of waxed paper in an airtight container and store at room temperature. Or, they can be frozen for up to 2 weeks.)

Makes about 5 dozen cookies

cocoa clouds

This recipe comes from my good friend Roxane Huang. She bakes multiple batches of these cookies every Christmas and I receive a towering plateful. They are irresistible cocoa-scented puffs, crisp on the outside and slightly chewy inside, and loaded with tiny semisweet chocolate chips. Consider these the "low-fat" cookie for the holiday exchange party!

3 LARGE EGG WHITES, AT ROOM TEMPERATURE

1/8 TEASPOON CREAM OF TARTAR

1/8 TEASPOON KOSHER OR SEA SALT

1 CUP SUPERFINE SUGAR

3 TABLESPOONS SIFTED UNSWEETENED NATURAL COCOA POWDER

1 1/2 CUPS (ABOUT 9 OUNCES) MINIATURE SEMISWEET CHOCOLATE CHIPS

Position one rack in the center and another rack in the lower third of the oven. Preheat the oven to 250°F. Line 2 rimmed baking sheets with parchment paper or nonstick baking liners, or use nonstick baking sheets.

In the bowl of a stand mixer fitted with the whip attachment, beat the egg whites on medium speed until foamy. Add the cream of tartar and salt and beat on medium-high speed until soft peaks form. Add the superfine sugar 1 tablespoon at a time, beating on medium-high speed until a strong, shiny meringue forms with stiff, glossy peaks. Using a small fine-mesh sieve, sift the cocoa over the meringue and then beat in on medium-low speed until well blended, about 1 minute, stopping to scrape down the sides of the bowl once, if needed. Using a rubber spatula, fold in the chocolate chips.

Drop by rounded teaspoons onto the prepared baking sheets, spacing the cookies about 3/4 inch apart. (The cookies don't spread as they bake.)

Bake the cookies until crisp, 25 to 30 minutes. Let the cookies cool on the pans on wire racks for 5 minutes. Transfer to wire racks and let cool completely. (The cookies can be made up to 3 days ahead. Layer the cookies between sheets of waxed paper in an airtight container and store at room temperature. The cookies cannot be frozen.)

Makes about 6 dozen cookies

8 food gifts from the kitchen

Homemade gifts from the kitchen are, first and foremost, gifts from the heart. They come in tins, jars, boxes, on paper plates, and in holiday-themed cellophane bags tied with a grosgrain bow. As a special holiday gift to you, I am sharing for the first time my recipe for Diane's Christmas Pecans. Nothing would make me happier than for these spectacular meringue-crusted nuts to become part of your own holiday gift-giving tradition. Also enjoy making and giving Chocolate-and-Caramel-Dipped Pretzel Logs, and Apricot, Ginger, and Walnut Tea Bread. Merry Christmas!

diane's christmas pecans

This recipe is a very personal gift to my friends, family, and colleagues who have been on the receiving end of my highly anticipated Christmas pecans every December. These coated nuts are sweet, crunchy, buttery gems of goodness—practically irresistible. Served along with dessert, they are a superb finish to a holiday meal, and if you ask my husband, he'll tell you they are perfection served with a tumbler of bourbon straight-up. One colleague tosses a handful of these nuts, along with sweetened dried cranberries and crumbled blue cheese, into a mesclun salad to serve as the first course for her Christmas Eve dinner. ❋ Over the years, many people have asked for the recipe and I have never given it out. In fact, I believe this is the only recipe I have never shared. Twenty years ago, I started baking these pecans as a food gift to give at Christmastime. I took them to holiday cocktail parties and open houses as a hostess gift, I made some to put out at my own Christmas parties, and then I started mailing them to friends and colleagues around the country. Pretty soon the list grew longer, and what started as a morning of baking a couple of pounds of pecans turned into a production schedule of baking almost twenty pounds. If it sounds like a chore, it isn't. In fact, quite the opposite, as it now feels like my special yearly tradition. Every fall, I order white laminated candy boxes that hold about a half pound of nuts, look for fun Christmas ribbons and gift tags, and make my list—checking it twice—to make sure I'm not missing anyone. Now, I am sharing this gift recipe with everyone!

1/2 CUP (1 STICK) UNSALTED BUTTER

2 EGG WHITES, AT ROOM TEMPERATURE
(SEE COOK'S NOTE, PAGE 186)

1/8 TEASPOON KOSHER OR SEA SALT

1 TEASPOON PURE VANILLA EXTRACT

1 CUP PACKED GOLDEN BROWN SUGAR

1 POUND SHELLED LARGE OR JUMBO
PECAN HALVES

Position a rack in the center of the oven. Preheat the oven to 300°F. Have ready a large rimmed baking sheet, preferably nonstick for easier cleanup.

Melt the butter on the baking sheet in the oven. Be careful not to let the butter brown. Set aside.

In the bowl of a stand mixer fitted with the whip attachment, beat the egg whites on medium speed until foamy. Add the salt and beat on medium-high speed until soft peaks form. Pour the vanilla over the brown sugar. Add the sugar 2 tablespoons at a time to the egg whites, beating on high speed to form a strong, shiny meringue with stiff, glossy peaks. Using a rubber spatula, gently fold in the nuts until they are well coated. **>>>**

diane's christmas pecans

Carefully tip the rimmed baking sheet so the butter evenly coats the bottom of the pan. Using a rubber spatula, spread the nuts over the butter, without stirring, to form an even layer without deflating the meringue.

Bake the nuts for 20 minutes. Remove from the oven and stir with the spatula, moving the nuts at the center of the pan to the edges and the nuts at the edges closer to the center. Return the pan to the oven, bake the nuts for 15 minutes longer, and stir them again. Continue baking, stirring every 15 minutes, until the nuts are separated, have absorbed the butter and glisten, and are beautifully browned but not dark brown, 45 minutes to 1 hour.

Immediately turn the nuts out on a counter lined with a long sheet of aluminum foil, spread them out, and let cool completely. (Store in an airtight tin or a covered glass container, or wrap in gift boxes lined with decorative waxed paper. The nuts will keep at room temperature for 2 to 3 weeks.)

Makes 1 pound

COOK'S NOTES

A couple of years ago, I tried making a test batch of the pecans using liquid egg whites sold in refrigerated cartons, thinking how much easier it would be to just measure egg whites and not waste egg yolks or try to find a use for them. I wasn't happy with the results. The meringue wasn't as lofty as when I used whites from freshly cracked eggs. ❋ As you can imagine, if I am making twenty pounds of pecans for the holidays, I have figured out a way to make larger batches. You can double the recipe, but you'll need to divide the coated nuts between two rimmed baking sheets and melt a stick of butter in each pan. My oven is wide enough to accommodate restaurant-grade hotel pans that are long and shallow. In those pans I can bake two pounds of nuts at a time. With two pans, I put one on the center rack and the other on a rack in the lower third of the oven, and I switch the pans every time I stir the nuts, baking four pounds of nuts at one time.

janine's curry-ginger walnuts

My friend and colleague Janine MacLachlan lives in Chicago and sends incredibly creative and unique Christmas cards every year. Several years ago, her card included "wishes for a warm and wonderful season from the Rustic Kitchen," her business, and was printed on elegant card stock mounted on shimmery bronze paper. Just below the greeting was a recipe for these walnuts. I have made them on numerous occasions and wanted to share her recipe. They have a caramelized, crackly sugar coating with a forward hit of curry and ginger, and a lingering kick from the cayenne pepper. Janine suggests serving them with a glass of sherry before dinner, or adding them to an arugula salad dressed with olive oil and a whisper of honey.

ROOM-TEMPERATURE BUTTER FOR PREPARING THE WAXED PAPER

1 CUP GRANULATED SUGAR

1/4 CUP WATER

1 TEASPOON CURRY POWDER

1 TEASPOON GROUND GINGER

1/2 TEASPOON KOSHER OR SEA SALT

1/4 TEASPOON CAYENNE PEPPER

2 CUPS WALNUT HALVES

Line a rimmed baking sheet with waxed paper and butter the paper. In a 10-inch sauté pan over medium-high heat, combine the sugar and water and stir to dissolve the sugar, about 1 minute. Add the curry powder, ginger, salt, and cayenne and bring the mixture to a boil. Add the walnuts and sauté, stirring frequently so the nuts don't burn. The sugar mixture will form crystals around the nuts as you stir. Lower the heat to medium and continue to stir until the crystallized sugar coating turns to a caramel-colored liquid, about 5 minutes.

Immediately transfer the nuts to the buttered waxed paper, separate them with a fork, and let cool completely. (Store in an airtight tin or a covered glass container, or wrap in gift boxes lined with decorative waxed paper. The nuts will keep at room temperature for about 10 days.)

Makes 2 cups

cinnamon-honey truffles with cocoa dust

These are for your chocoholic friends. To make them, I blend bittersweet chocolate with cream that has been steeped with honey, vanilla, cinnamon, and cloves. A touch of butter gives the truffles a creamy, smooth texture. Double the recipe if you have a lot of chocolate lovers on your gift list.

8 OUNCES DARK BITTERSWEET CHOCOLATE (AT LEAST 64% CACAO), VERY FINELY CHOPPED (SEE COOK'S NOTE, PAGE 136)

1/2 CUP HEAVY (WHIPPING) CREAM

1 TABLESPOON HONEY

1/2 TEASPOON PURE VANILLA EXTRACT

1/2 CINNAMON STICK, ABOUT 1 1/2 INCHES LONG

2 WHOLE CLOVES

PINCH OF KOSHER OR SEA SALT

2 1/2 TABLESPOONS UNSALTED BUTTER, AT ROOM TEMPERATURE

1/3 CUP UNSWEETENED DUTCH-PROCESS COCOA POWDER, SIFTED

Place the chocolate in a medium heatproof bowl.

In a small saucepan over medium heat, combine the cream, honey, vanilla, cinnamon stick, cloves, and salt. Bring to a boil, reduce the heat to low, and simmer for 5 minutes. Remove from the heat. Pour the cream through a fine-mesh sieve held over the chocolate, discarding the contents of the sieve, and let stand for 2 minutes. Using a rubber spatula, gently stir the chocolate mixture in a circular motion until it has completely melted. Add the butter and stir until incorporated. Cover the bowl with plastic wrap and set aside at room temperature for 30 minutes to set the chocolate. (If the chocolate is still too soft to scoop balls, refrigerate it for 10 minutes.)

Line a rimmed baking sheet with parchment or waxed paper. Using a melon baller, a tiny ice cream scoop, or a spoon, scoop out 1-inch balls of chocolate and place them 1 inch apart on the prepared baking sheet. Then roll each ball between your palms into an irregularly shaped truffle. Return the truffles to the refrigerator and chill until firm, about 1 hour.

Place the cocoa in a small, shallow bowl. One at a time, roll the truffles in the cocoa, coating them evenly. (The truffles can be made up to 2 weeks ahead. Layer them between sheets of waxed paper in a flat airtight container and store in the refrigerator.)

Makes about thirty 1-inch truffles

white chocolate—dipped pretzel logs

Turn pretzel rods into brightly coated Christmas delights by first dipping them in white chocolate and then picking your favorite holiday sprinkles to decorate. I like to use nonpareils, the tiny sugar balls that are commonly sold white but are packaged in a combination of red, green, and white at Christmastime. This is another fun cooking project with kids and a delightful gift to give to children. Long, clear cellophane bags work best for wrapping the logs.

4 OUNCES WHITE CHOCOLATE, CHOPPED

12 PRETZEL RODS

1/3 TO 1/2 CUP MIXED RED, GREEN, AND WHITE NONPAREIL SPRINKLES

To melt the chocolate, place three-fourths of the chocolate in the top of a double boiler over barely simmering water in the lower pan, or in a heatproof bowl set over barely simmering water in a saucepan. Slowly melt the chocolate, stirring occasionally. Remove the top of the double boiler or the bowl and wipe the bottom to prevent any water from coming in contact with the chocolate. Stir in the remaining chocolate. Continue to stir until all the chocolate is melted.

Line a rimmed baking sheet with waxed paper or parchment paper. (Do not spray the paper with cooking spray.) Working with 1 pretzel at a time, dip the top half in the melted chocolate and allow the excess chocolate to drip back into the pan. You can also use the back of a spoon to remove the excess. Place the dipped pretzels on the prepared baking sheet. Allow the chocolate to cool and set slightly, about 5 minutes. Sprinkle the chocolate-covered half of each pretzel with the sprinkles, turning to coat all sides.

Refrigerate until the chocolate is hardened, about 20 minutes. The pretzels will release from the paper once dry. (The dipped pretzels can be made up to 1 week ahead. Layer them, without touching, between sheets of waxed paper in a flat airtight container and store at room temperature.)

Makes 12 pretzels

chocolate-and-caramel-dipped pretzel logs

While I was developing the recipes for this book, the Starbucks in my neighborhood was selling pretzel rods dipped in caramel and chocolate as a Christmastime treat. My husband bought a package and we tried them. They were addictive—a winning match of salty and sweet. I said, "I can duplicate these." And I did. Think of this recipe as a fun cooking project to make with children and a fanciful food gift to give to children. I bought long cellophane packages for wrapping the pretzel logs and tied them with bright ribbons and gift tags.

25 INDIVIDUALLY WRAPPED CARAMELS SUCH AS KRAFT BRAND CARAMELS, UNWRAPPED

1 1/2 TEASPOONS WATER

VEGETABLE-OIL COOKING SPRAY FOR PREPARING THE WAXED PAPER

12 PRETZEL RODS

4 OUNCES BITTERSWEET CHOCOLATE, CHOPPED

To melt the caramels, fill the bottom pan of a double boiler or a medium saucepan one-third full of water and bring to a simmer over medium heat. Place the caramels and water in the top of the double boiler or in a heatproof bowl that will fit snugly on top of the pan without touching the water and place over the water. Reduce the heat to low. Stir to melt the caramels, about 5 minutes. Remove from the heat.

Spray a sheet of waxed paper with vegetable-oil cooking spray. Working with 1 pretzel at a time, dip the top half in the melted caramel and allow the excess caramel to drip back into the pan. You can also use the back of a spoon to remove the excess. Place the dipped pretzels on the prepared waxed paper. Allow the caramel to set, about 30 minutes.

To melt the chocolate, place three-fourths of the chocolate in the top of a double boiler over barely simmering water in the lower pan,

or in a heatproof bowl set over barely simmering water in a saucepan. Slowly melt the chocolate, stirring occasionally. Remove the top of the double boiler or the bowl and wipe the bottom to prevent any water from coming in contact with the chocolate. Stir in the remaining chocolate. Continue to stir until all the chocolate is melted. Use an instant-read thermometer to check the temperature of the chocolate. It will stay glossy without any white streaking if the temperature is between 86° and 90°F when the pretzels are dipped.

Have ready a fresh sheet of waxed paper or use parchment paper. (Do not spray the paper with cooking spray.) Dip 1 caramel-coated pretzel at a time, coating the chocolate over the caramel, but leaving about 1/4 inch of the caramel showing. Let the excess chocolate drip back into the bowl. Carefully place the pretzel on the paper and let dry for 1 hour. The pretzels will release from the paper once dry. (The dipped pretzels can be made up to 1 week ahead. Layer them, not touching, between sheets of waxed paper in a flat airtight container and store at room temperature.)

Makes 12 pretzels

"morgan's own" house vinaigrette

If Paul Newman can make his own salad dressing, bottle it, and call it Newman's Own, I figure that I can bottle my favorite vinaigrette, call it Morgan's Own, and turn it into a food gift at Christmastime. I don't have a single bottle of store-bought salad dressing on my pantry shelf or in my refrigerator. I always make my own—it's so easy. Buy handsome tall bottles with tight-fitting caps that will hold 2 to 2½ cups of dressing. Fill the bottles with this vinaigrette, and tie a gift tag onto the bottle neck with the recipe and the variations I give below.

2 TEASPOONS KOSHER OR SEA SALT

1 TEASPOON GRANULATED SUGAR

1 TEASPOON FRESHLY GROUND PEPPER

1/2 CUP UNSEASONED RICE VINEGAR

1 1/2 CUPS EXTRA-VIRGIN OLIVE OIL

Place a funnel in the top of a glass bottle large enough to hold 2 cups of dressing. Add the salt, sugar, and pepper through the funnel into the bottle. Pour the vinegar and olive oil through the funnel into the bottle. Secure the cap on the bottle and shake vigorously to combine. Store the dressing on the pantry shelf at room temperature. Shake vigorously before each use. (Use 1/4 cup vinaigrette to dress a salad to serve 4, assuming you use about 1 cup lightly packed salad greens per person.) The vinaigrette will keep for 3 months.

Makes 2 cups

VARIATIONS

Dijon Vinaigrette: Add 1 teaspoon Dijon mustard to 1/4 cup vinaigrette.

Herb Vinaigrette: Add 2 teaspoons minced fresh herbs such as flat-leaf parsley, basil, oregano, and tarragon to 1/4 cup vinaigrette.

Mustard-Herb Vinaigrette: Add 1 teaspoon Dijon mustard and 2 teaspoons minced fresh herbs such as flat-leaf parsley, basil, oregano, and tarragon to 1/4 cup vinaigrette.

Creamy Vinaigrette: Add 1 tablespoon heavy (whipping) cream to 1/4 cup vinaigrette.

Creamy Herb Vinaigrette: Add 1 tablespoon heavy (whipping) cream and 2 teaspoons minced fresh herbs such as flat-leaf parsley, basil, oregano, and tarragon to 1/4 cup vinaigrette.

Creamy Dijon-Herb Vinaigrette: Add 1 tablespoon heavy (whipping) cream, 1 teaspoon Dijon mustard, and 2 teaspoons minced fresh herbs such as flat-leaf parsley, basil, oregano, and tarragon to 1/4 cup vinaigrette.

Creamy Blue Cheese Vinaigrette: Add 1 tablespoon heavy (whipping) cream, 1 teaspoon minced fresh flat-leaf parsley, and 1 rounded tablespoon crumbled blue cheese to 1/4 cup vinaigrette.

apricot, ginger, and walnut tea bread

This is my family's favorite quick bread, and it is also an excellent gift for a friend hosting a holiday party. A loaf quickly disappears if sliced and set out for breakfast on a lazy weekend. Toasting the bread and smearing it with a little butter is also divine. ❋ The recipe yields two standard loaves. But you can buy lovely Italian-made heavy waxed-paper loaf pans in two sizes, 6 by 3 inches or 2 by 4 inches, and bake three small loaves or six miniature loaves. After baking the loaves, leave them in their attractive paper pans, which are brown with a decorative gold pattern, and wrap them with clear cellophane and a bright bow. Buy these paper pans at well-stocked cookware stores, or order them from King Arthur Flour online at www.bakerscatalogue.com or by calling 800-827-6836.

VEGETABLE-OIL COOKING SPRAY
FOR PREPARING THE PANS

3 1/2 CUPS UNBLEACHED ALL-PURPOSE FLOUR

4 TEASPOONS BAKING POWDER

1 TEASPOON KOSHER OR SEA SALT

1/2 TEASPOON BAKING SODA

1/2 TEASPOON GROUND CINNAMON

1/8 TEASPOON FRESHLY GRATED NUTMEG

2/3 CUP (1 STICK PLUS 3 TABLESPOONS)
UNSALTED BUTTER

1 1/3 CUPS GRANULATED SUGAR

4 LARGE EGGS, AT ROOM TEMPERATURE

2 CUPS MASHED RIPE BANANAS (ABOUT 4 BANANAS)

3/4 CUP CHOPPED WALNUTS, TOASTED
(SEE PAGE 23)

1 CUP FINELY CHOPPED DRIED APRICOTS,
TOSSED WITH 1 TABLESPOON FLOUR TO SEPARATE

1/3 CUP DICED CRYSTALLIZED GINGER
(SEE COOK'S NOTE, PAGE 118)

Position a rack in the center of the oven. Preheat the oven to 350°F. Spray the bottom and sides of two 9-by-5-inch loaf pans with vegetable-oil cooking spray. Set aside.

In a large mixing bowl, sift together the flour, baking powder, salt, baking soda, cinnamon, and nutmeg. Set aside.

In the bowl of a stand mixer fitted with the paddle attachment, cream together the butter and sugar on medium speed until fluffy, about 3 minutes. Add the eggs one at a time, beating well after each addition. Beat in the bananas, stopping and scraping down the sides of the bowl once with a rubber spatula.

With the mixer on low speed, add the sifted ingredients in 3 batches, beating after each addition until the flour disappears. Do not overmix. Using a rubber spatula, fold in the walnuts, apricots, and ginger.

Divide the batter evenly between the prepared pans. Bake the breads until nicely browned, puffed at the center, and a toothpick inserted in the center comes out clean, about 45 minutes. Let cool in the pans on wire racks for 10 minutes. Turn the loaves out of the pans and let cool completely on the racks before wrapping. (The breads can be made up to 2 days ahead. Wrap them tightly in plastic wrap or place in lock-top plastic bags, forcing out all the air before securing closed. The breads can be frozen up to 1 month.)

Makes 2 loaves

9 leftover favorites

Joy to a refrigerator well stocked with cooked food! Having worked hard preparing the Christmas feast (or multiple feasts), you've earned your place sitting in front of the fire instead of standing over it. Leftovers, especially at this time of year, are truly gifts that keep on giving. So don't just settle for a warmed-up version of Christmas dinner past, as good as that might be. Think instead of nesting Santa dolls that reveal yet another Santa (or two or three!) inside. In this case, it's the Christmas turkey that yields Turkey Potpie with a Puff Pastry Crust or the prime rib that's concealing a Mediterranean Beef Salad. Hallelujah!

hot beef borscht

Wintry days make me hungry for comfort foods, and nothing satisfies more than this hearty eastern European–style soup. I use either leftover brisket from Diane Cohen's Brisket on page 94 or some of the beef from Salt and Garlic-Crusted Prime Rib of Beef on page 80.

3 TABLESPOONS UNSALTED BUTTER

1 LARGE YELLOW ONION, CUT INTO 1/2-INCH DICE

2 RIBS CELERY, TRIMMED AND CUT INTO 1/2-INCH DICE

1 FENNEL BULB, STALKS AND BULB CUT INTO 1/2-INCH DICE, FEATHERY FRONDS CHOPPED AND RESERVED FOR GARNISH

1 TEASPOON GROUND CORIANDER

1 TEASPOON GROUND CUMIN

1 TEASPOON CARAWAY SEEDS

1 TEASPOON FRESHLY GROUND PEPPER

3 BEETS, PEELED AND CUT INTO 1/2-INCH DICE (SEE COOK'S NOTE)

1/2 SMALL GREEN CABBAGE, CUT INTO 1/2-INCH DICE

7 CUPS HOMEMADE CHICKEN STOCK OR CANNED LOW-SODIUM CHICKEN BROTH

12 OUNCES COOKED BRISKET OR ROAST BEEF, CUT INTO 1/2-INCH DICE

KOSHER OR SEA SALT

1/2 CUP SOUR CREAM

In a heavy soup pot over medium heat, melt the butter and swirl to coat the pan. Add the onion, celery, and diced fennel and sauté, stirring constantly, for 1 minute. Cover, reduce the heat to low, and cook until the vegetables are softened but not brown, about 5 minutes. Add the coriander, cumin, caraway seeds, and pepper and sauté, stirring constantly, until the spices are fragrant, about 1 minute. Add the beets, cabbage, and chicken stock and bring to a simmer. Partially cover the pot and simmer until the beets are tender, about 35 minutes.

When the beets are tender, add the beef and heat through. Season to taste with salt. Ladle into warmed soup bowls. Serve with a dollop of sour cream and garnish with the chopped fennel fronds.

Serves 6 to 8

COOK'S NOTE
I use disposable surgical gloves when I am working with beets to keep my fingers from being stained red. Look for them at a pharmacy or in a supermarket where bandages and first-aid supplies are sold.

lamb and pita sandwiches with yogurt-mint sauce

Here is a fun, casual sandwich supper utilizing leftover roast lamb from the Herb and Garlic—Stuffed Roast Leg of Lamb on page 84. Using romaine and roasted red peppers is one way to stuff the pita sandwiches, but use whatever vegetables you like— sliced cucumbers, sliced sweet onions, sliced tomatoes, a mixture of romaine lettuce and fresh mint leaves, pan-grilled zucchini slices—the possibilities are endless. Serve with plenty of napkins. Buy some hummus and cut some vegetables for a crudité platter to serve with the sandwiches.

4 PITA BREADS, HALVED

8 SLICES ROAST LEG OF LAMB

1/2 CUP WHOLE-MILK OR LOW-FAT PLAIN YOGURT, PREFERABLY GREEK YOGURT

3 TABLESPOONS SOUR CREAM

2 TABLESPOONS FINELY CHOPPED FRESH MINT

1 TEASPOON FRESH LIME JUICE

1/2 TEASPOON MINCED GARLIC

1/4 TEASPOON KOSHER OR SEA SALT

1/8 TEASPOON FRESHLY GROUND PEPPER

4 ROMAINE LETTUCE LEAVES, ENDS TRIMMED AND CUT CROSSWISE INTO NARROW RIBBONS

4 JARRED ROASTED RED PEPPERS, DRAINED AND BLOTTED DRY, CUT INTO NARROW STRIPS

Position a rack in the center of the oven. Preheat the oven to 250°F. Wrap the pita breads in aluminum foil. Wrap the lamb slices in another foil package, or arrange them in a baking dish and cover with foil. Heat the pitas and lamb until warmed, about 20 minutes.

Meanwhile, in a small bowl, combine the yogurt, sour cream, mint, lime juice, garlic, salt, and pepper. Stir to combine and set aside.

To assemble the sandwiches, stuff a slice of lamb into each pita half. Stuff some lettuce and pepper strips inside the pita and top with a dollop of the sauce. Serve immediately.

Serves 4

asian noodle bowl with pork, watercress, and shiitake mushrooms

Take a walk through the Asian-foods section of a well-stocked supermarket and look for rice stick noodles. They are thin, dry white noodles made from rice flour and are typically packaged in cellophane bags. The noodles are available in assorted widths, anywhere from $1/16$ to $1/4$ inch wide; any width will work fine for this recipe. Pick up some dried black (shiitake) mushrooms as well (they are a handy pantry item if you like to make Asian-style recipes), rehydrate them, and add them along with the pork to the soup. Use leftover roast pork from either Garlic and Herb-Rubbed Crown Roast of Pork (page 77) or Roast Loin of Pork Stuffed with Apricots and Dried Plums (page 87).

4 OUNCES RICE STICK NOODLES

10 DRIED BLACK (SHIITAKE) MUSHROCMS

8 CUPS HOMEMADE CHICKEN STOCK OR CANNED LOW-SODIUM CHICKEN BROTH

1 LARGE CARROT, PEELED AND CUT ON THE DIAGONAL INTO $1/8$-INCH-THICK OVALS

1 TABLESPOON PEELED AND FINELY MINCED FRESH GINGER

1 TABLESPOON LOW-SODIUM SOY SAUCE

$1 1/2$ CUPS JULIENNED ROAST PORK

1 BUNCH FRESH WATERCRESS, INCLLDING TENDER STEMS, CUT INTO 2-INCH LENGTHS

2 GREEN ONIONS, INCLUDING GREEN TOPS, CUT INTO 1-INCH LENGTHS

In a large bowl, combine the rice noodles with warm water to cover. Place the dried mushrooms in a small container with a tight-fitting lid, add warm water to the top, and close the container. (Dried mushrooms float; placing them in a covered container ensures they will be submerged.) Soak the noodles and mushrooms for 20 minutes. Drain the noodles in a colander and set aside. Drain the mushrooms, pat dry with paper towels, trim and discard the stems, and cut the tops into thin strips.

Meanwhile, in a $3 1/2$- to 4-quart saucepan, bring the stock to a boil. Reduce the heat to a simmer, add the carrot and ginger, and cook until the carrot is crisp-tender, 12 to 15 minutes. Add the soy sauce, pork, watercress, green onions, drained rice noodles, and mushrooms. Stir to combine and heat through. Ladle into warmed soup bowls and serve immediately.

Serves 4 to 6

macaroni and cheese with ham

Go ahead and call me old-fashioned because one of my favorite ways to use leftover ham is in a homey casserole of macaroni and cheese. This classic comfort food has been maligned over the years by school cafeterias and hospital kitchens, let alone food manufacturers trying to convince children with clever advertising that what comes out of a blue box is honest-to-goodness macaroni and cheese. Truly, what was intended was a bubbly-hot dish of al dente macaroni covered with a silken cheese sauce under a crusty topping of mixed bread crumbs and Parmesan. I've added diced holiday ham to make this a sublime leftover favorite.

5 TABLESPOONS UNSALTED BUTTER, PLUS 1 TABLESPOON, AT ROOM TEMPERATURE, FOR PREPARING THE DISH

5 TABLESPOONS ALL-PURPOSE FLOUR

3¹/4 CUPS MILK

¹/2 TEASPOON KOSHER OR SEA SALT

1 TEASPOON DRY MUSTARD

¹/2 TEASPOON HOT-PEPPER SAUCE

5 CUPS (12 OUNCES) SHREDDED EXTRA-SHARP CHEDDAR CHEESE

12 OUNCES SMALL ELBOW MACARONI

3 CUPS ¹/2-INCH-DICE BOURBON AND BROWN SUGAR–CRUSTED HAM (PAGE 93)

¹/2 CUP *PANKO* (JAPANESE BREAD CRUMBS) OR OTHER UNSEASONED BREAD CRUMBS

¹/2 CUP (2 OUNCES) FRESHLY GRATED PARMESAN CHEESE, PREFERABLY PARMIGIANO-REGGIANO

Position a rack in the center of the oven. Preheat the oven to 350°F. Use the 1 tablespoon butter to butter a 9-by-13-inch flameproof baking dish.

In a 4-quart saucepan over medium heat, melt the remaining 5 tablespoons butter. Stir in the flour and cook, stirring constantly, until the mixture is very lightly browned, 1 to 2 minutes. Gradually whisk in the milk about 1 cup at a time. Whisk in the salt, mustard, and hot-pepper sauce. Bring to a simmer, whisking frequently, and cook, continuing to whisk, until the sauce thickly coats a spoon, about 5 minutes. Add the Cheddar cheese and cook, stirring constantly, until it melts. Remove from the heat and set aside.

Fill a 4-quart or larger pot with water and bring to a rolling boil over high heat. Add the macaroni and cook, stirring occasionally, until cooked through but still quite chewy, about 6 minutes. (Do not overcook the pasta; it will continue to cook while baking.) Drain in a colander, shaking out as much water as possible.

Mix the macaroni with the ham and spread in the prepared baking dish. Pour the sauce evenly over the top. In a small bowl, stir together the bread crumbs and Parmesan cheese. Sprinkle the mixture evenly over the macaroni.

Bake until bubbly and crispy brown at the edges, about 30 minutes. If the crumbs have not browned handsomely, place the casserole under the broiler for a few seconds before serving.

Serves 6 to 8

shrimp and ham jambalaya

Louisiana, home to French-influenced Creole and Cajun cooking, is also home to jambalaya, a rice dish combining seafood and ham. I've made a colorful version that combines shrimp, ham, and Garnet yams. The yams add a subtle sweetness that pairs delectably with the peppers, tomatoes, and smokiness of the meat. For holiday entertaining, this is an easy, do-ahead, one-pot main course, either for a sit-down dinner or a buffet. The day of the party, or even a day ahead, prepare the jambalaya up to the point of adding the rice. Set aside, covered, for up to 6 hours or refrigerate overnight, and then bring to a simmer 30 minutes before you plan to serve. Have the rice, shrimp, ham, and parsley measured and ready to be added. Add the rice and proceed as directed to complete the dish. If you have ham for Christmas, this is a great way to use up some of the leftovers.

2 TABLESPOONS UNSALTED BUTTER

2 TABLESPOONS EXTRA-VIRGIN OLIVE OIL

1 1/2 POUNDS GARNET YAMS, PEELED AND CUT INTO 3/4-INCH DICE (ABOUT 4 CUPS)

2 LARGE CLOVES GARLIC, MINCED

1 YELLOW ONION, CUT INTO 1/2-INCH DICE

1 LARGE GREEN BELL PEPPER, SEEDED, DERIBBED, AND CUT INTO 1/2-INCH DICE

PINCH OF GROUND CLOVES

1/4 TEASPOON CAYENNE PEPPER

1 TABLESPOON MINCED FRESH THYME

1 BAY LEAF

1 1/2 CUPS WATER

1 CAN (28 OUNCES) DICED TOMATOES IN JUICE

1/2 CUP SHORT-GRAIN WHITE RICE

1 POUND LARGE (21/30 COUNT) UNCOOKED SHRIMP, PEELED AND DEVEINED

12 OUNCES SMOKED HAM STEAK, ABOUT 1/4-INCH THICK, CUT INTO 1/2-INCH DICE

1/3 CUP MINCED FRESH FLAT-LEAF PARSLEY

HOT-PEPPER SAUCE (OPTIONAL)

In a deep, 12-inch sauté pan over medium-high heat, melt the butter with the olive oil and swirl to coat the pan. Add the yams and sauté, stirring frequently, until well coated with the butter mixture, about 2 minutes. Add the garlic, onion, and bell pepper and sauté, stirring frequently, until the vegetables are crisp-tender, about 3 minutes longer. Add the cloves, cayenne pepper, thyme, bay leaf, water, and the tomatoes and their juice and stir to combine. Bring to a simmer and stir in the rice. Partially cover the pan and simmer over low heat until the rice is almost tender, about 12 minutes.

Add the shrimp and ham and simmer just until the shrimp turn pink and are cooked through, about 5 minutes longer. Remove the bay leaf and stir in the parsley. Taste and adjust the seasoning. Add the hot-pepper sauce to taste. Ladle into warmed shallow bowls and serve immediately.

Serves 8

turkey potpie with a puff pastry crust

This is a terrific way to use up leftover turkey. Potpies are a great do-ahead main course for a brunch, lunch, or simple supper with friends and family. They can be made a day in advance, covered, and refrigerated, and then can go straight from the refrigerator to the oven to the table without last-minute fussing. I like to serve individual potpies when entertaining a group of six. For single-serving potpies, you'll need 1½ sheets of puff pastry to cut 6 circles of dough, so plan accordingly.

1 TO 2 SHEETS FROZEN PUFF PASTRY DOUGH, FROM A 17.3-OUNCE PACKAGE

1½ CUPS HOMEMADE CHICKEN STOCK OR CANNED LOW-SODIUM CHICKEN BROTH

1 LARGE CARROT, PEELED, HALVED LENGTHWISE, AND THINLY SLICED

3 TABLESPOONS UNSALTED BUTTER

2 TABLESPOONS CANOLA OIL

1 SMALL YELLOW ONION, DICED

8 OUNCES CREMINI MUSHROOMS, WIPED OR BRUSHED CLEAN, STEMS TRIMMED, AND QUARTERED

2 TABLESPOONS ALL-PURPOSE FLOUR

½ CUP HEAVY (WHIPPING) CREAM

3 CUPS ½-INCH-DICE ROAST TURKEY

½ CUP FINELY CHOPPED FRESH FLAT-LEAF PARSLEY

KOSHER OR SEA SALT

FRESHLY GROUND PEPPER

Remove 1 or 2 pastry sheets from the package (you will need 1 sheet if making a single large pie and 1½ sheets if making 6 individual pies) and thaw the pastry at room temperature for 30 minutes. If using only 1 pastry sheet, tightly seal the remaining pastry and return to the freezer for another use.

Meanwhile, make the filling. Position a rack in the center of the oven. Preheat the oven to 400°F. Have ready an 8-cup baking dish about 2 inches deep, or use a 10-inch cast-iron skillet with 2-inch sides, and make the filling right in the skillet. For individual potpies, set six 10-ounce ramekins each about 4 inches in diameter on a rimmed baking sheet.

In a 1-quart saucepan over medium heat, bring the chicken stock to a boil. Add the carrot and cook until crisp-tender, about 10 minutes. Remove from the heat. Using a slotted spoon, transfer the carrot to a plate and set aside. Reserve the stock.

In a 10-inch skillet (cast iron, if you will be using it for baking), melt the butter with the oil over medium heat until the butter foams. Add the onion and sauté until it begins to soften, about 2 minutes. Add the mushrooms and sauté until they just begin to brown, about **>>>**

turkey potpie with a puff pastry crust
CONTINUED

3 minutes longer. Sprinkle the flour over the onion-mushroom mixture and stir to blend in. Slowly stir in the reserved stock, bring to a simmer, and stir until smooth and thickened, about 2 minutes. Add the cream, stir to blend, and bring to a simmer. Add the reserved carrot, the turkey, and the parsley and stir to combine. Return the mixture to a simmer and season to taste with salt and pepper. Remove from the heat. Divide the filling among the ramekins, spoon it into the baking dish, or leave it in the cast-iron skillet in which you cooked it.

Unfold the sheet(s) of puff pastry and lay them flat on a lightly floured work surface. For individual potpies, roll out each pastry sheet to a 12-inch square. Using a 5- or 6-inch plate, cut out 4 rounds from 1 sheet and 2 rounds from the second sheet. Cut two 2-inch-long slits in the center of each round. For 1 large potpie, roll out the pastry sheet to an 11-inch square and then trim the edges with a paring knife to form a circle. Cut three 2-inch-long slits in the center of the dough. Carefully center the dough over the filling and firmly press the edges of the dough against the sides of the ramekins, baking dish, or cast-iron skillet.

Bake the potpie(s) until the dough is nicely browned and puffed, about 25 minutes. Serve immediately.

Serves 6

mediterranean beef salad

People are divided into two camps on how to spend the days after Christmas: those who can't wait to hit the ground running for post-holiday sales, and those who want to curl up with a book, see a movie, or take leisurely walks with family and friends. No matter which group you fall into, it is likely that you've eaten too much, and cooking another elaborate meal is the last thing on your mind. ❋ After Christmas, my refrigerator often holds leftover roast beef. When it does, I like to pull a few condiments from my pantry shelf, whip together a simple vinaigrette, cube some of the cold roast beef, and put together this hearty main-course salad. All you need to complete this meal is some crusty bread and a glass of full-bodied red wine, and then put up your feet and relax.

VINAIGRETTE

1/2 CUP EXTRA-VIRGIN OLIVE OIL

3 TABLESPOONS BALSAMIC VINEGAR

2 TEASPOONS DIJON MUSTARD

1 CLOVE GARLIC, MINCED

1/2 TEASPOON KOSHER OR SEA SALT

FRESHLY GROUND PEPPER

4 TO 4 1/2 CUPS (ABOUT 1 1/2 POUNDS) COLD, 1/2-INCH-CUBED ROAST BEEF

1 1/2 CUPS COOKED GREEN BEANS, CUT INTO 1-INCH LENGTHS

1 LARGE RED BELL PEPPER, SEEDED, DERIBBED, AND CUT INTO 1/2-INCH DICE

1/2 CUP THINLY SLICED GREEN ONIONS, INCLUDING GREEN TOPS

1/2 CUP PIMIENTO-STUFFED GREEN OLIVES, HALVED

2 TABLESPOONS SMALL CAPERS, RINSED AND BLOTTED DRY

1/2 CUP CHOPPED FRESH FLAT-LEAF PARSLEY

1 PINT CHERRY TOMATOES, STEMMED

To make the vinaigrette, in a small bowl, whisk together the olive oil, vinegar, mustard, garlic, salt, and pepper to taste. Taste and adjust the seasoning. Set aside.

In a large bowl, combine the beef, green beans, bell pepper, green onions, olives, capers, parsley, and tomatoes. Toss lightly to combine. Add the vinaigrette, toss to coat evenly, and serve immediately.

Serves 6

10 christmas menus + timetables

To ensure that your holiday is full of comfort and joy, build in careful planning, good organization, and assignments for your seasonal elves. Make lots of lists—for shopping, cooking, and decorating—and check them twice. Constantly remind yourself that holiday entertaining is fun! Above all, enjoy the sheer pleasure of being in the kitchen or deciding where to place the birch-bark reindeer this year. I've included many sample menus to help guide the way, but trust your own ingenuity, too. After all, someone created *Seinfeld*'s cult-status Festivus and the interfaith Chrismukkah!

deck-the-halls decorating party

A decorating party is a lively, casual affair with family and close friends gathered to trim the tree, accent the mantle with greens, and, perhaps, hang a garland or ribbon on the staircase banister. Set up a buffet in the kitchen where everyone can gather and nibble finger foods, fill oversized mugs with steaming salmon chowder, and munch a crisp salad. Later, after the house is scented with fresh evergreens and the lights are twinkling on the tree, bring out the decadently delicious chocolate brownies for everyone to devour. Have bottles of chilled French or California Chardonnay on hand—the ideal complement to the salmon chowder.

❋ *Nuts, olives, marinated mushrooms*

❋ *Crudités with store-bought herbed goat cheese*

❋ *Polenta Crostini with Fig and Kalamata Olive Tapenade (page 44)*

❋ *Wild Salmon Chowder with Leeks and Celery Root (see Note, facing page) (page 59)*

❋ *Basket of artisanal breads and rolls*

❋ *Butter Lettuce Salad with Satsuma Tangerines and Pomegranate Seeds (page 66)*

❋ *Fudgy Chocolate Walnut Brownies (page 177)*

timetable

TWO WEEKS AHEAD
Make the brownies and freeze.

FIVE DAYS AHEAD
Make the fig tapenade and refrigerate.

TWO DAYS AHEAD
Make the polenta crostini and refrigerate.

EIGHT HOURS AHEAD
Cut and arrange the crudités on a serving platter, cover with damp paper towels and then plastic wrap, and refrigerate.

Wash and dry the butter lettuce. Roll the leaves in a dry cotton towel, place in a large plastic bag, and refrigerate.

Make the salad dressing and set aside at room temperature.

Prepare the tangerines and pomegranate seeds for the salad and set aside at room temperature.

FIVE HOURS AHEAD
Remove the brownies from the freezer. Cut into squares while frozen and arrange on a serving platter. Set aside at room temperature.

Make the salmon chowder up to the point of simmering the celery root. Set aside at room temperature. Cut the salmon and chop the herbs. Refrigerate until ready to finish the soup.

THREE HOURS AHEAD
Cut and broil the polenta crostini and set aside at room temperature.

Set out the nuts, olives, and marinated mushrooms in serving bowls.

ONE HOUR AHEAD
Remove the fig tapenade from the refrigerator. Assemble the polenta crostini appetizers.

Remove the crudités from the refrigerator. Place the herbed goat cheese in a serving dish.

Arrange the breads and rolls in a basket.

SHORTLY BEFORE SERVING
Finish the soup and keep warm.

Toss the salad just before serving.

Note: The salmon chowder serves 6. If you are serving a larger group, then double the recipe.

christmas open house

What a jolly time of year to entertain on a large scale. For many, hosting a Christmas open house is a way of returning thanks for being invited to cocktail and dinner parties throughout the year. With my children away at college, Christmastime entertaining is also an opportunity for them to see their friends when everyone is home on holiday break. An open house takes planning, and I have scaled the party and menu to make it easy on the cook. Divide and conquer with someone watching over the kitchen duties and someone else working at the bar. I suggest the Wassail Bowl and Pomegranate Martinis for the adults and sparkling apple cider for the children. You can also offer wine, beer, and other liquor, depending on whether or not you want to assemble a full bar. A buffet of several hors d'oeuvres and a few sweets is a good mix for an afternoon open house.

❋ *Wassail Bowl, Pomegranate Martinis, and sparkling apple cider (pages 50; 53)*

❋ *Spicy Crab in Wonton Cups (page 36)*

❋ *Blue Cheese Pastry Buttons (page 38)*

❋ *Cucumber Cups with Smoked Salmon and Chive Pâté (page 43)*

❋ *Wild Mushroom Croustades with Caraway and Dill (page 46)*

❋ *Polenta Crostini with Fig and Kalamata Olive Tapenade (page 44)*

❋ *Coconut–Orange Snowballs (page 169)*

❋ *Grandma Becky's Rugelach (page 178)*

❋ *Cinnamon–Honey Truffles with Cocoa Dust (page 189)*

timetable

TWO WEEKS AHEAD
Make the truffles and refrigerate.

Make the rugelach and freeze.

Make the snowball cookies and freeze.

THREE DAYS AHEAD
Make the pastry buttons and store at room temperature.

Make the croustades and store at room temperature.

Make the mushroom filling for the croustades and refrigerate.

Make the fig tapenade and refrigerate.

TWO DAYS AHEAD
Make the wonton cups and store at room temperature.

Make the blue cheese butter and refrigerate.

Make the smoked salmon pâté and refrigerate.

Make the polenta crostini and refrigerate.

ONE DAY AHEAD
Set up the buffet and bar. Organize glassware, plates, and napkins at the bar and buffet.

Thaw the rugelach and dust with confectioners' sugar. Arrange on a serving plate and store at room temperature.

Thaw the snowball cookies and roll in confectioners' sugar. Arrange on a serving plate and store at room temperature.

Chill the sparkling cider.

Make the crab filling and refrigerate.

Make the cucumber cups and refrigerate.

FIVE HOURS AHEAD
Refresh the pastry buttons in the oven for 3 minutes and set aside at room temperature.

Bake the Lady apples for the Wassail Bowl and set aside at room temperature.

Simmer the spices and citrus for the Wassail Bowl and set aside at room temperature.

Prepare the ingredients for the martinis and arrange at the bar.

TWO HOURS AHEAD
Remove the blue cheese butter from the refrigerator.

Assemble the cucumber cups.

Cut and broil the polenta crostini. Set aside at room temperature.

ONE HOUR AHEAD
Remove the truffles from the refrigerator and place in a candy dish.

Assemble the pastry buttons.

Warm the mushroom filling and assemble the croustades.

Remove the fig tapenade from the refrigerator. Assemble the crostini appetizers.

SHORTLY BEFORE SERVING
Assemble the crab appetizer.

Add the ale and apple cider to the wassail. Transfer to a heatproof punch bowl and add the roasted Lady apples.

christmas eve supper

Christmas Eve dinner is often an intimate affair, with just the immediate family gathered around the table. Following the Italian tradition, I like to serve seafood, and Saffron-Scented Fish Stew is the perfect dish to serve: special, warming, and comforting all at the same time. The family typically gathers in the kitchen, where I offer a few nibbles to start. I like to serve a salad after the main course, but you can serve it first, while the seafood is simmering. End the meal with a wedge of almond torte accompanied by the jewel-toned blood orange compote. Serve a Pinot Grigio or a Spanish Albariño with the seafood stew. You can also easily double the fish stew for a larger group.

❋ *Olives, nuts, baby carrots, cherry tomatoes*

❋ *Pistachio and Chive Goat Cheese on Puff Pastry Wafers (page 41)*

❋ *Saffron-Scented Fish Stew (page 56)*

❋ *Radicchio Caesar Salad (page 63)*

❋ *Almond Torte with Blood Orange Compote (page 140)*

timetable

THREE DAYS AHEAD
Make the torte. Cover
and store at room
temperature.

TWO DAYS AHEAD
Make the pistachio and
chive goat cheese and
refrigerate. Prepare the
radicchio for the salad
and refrigerate.

ONE DAY AHEAD
Make the blood orange
compote and refrigerate.

Make the puff pastry
wafers and store at room
temperature. Make the
dressing for the salad
and refrigerate.

Make the croutons for
the salad and store at
room temperature.

EIGHT HOURS AHEAD
Make the shellfish
broth. Cool, cover, and
refrigerate.

TWO HOURS AHEAD
Arrange the olives,
nuts, carrots, and
cherry tomatoes in
serving bowls.

Remove the compote
from the refrigerator.

Dust the torte with
confectioners' sugar.

Remove the pistachio
and chive goat cheese
from the refrigerator.

ONE HOUR AHEAD
Assemble the goat
cheese appetizers.

Make the bruschetta
and set aside at room
temperature.

Soak the saffron threads
for the fish stew.

**THIRTY MINUTES
AHEAD**
Finish preparing the fish
stew up to the point of
adding the seafood.

**SHORTLY BEFORE
SERVING**
Add the seafood to the
stew, cook, and garnish.

Assemble the salad.

the magic of christmas brunch

Anticipation, laughter, and smiles fill the house on Christmas morning. Wrapping paper is strewn about, Christmas ribbons are untied, and the hoped-for presents are exchanged. It's a jolly time and a hungry time, too. Hopefully, mugs of hot chocolate and coffee can stave off hunger long enough for brunch to be served. (If not, serve fruit and muffins first!) It's hard to decide between a brunch menu filled with sweet foods, savory foods, or a union of both, which is what I chose for this menu. I've paired subtly cured salmon, a Scandinavian specialty, with a deeply savory bread pudding accented with sausage and ham. Hit the sweet spots with fresh fruit and a basketful of warm streusel-topped cranberry muffins. Toast the family with mimosas for the adults and freshly squeezed orange juice for the children. It's a merry Christmas Day.

※ *Blood Orange Mimosas and freshly squeezed orange juice (page 53)*

※ *Fresh fruit platter*

※ *Gravlax (page 155)*

※ *Pumpernickel bread, butter, and cream cheese*

※ *Savory Bread Pudding with Sausage and Ham (page 162)*

※ *Cranberry Muffins with Brown Sugar—Almond Streusel (page 160)*

※ *Coffee, tea, and hot chocolate*

timetable

THREE DAYS AHEAD
Make the gravlax.

ONE DAY AHEAD
Refrigerate the Champagne for the mimosas.

Assemble the bread pudding and refrigerate.

Make the streusel topping for the muffins and store at room temperature.

Mix the dry ingredients and orange zest for the muffins and store at room temperature.

Toast the almonds for the muffins and store at room temperature.

Measure all the wet ingredients for the muffins and refrigerate.

THREE HOURS AHEAD
Preheat the oven to 425°F for the muffins.

Assemble and bake the muffins.

TWO HOURS AHEAD
Reduce the oven to 350°F for baking the bread pudding.

Arrange the bread and muffins in baskets. Place the butter and cream cheese on plates or fill ramekins.

Cut fruit and arrange on a serving platter. Cover and set aside until ready to serve.

ONE AND ONE-HALF HOURS AHEAD
Remove the bread pudding from the refrigerator.

ONE HOUR AHEAD
Bake the bread pudding.

Slice the gravlax and assemble on a platter.

SHORTLY BEFORE SERVING
Squeeze blood oranges for the mimosas.

Squeeze oranges for juice.

Make coffee, tea, and hot chocolate.

a grand christmas dinner for a dozen

Planning is everything for a spectacular Christmas feast, and with a timeline for tasks, this elaborate menu is completely doable. I have designed a showstopper dinner complete with a grand beef tenderloin for the main course and Bûche de Noël for the breathtaking finale. Divided into steps, you have a game plan that keeps you, and maybe a few elves, busy but not taxed in the kitchen. Pick a different dessert if baking doesn't interest you. However, if you love to bake and decorate, then have a camera ready when you present this enchanting dessert, because you'll have the biggest smile ever, and your guests will, too.

❋ *Nuts, olives, pickled vegetables*

❋ *Crudités with store-bought herbed goat cheese*

❋ *Cucumber Cups with Smoked Salmon and Chive Pâté (page 43)*

❋ *Sake Oyster Shooters (page 39)*

❋ *Roast Tenderloin of Beef with Bordelaise Sauce (page 89)*

❋ *Potatoes au Gratin with Fresh Thyme and a Parmesan Crust (page 116)*

❋ *Roasted Carrots and Parsnips with Fresh Dill (page 102)*

❋ *Creamed Spinach (page 111)*

❋ *Bûche de Noël (page 131)*

timetable

THREE WEEKS AHEAD
Make the meringue mushrooms for the Bûche de Noël and store at room temperature.

TWO WEEKS AHEAD
Make the sponge cake and buttercream for the Bûche de Noël.

Spread the buttercream, roll the cake, and freeze.

TWO DAYS AHEAD
Make the smoked salmon pâté and refrigerate.

Make the Bordelaise sauce and refrigerate.

ONE DAY AHEAD
Thaw the cake in the refrigerator.

Make the cucumber cups and refrigerate.

TWELVE HOURS AHEAD
Glaze the cake for the Bûche de Noël.

EIGHT HOURS AHEAD
Cut and arrange the crudités on a serving platter, cover with damp paper towels and then plastic wrap, and refrigerate.

Mix the wasabi and cut the cucumber and chives for the oyster shooters and refrigerate.

Chop the garlic and thyme for the beef tenderloin and set aside at room temperature.

Wash and chop the spinach. Refrigerate until ready to sauté.

Assemble the carrots and parsnips dish and set aside at room temperature to roast later.

THREE HOURS AHEAD
Assemble the potatoes au gratin and set aside at room temperature.

Make the rosemary and cranberry garnishes for the Bûche de Noël. Finish decorating the dessert.

TWO HOURS AHEAD
Bake the potatoes au gratin.

Arrange the nuts, olives, and pickled vegetables in serving bowls.

Assemble the cucumber cups.

Remove the beef tenderloin from the refrigerator and prepare it for roasting.

Make the béchamel sauce for the spinach.

ONE HOUR AHEAD
Remove the crudités from the refrigerator. Place the herbed goat cheese in a serving dish.

FORTY-FIVE MINUTES BEFORE SERVING
Roast the beef tenderloin.

Roast the carrots and parsnips.

THIRTY MINUTES BEFORE SERVING
Remove the Bordelaise sauce from the refrigerator and place it in a saucepan to warm.

Make the spinach and keep warm.

SHORTLY BEFORE SERVING
Arrange the ingredients for the oyster shooters.

Carve the beef tenderloin and arrange on a warmed platter.

chrismukkah—the hybrid holiday meal

Not only is this a blended holiday menu celebrating Christian and Jewish traditions, but it is also, more often than not, a joyous hybrid occasion reaching across a handful of cultures. So it seems fitting to add some Asian and Italian flavors to the menu. After all, celebrating the holiday season with Chrismukkah as the gathering feast is all about family-building, community-building, and pleasurable meals as a means to closer human relationships. Joy to the foods of the world and joy to the cook or cooks who make this blessed repast. (Depending on family preferences, Christmas Kugel, on page 105, could trump latkes on your menu. Oy vey.)

❋ *Spicy Crab in Wonton Cups (page 36)*

❋ *Sake Oyster Shooters (page 39)*

❋ *Crudités with store-bought hummus dip*

❋ *Blood Orange Salad with Mâche and Salt-Cured Black Olives (page 65)*

❋ *Diane Cohen's Brisket (page 94)*

❋ *Roasted Carrots and Parsnips with Fresh Dill (page 102)*

❋ *Sautéed Brussels Sprouts with Garlic and Parmesan (page 113)*

❋ *Fa-La-La-La Latkes (page 114)*

❋ *Gingerbread Bundt Cake with Crème Anglaise (page 137)*

timetable

TWO WEEKS AHEAD
Make the gingerbread cake and freeze.

TWO DAYS AHEAD
Make the crème anglaise and refrigerate.

Make the brisket. Cool, cover, and refrigerate.

Make the wonton cups and store at room temperature.

ONE DAY AHEAD
Thaw the gingerbread cake at room temperature.

Make the potato latkes. Cool, layer between sheets of waxed paper, cover, and refrigerate.

Make the salad dressing and refrigerate.

Make the crab filling and refrigerate.

EIGHT HOURS AHEAD
Cut and arrange the crudités on a serving platter, cover with damp paper towels and then plastic wrap, and refrigerate.

Mix the wasabi and cut the cucumber and chives for the oyster shooters and refrigerate.

Wash and trim the Brussels sprouts. Refrigerate until ready to sauté.

Assemble the carrots and parsnips dish and set aside at room temperature to roast later.

TWO HOURS AHEAD
Remove the brisket from the refrigerator.

Assemble the ingredients for the Brussels sprouts.

Remove the salad dressing from the refrigerator.

Prepare the ingredients for the salad.

ONE AND ONE-HALF HOURS AHEAD
Roast the carrots and parsnips.

ONE HOUR AHEAD
Heat the brisket in a 250°F oven until hot.

Remove the crudités from the refrigerator. Place the hummus in a serving dish.

TWENTY MINUTES AHEAD
Heat the potato latkes in a 350°F oven until crisp and hot.

Put the sour cream and applesauce in serving bowls for the latkes.

Assemble the crab appetizer.

SHORTLY BEFORE SERVING
Arrange the ingredients for the oyster shooters.

Slice the brisket and arrange on a warmed platter.

Sauté the Brussels sprouts.

Dust the gingerbread cake with confectioners' sugar.

Assemble the salad.

11 holiday decor

Set the scene at Christmastime. Decorating is a personal expression of your style and traditions. Simple, seasonal elements make your house feel welcoming and special. For instance, every year, I decorate the mantle with garland, weaving gathered, moss-covered twigs into faux garland and adding pinecones and Christmas balls. The Christmas stockings, however, are traditional—the ones we've had since the children were toddlers. The table is set with the china and silver flatware I inherited from my grandmother, and I add fun, modern elements such as the glass cubes with fresh flowers and twisted wire. The ideas in this chapter aren't elaborate—just fun projects to create a warm, inviting ambience.

mantle garland

Floral designers David and Leanne Kesler showed me a great way to decorate a mantle and keep it looking fresh throughout the holiday season. Use a faux garland and weave gathered twigs, preferably ones covered with some moss, decoratively through it. Add pinecones and Christmas balls. For a party, insert fresh flowers and greens. Look for the wire at your local crafts store.

ONE 4-BY-8-INCH BRICK FLORIST FOAM

1 RECTANGULAR DISH, LARGE ENOUGH
TO HOLD THE FLORIST FOAM

FLORIST WATERPROOF TAPE

ONE 9-FOOT-LONG FAUX GARLAND

ASSORTED GATHERED STICKS, ONE-THIRD
TO ONE-HALF THE LENGTH OF YOUR MANTLE

SIX 4-INCH-LONG WOOD FLORAL PICKS

12 NATURAL PINECONES OR GLISTENING SNOW
PINECONES (PAGE 234)

TWELVE 18-INCH PIECES 18-GAUGE WIRE

TWELVE 50-MM OR 2-INCH CHRISTMAS BALLS
WITH WIRES ATTACHED

FRESH CHRISTMAS GREENS AND
FLOWERS (OPTIONAL)

Presoak the florist foam and then anchor it in the dish with waterproof tape.

Center the garland on the front of the dish and anchor it at 2 points using 2 of the floral picks. Fasten the garland to the ends of the florist foam using 2 more floral picks. This securely fastens the garland to the foam base in 4 places.

Place the gathered sticks into the foam, following the line of the garland. Weave them decoratively to create a natural look.

To attach the pinecones, wrap each one near the base with a piece of the wire. Twist the wire to bring it together and leave the excess length for insertion into the foam. Place the pinecones in the center of the garland in a balanced, symmetrical fashion.

Group Christmas balls in the bottom center and top center of the design.

If you want to add fresh flowers or greens to the garland, cut the stems of the greens or flowers and secure them to the florist foam. Add water to the dish every 2 or 3 days to keep the florist foam moist.

glass cubes with fresh flowers and twisted wire

Bring a minimalist modern motif to your holiday table using glass cubes filled with twisted, colored aluminum wire and a single holiday flower. These vases look fabulous interspersed with votive candles running the length of your holiday table. Look for the aluminum wire at your local crafts store or online at www.floraldesigninstitute.com.

3 YARDS GREEN OR RED ALUMINUM WIRE

THREE 4-INCH-SQUARE GLASS CUBES

3 CYMBIDIUM ORCHIDS OR OTHER HOLIDAY FLOWERS SUCH AS RED ROSES, RED OR WHITE CARNATIONS, OR WHITE CHRYSANTHEMUMS

Use 1 yard aluminum wire per cube. Twist and bend the wire to form an irregular wad that will fit inside the cube. Repeat for each cube. Fill the cubes with water and place a single flower in the cube.

individual glass cubes

Wrap wired ribbon around individual glass cubes, tie a classic or fanciful knot, and run the cubes along the length of your holiday table. You can even mix the sizes, using some small and some large cubes. Fill the cubes with flowers, tiny Christmas ornaments, or sprayed nuts and cranberries (page 233). To coordinate the table, tie napkins with the same ribbons, using the same style knot. If desired, tie a small ornament onto the ribbon on each napkin as a gift for each guest.

THREE TO FIVE 4-INCH-SQUARE GLASS CUBES

2 TO 3 YARDS HOLIDAY WIRED RIBBON, 2 1/2 INCHES WIDE

2 TO 3 YARDS HOLIDAY WIRED RIBBON, 1 1/2 INCHES WIDE

Lay a glass cube on its side. Use about 20 inches of wide ribbon and 20 inches of narrow ribbon for each cube. Center the narrow ribbon along the length of the wide ribbon. Wrap the ribbons around the circumference of the cube, centering them, and tie together to form a decorative double knot. Dovetail the ends of the ribbons by folding them in half lengthwise and then cutting them at an angle.

leaf-wrapped votive holder with gold ribbon

Floral expert Leanne Kesler showed me how to transform inexpensive glass votive holders into festive table lights. She uses galax leaves or other small leathery leaves such as salal, sprays them with adhesive spray, and then attaches the leaves to the votive holder and wraps them with twinkling gold bullion wire. For a spectacular holiday table, alternate the votives with several Individual Glass Cubes (page 225) wrapped with metallic gold ribbon. Look for the leaves at a florist shop and the wire at a crafts store.

15 TO 25 GALAX LEAVES, STEMS REMOVED

3M SUPER 77 SPRAY ADHESIVE

3 TO 5 VOTIVE HOLDERS, EACH ABOUT
2 1/2 INCHES HIGH

3 TO 5 YARDS GOLD BULLION WIRE

3 TO 5 WHITE VOTIVE CANDLES, EACH ABOUT
1 1/2 INCHES HIGH

Spread newspapers on a porch, in your garage, or in a well-ventilated room. Arrange the leaves upside down on the newspapers so they don't touch, and allow plenty of room for overspray. Lightly spray the leaves with the spray adhesive. Wait about 30 seconds, or until sticky enough to pick up a leaf with your finger. Place 1 leaf on the votive holder, so the top of the leaf stands 1/3 to 1/2 inch above the rim. Attach 4 additional leaves, overlapping them slightly, so the sides of the holder are covered. Using scissors, trim the leaves flush with the base of the votive holder. Using about 1 yard of bullion wire for each votive holder, wrap the wire around the center of the holder, overlapping it and then twisting the ends together to secure it. Trim any excess wire. Place a votive candle in each holder. The decorated holders will keep for about 1 month.

lighted glass presents

Lorinda Moholt, one of the most talented calligraphy artists I know, gets full credit for this enchanting Christmas decoration. My husband and I attended an intimate holiday dinner with mutual friends at Ray and Lorinda's home and admired a two-tiered stack of lighted glass blocks tied beautifully with gold metallic ribbon on the dining-room buffet. Everyone wanted to know where she bought it, and Lorinda smiled and told us she made the glass presents. Now, I'm not a handy-dandy tool gal, and working with kitchen tools comes much more naturally to me than working with shop tools, but even I could drill the glass and make this sensational decoration following her directions. Look for the glass tile blocks at home-improvement stores.

TWO 7-BY-7-BY-2-INCH GLASS TILE BLOCKS

1 MEDIUM-SIZED CORRUGATED CARTON

1 ELECTRIC DRILL

ONE $1/2$-INCH GLASS AND TILE DRILL BIT

SAFETY GOGGLES

DUST MASK (OPTIONAL)

2 CHRISTMAS MINIATURE-LIGHT SETS, EACH WITH WHITE WIRE AND 25 WHITE LIGHTS

4 TO 5 YARDS SHEER WIRED METALLIC GOLD, SILVER, RED, OR MIDNIGHT BLUE RIBBON

SCOTCH TAPE

EXTENSION CORD

Place 1 glass block upright inside the carton. (The carton helps contain the dust.)

Fit the drill with the drill bit. Positioning the glass block so that you are facing a 2-inch-high side, drill a hole through the glass about 2 inches in from the corner. This will take a few minutes, so be patient. Once the opening is formed, rotate the blade around the hole to widen it enough to thread the miniature lights inside. (The plug ends will not be inserted, so the hole only needs to be large enough to thread the lights and cord.) Repeat with the second glass block. Tap the block to remove any dust from the inside.

Test the light sets before threading them into the cubes! Then thread 1 set of lights into each cube, leaving the two plug ends on the outside.

Wrap the bottom glass block with ribbon on all four sides and tape the ends together to secure them. (Taping the ribbon keeps the surface flat. If you tie a knot, then the top block will wobble when placed on top of the bottom block.) Repeat with the second block, this time tying a knot to secure the ribbon on top. Leave the excess ribbon to help secure the bow.

Create a bow for the top block, forming 6 to 8 loops if possible. Carefully secure the bow to the top cube. Arrange the cubes near an outlet, or attach an extension cord, and plug in the lights.

holiday wreath

Every year I order a stunning holiday wreath from Christine Belluschi, my gardening expert and landscape designer. She builds them from scratch, shaping the wire frame and arranging evergreens and beautiful magnolia leaves into a large, lush wreath. I asked Christine to share her creativity and techniques. Pick the color or colors you like for the ornaments. Last year, Christine decorated the wreath with gold-sprayed pinecones, mossy twigs, and dazzling, effervescent green glass balls that harmonized beautifully with the natural greens.

15 TO 20 REGULAR-SIZE NATURAL PINECONES

1 CAN RUST-OLEUM BRIGHT GOLD METALLIC SPRAY PAINT

HOT-GLUE GUN AND GLUE STICKS

1 EVERGREEN WREATH, 24 OR 30 INCHES IN DIAMETER

25 TO 40 GLASS OR PLASTIC BALL ORNAMENTS, IN VARIOUS SIZES (SEE DECOR NOTE)

TINY NATURAL PINECONES

GATHERED TWIGS OR SMALL BRANCHES, PREFERABLY WITH SOME MOSS ATTACHED

HANGING WREATH HOOK

Spread newspapers on a porch, in your garage, or in a well-ventilated room. Arrange the regular-sized pinecones on the newspapers so they do not touch, and allow plenty of room for overspray. Lightly spray the balls with the gold spray paint. Allow to dry on one side, about 10 minutes, and then turn the pinecones to spray the underside.

Heat a hot-glue gun and place it on its stand with a disposable plate underneath the tip to catch drips. Place the wreath on a counter protected with newspapers or craft paper. Working with one gold pinecone at a time, apply glue to the base of the cone and nestle it into the greens. Repeat with the remaining sprayed pinecones, decoratively arranging them around the wreath.

Working with 1 ball ornament at a time, apply glue to the base of the ball and nestle it into the greens on the wreath. Repeat with the remaining ornaments, clustering several together. Apply glue to the small pinecones and arrange them randomly around the wreath. Once all the glued decor is dry, artfully nestle the twigs or small branches around the wreath with some of the stems reaching beyond the edges of the evergreens. Use a wreath hook to secure the wreath to your front door.

DECOR NOTE

You will need 25 to 28 ball ornaments for a 24-inch wreath and about 40 ornaments for a 30-inch wreath. ❄ *If your front door is unprotected by an overhang, spray the glass balls with Varathane brand water-based, crystal clear spray polyurethane before gluing them to the wreath. This will protect the finish from moisture. (This step is not necessary if you use plastic ball ornaments.) Spread newspapers on a porch, in your garage, or in a well-ventilated room. Arrange the ball ornaments, not touching, on the newspapers and allow plenty of room for overspray. Lightly spray the balls with the polyurethane.* ❄ *Allow to dry completely before attaching the balls to the wreath.*

metallic sprayed fruits and nuts

Decorating a mantle, holiday buffet, or table centerpiece with winter greens, glistening sprayed fruits, dark green acorn squash dusted with antique brass, and whole nuts sparkling with gold adds a welcome touch of drama. Landscape designer Christine Belluschi and I spent a morning experimenting with different sprayed fruits and squashes.

SEVERAL CORRUGATED CARTONS
RUST-OLEUM BRIGHT GOLD METALLIC SPRAY PAINT
RUST-OLEUM ANTIQUE BRASS SPRAY PAINT
RUST-OLEUM LEATHER BROWN GLOSS SPRAY PAINT
RUST-OLEUM CRYSTAL CLEAR ENAMEL SPRAY PAINT
KOSHER SALT

SUGGESTED FRUITS, SQUASH, AND NUTS TO SPRAY
SMALL, HARD RED DELICIOUS APPLES
LADY APPLES
LEMONS WITH PEBBLY SKIN
NAVEL ORANGES WITH LOTS OF RIDGES AND PEBBLY SKIN
STAR FRUITS, UNDERRIPE
UGLI FRUITS
POMEGRANATES
CRANBERRIES
SMALL ACORN SQUASHES
ASSORTED NUTS IN THE SHELL SUCH AS WALNUTS, ALMONDS, AND CHESTNUTS

Line several corrugated cartons with newspapers and place on a porch, in your garage, or in a well-ventilated room. Dividing them according to the paint color you are using, arrange the fruits, squashes, and nuts in the boxes, placing them, not touching, on the newspapers and allowing plenty of room for overspray. Use a light touch on the paint nozzle and move your hand back and forth to spray the fruits, squashes, and nuts with paint. Apply several light coats rather than a single heavy coat. Allow to dry completely before turning to spray the undersides.

Apples: Lightly dust the tops with gold or antique brass spray paint. Or, for a just-fallen-snow look, spray the apples with crystal clear enamel, wait 1 minute for the paint to set, and then dust the apple with kosher salt.

Lemons: Spray first with gold spray paint and then spray with antique brass. Or, spray only with gold, allowing some of the yellow to come through.

Oranges: Spray first with leather brown spray paint and then spray an overcoat of gold.

Star fruits: Spray with gold spray paint. Or, spray first with leather brown paint and then with antique brass.

Ugli fruits: Spray first with antique brass paint and then spray an overcoat of gold.

Cranberries and pomegranates: Lightly dust with gold spray paint.

Small acorn squashes: Spray with antique brass, allowing some of the green to show through on the sides. Or, spray completely with leather brown paint and then spray an overcoat of gold.

Assorted nuts: Spray with gold or antique brass paint.

wired twig candle wrap

For holidays at a winter lodge house or cabin, or even in your home or apartment with a country-style decor, building twig wraps for pillar candles is an inexpensive and country-chic way to decorate. After the holidays, think about building candle wraps with thin pieces of bamboo for an Asian look. Look for the wire at your local crafts store or online at www.floraldesigninstitute.com.

GATHERED STICKS ABOUT 1/4 INCH THICK

SPOOL OF 20-GAUGE RED METAL WIRE

2 OR 3 WHITE, DARK GREEN, OR RED PILLAR CANDLES

Cut the sticks into 2 1/2- to 3-inch lengths. To make a wrap for 1 candle, twist the wire around the center of each stick, leaving about 1 1/2 inches of wire between the sticks. Build a length of wire-wrapped twigs long enough to encircle the base of the candle at least 4 or 5 times, for a rustic holiday look. Repeat to create twig wraps for as many pillar candles as you plan to use.

glistening snow pinecones

Here's an easy way to add glistening snow to pinecones or foliage.

NATURAL PINECONES

FRESH OR FAUX GREENS

3M SUPER 77 SPRAY ADHESIVE

TABLE SALT

Spread newspapers on a porch, in your garage, or in a well-ventilated room. Arrange the pinecones and greens on the newspapers, allowing plenty of room for overspray. Lightly spray the pinecones and greens with the spray adhesive. Evenly sprinkle with salt to mimic snow. Set aside until dry.

index

table of equivalents

The exact equivalents in the following tables have been rounded for convenience.

LIQUID / DRY MEASUREMENTS

U.S.	METRIC
¼ teaspoon	1.25 milliliters
½ teaspoon	2.5 milliliters
1 teaspoon	5 milliliters
1 tablespoon (3 teaspoons)	15 milliliters
1 fluid ounce (2 tablespoons)	30 milliliters
¼ cup	60 milliliters
⅓ cup	80 milliliters
½ cup	120 milliliters
1 cup	240 milliliters
1 pint (2 cups)	480 milliliters
1 quart (4 cups, 32 ounces)	960 milliliters
1 gallon (4 quarts)	3.84 liters
1 ounce (by weight)	28 grams
1 pound	448 grams
2.2 pounds	1 kilogram

LENGTHS

U.S.	METRIC
⅛ inch	3 millimeters
¼ inch	6 millimeters
½ inch	12 millimeters
1 inch	2.5 centimeters

OVEN TEMPERATURE

FAHRENHEIT	CELSIUS	GAS
250	120	½
275	140	1
300	150	2
325	160	3
350	180	4
375	190	5
400	200	6
425	220	7
450	230	8
475	240	9
500	260	10